TANS

THE TANS COLLECTION

VOLUME III

You called. We Went.

D1287864

Edited by Wayne Munkel

TANS
The TANS Collection, Volume III

Cover Design by Lea Koesterer
Cover Photo Courtesy of Pete Komada

ISBN: 978-1-938674-09-9

DoubleSpin

DoubleSpin Publishing
A Division of Dancing Bear Ent. LLC
John *Mad Jack* Klawitter
Printed in the United States of America
Published 30 April 2014

Dedicated to
Arthur Wayne Glover
An ASA trooper
Who gave everything
In the service of our country.

CONTENTS

Chapter 1
How I ended up in the ASA;
Explanations and Excuses

Harlan Olson, Andy Anderson, John Standish, Terry Hester, Paul Neimeyer, Dave Ulm, Jerry Frankenburger, Lee Hendley, Skip Saurman, James 'Barney' Reynolds, Lon Ludwig, Ivan Riggle, Lucky Rupp, and Robert Flanagan
pp. 1 - 17.

Chapter 2
The Early Years 1961-1965

Chapter 3
The Middle 60s

Chapter 4
1968

Chapter 5
1969

Chapter 6
The 1970s

Epilogue
After The War

Preface

The stories in this book were written in response to a yearly writing contest of the Southeast Asia Army Security Agency Association. A panel of judges rated the stories and recognition was given to the authors of these stories. The winner each year was recognized with his name engraved on a brass plate that was attached to a traveling trophy. The trophy was given to the Association by Mike Conaghan from Australia. Mike was a member of the Australian 547th Signal Troop in Vietnam. Two of Mike's stories appear in this book. Other stories deemed worthy of merit were given recognition in the form of a totally worthless piece of paper suitable for framing.

The involvement of the Army Security Agency (ASA) in the Vietnam War began in May, 1961, and ended by March, 1973. The Agency was awarded all seventeen campaign streamers. The tour of duty was a year but some soldiers extended their tours and some served years during the war. Some soldiers made repeat tours in ASA or in other units. Because of the long duration of the war, numerous cycles of ASA personnel were needed. There were an increasing number of forces to fight the war and likewise, an increasing number of ASA units. The book is divided into a chronology based on the years the authors were in Viet Nam. In some cases I did not know when an author was there and I put stories where I saw the best fit.

This book, more than the previous two, reflects a darker side of the war. By the mid to late sixties American combat units were heavily engaged with the Viet Cong and North Vietnamese Army. There was no safe place for the military or civilians. Soldiers of the ASA were just as vulnerable as anyone and some paid the ultimate price. Others were wounded.

While ASA was not a combat arm, combat was all around them. It could be seen, heard and felt at times. These soldiers experienced vicarious trauma just by being where they were and knowing the war was all around them and that they could be killed or wounded at any time. No one was safe from area weapons like rockets, mortars, artillery or bombs. Rank was no protection. Time and place were the deciders of death and injury.

Several stories speak of the terror and horror of bombardments. They also speak of the consequences of those experiences in a lifetime of dreams and nightmares. It is no small wonder that PTSD is the consequence of the experiences of war. Losing a friend or buddy in war is one of the most devastating experiences and one carries that experience forever. You can almost feel the pain the authors experienced as they tell their stories.

Some of the stories reveal the personalities of the authors as they reflect on their youthful experiences in Viet Nam. Sexual encounters and drinking are prominent. Relating to other soldiers often took on a humorous bent with nick names, name calling, and practical jokes.

Life in the boonies was just as difficult for ASA troops as other soldiers. Those who were attached to combat units could find themselves fighting for their lives along with the combat units.

After exiting Vietnam, ASA still had a worldwide mission to monitor communications of our enemies. The Cold War was still on and there were several hot items in the ensuing years. China, Taiwan, Iran, Russia and North Korea were a few of the hot spots and ASA was in the thick of it.

— Wayne Munkel

Sacred Stones
By Marty Noland

Here I walk among white stones.
On some are names, some marked 'Unknown.'
The cost of war here for all to see,
This field our children's final home.

Stones with peaks or rounded tops
From an 'un-Civil War', a nation's shame
Mark young men's graves from so long ago
Brother 'gainst brothers, to both, death came.

Stones with names of our progeny,
Who died in our 'World Wars' afar?
Stationed now for eternity 'neath
Granite stones with cross or star.

Similar stones mark hero's graves,
From a 'forgotten' war on Korean soil.
Those stalwart soldiers, forever young,
Stilled hearts once bold, but ever loyal.

Brass plaques I see with names I know.
Childhood friends by their leaders damned
Young warriors who answered their nation's call,
Their lives were taken in Viet Nam.

Politicians send the young to die in war.
They hold our daughters and sons as shields.
For their egos, their power, and earthly goods
Are reasons to fill the stone-marked fields.

God grant that I, as I come to you,
May it never be said of me.
That I sent my precious children to die
For simple possession, or what I needed to be.

Chapter 1
How I ended up in the ASA: Explanations and Excuses

In the early 1960s the draft was providing men for the Armed Forces. Young men coming out of high school knew they could be drafted at some time. Registering for the draft was mandatory for 18-year-olds. Some men went out of high school into the military to get it over with. Others went into the service for specific training, schools, or for experiences-like Airborne. As the Vietnam War intensified, more combat troops were needed. In order to avoid the draft consequences, young men of draft age sought out ways to avoid the draft by fleeing the country, fleeing to deferments in colleges and universities or seeking roles in the military where they would have some choice about what their service would be. The ASA was one of those choices for those who qualified. They were considered the top ten percent of the Army. These were intelligent young men often with some college experience or post high school training. Others were bright enough to score high on the battery of tests. The ASA needed bright students for the highly technical nature of the training and skills needed in electronic warfare. Most ASA schools were months long and some were even more than a year.

The ASA also needed men of character to be trusted with the secrets of the ASA and the nation. That is why security clearances were at the Top-Secret-Crypto or higher level. ASA needed not just Boy Scouts but people with squeaky clean records to receive these clearances. So how did Army recruiters find intelligent, crime free people? The tests were starters. Then they appealed to the macho image of secret agents, secret missions, far away exotic countries; buddy enlistment programs; promise of schools and training that would be career builders in the military or in civilian life. As the Vietnam War continued ASA became a ploy to avoid going to Vietnam which, in the end, often led there.

What follows are a selection of brief vignettes of how some soldiers ended up in the ASA. These stories come from a collection of stories submitted to Southeast Asia ASA Association by former ASA soldiers who served in Vietnam some time during their Army service.

Tired of Milking Cows and Intrigued by a Top-Secret Clearance

By Harlan Olson

I was fresh out of high school, living on a dairy farm ten miles east of Decorah, Iowa. I joined the Army to get away from milking those darn 80 Holsteins twice a day. I remember taking the bus to Des Moines, Iowa to the Army induction center for processing. I remember raising my right hand and standing in line for the medical exam and the shots. But what I focused on was being called to the office of the Sergeant. He came and got me out of the line and took me to his office and closed the door.

He said, "Mr. Olson, I see that you have enlisted for the Military Police".

I replied, "Yes, Sir."

He said, "Are you sure you want all that spit and polish?" He continued, "Your scores are pretty high so that I can make you a better offer. How about going into the Army Security Agency?"

I said, "What's that?"

He said, "I can't tell you a whole lot, but you will need a Top-Secret Clearance. Is there anything that would prevent you from getting one?"

That question alone intrigued me enough to say, "Sure, why not?"

Got My Draft Notice and Already in the NSA
By Andy Anderson

There I was in 1966 working as a civilian at the NSA's Headquarters at Fort Meade, Maryland. I was working alongside guys in the Army, Navy, Air Force, and the Marines, and never giving them a second thought. They were just guys that did the same kind of job that I did, except that they wore uniforms. Then my draft notice came! I talked to a couple of the military guys and started thinking. Here I am, working at NSA with my Top-Secret Clearance, what the hell, if I enlisted in one of the security groups, they would just send me right back here to do my same job with a uniform on. I started checking them out, and since I already got my draft notice, found out that the Army was the only branch that would accept me. I signed on the dotted line for four years, and was sent to Fort Dix, New Jersey for Basic Training. Then I went to Fort Gordon, Georgia for Signal School, and then to Fort Carson, Colorado after graduation. I spent a year there, and then volunteered for Vietnam. I spent 19 months in-country and then was assigned to Fort Devens, Massachusetts. I left the Army in August, 1970, and went back to NSA and my old job.

I Wanted to Be an Electrical Engineer
By John Standish AKA 'Double 00'

I enlisted in the Army for the Army Security Agency in December, 1962 to be an electrical engineering assistant, Military Occupation Specialty 309 or MOS - 309. I was guaranteed by the Army recruiter at Wilkes-Barre, Pennsylvania that I would go to Fort Huachuca, Arizona for military communication electronics training after completing Basic Training at Fort Dix, New Jersey. The Army recruiter was misinformed, unaware, overruled or fed me a story to recruit me.

After Basic Training I received orders to report directly to Vint Hill Farms Station Special Projects Unit in Warrenton, Virginia. I was assigned to work for a civilian electrical engineer from the NSA at Fort Meade. Everyone at the VHFS-SPU held Top-Secret Crypto Security Clearances. SPU was okay in my opinion, interesting work in a relaxed atmosphere except for frequent KP duty.

The VHFS was also near DC for weekend payday jaunts but, as time passed at VHFS-SPU, I had no rank, no stripes and was receiving very low E-2 or E-3 grade pay.

I asked, "What's up?"

The SPU Commandant, a colonel, said he couldn't promote me because MOS - 309 requires a BS EE and six months professional experience or an MS EE, which I didn't have, so I was being carried on the SPU organizational chart as an MOS - 006, a basic trainee. My moniker '006' came from the MOS - 006, later shortened to Double 0 in Vietnam.

I Wanted to Drink Beer and Chase Girls
By Terry Hester

My story sounds similar to Harlan's, but I never milked any Holsteins. This Tennessee boy got out of high school and went to college. I soon found that I liked drinking beer, partying and chasing after girls better than going to class. In 1965, after I finished my first quarter, I was put on probation and told that I must improve all my grades or be kicked out. By then, it was January, 1966.

I had a friend from high school who had just joined the Marine Corps, and I thought to myself, I'll do the same thing. I was never anti-draft but I just didn't know what I wanted to do except drink beer and chase girls. So I drove over to the recruiting office with the intention of joining the Marine Corps. When I got there, the only person there was a Sgt. First Class Army recruiter.

So, I thought what the heck, I'll talk to him. He said for me to tell him what I had been doing, and I said that I had been going to college. I did not tell him that I was about to be flunked out. He said okay, with your background the Army Security Agency would be perfect for you. However, I can't tell you a whole lot about it because it's super-secret. But, I know you would be perfect for it.

After Basic at Fort Jackson, South Carolina and then Signal School at Fort Gordon, I went to Korea and the 508th ASA group at wonderful Yong Dong Po. I immediately found myself drinking plenty of beer and now chasing Korean girls. I said, "Is this a great army or what!"

Army Guy Assured Me
There Was No ASA In Vietnam
By Paul Neimeyer

I was raised from birth to become a US Air Force fighter pilot by my father, who was the last enlisted pilot in the Army Air Corps. A good friend of mine was home on leave from Fort Campbell, Kentucky and he and I went out for a few drinks. I was impressed with the uniform and what he'd been doing as a tanker. Later the next evening at the dinner table, I casually mentioned to my father that I was thinking about possibly joining the Army.

My father laughed in my face and said, "Son, you'll never make it through Basic Training", to which I replied, "Dad I know for a fact that you were a pilot with TWA before you entered the Air Corps and immediately was commissioned as an Army aviator and never went through Basic Training."

The next day I joined the Army and was being talked to by this Army guy who assured me there was no ASA in Vietnam and did I want to join ASA. I did and put in for Germany and eventually ended up in Okinawa for 38 months on an 18 months tour. I was TDY to Vietnam and Udorn for 179 days each, where I found out that the recruiting guy was right. There was no ASA in Vietnam, only little things like RRG's, RRU's, and SOD's but certainly no ASA.

Opportunity to Fly in a Plane
and Get Further from Home
By Dave Ulm

I was registered for the fall term at the University of Dayton and enjoying my summer between high school graduation and college. I was pissed off because my friends had cars and I didn't. I decided to give my dad an ultimatum; buy me a car or I'm joining the service. I had two brothers and one had joined the Army and the other joined the Air Force after high school. My dad said he wasn't going to buy me a car and any time he wanted to he could cut off support for my college. My eldest brother was still in the Army and had been Airborne and was currently a helicopter pilot. My other brother had spent four years in the Air Force and had married a beautiful young French girl and was now working for an aviation company in California. That sounded like the road I wanted to take.

My buddy Ed and I enlisted in the Army and were sworn in at Fort Thomas, Kentucky. After we had taken the physical and battery of tests, we were called to the side and told that we had both scored very high on the test. We had an opportunity to join the ASA, and if we did, they would fly us to Columbia, South Carolina for Basic Training at Fort Jackson. They gave us all the assurances and that we would be able to stick together, but the only time we were together was for six months when Ed came TDY from Okinawa to Davis Station where I was permanently assigned.

I stayed in Vietnam for the remaining three years and three months of my ASA enlistment and got an early out on July 3, 1967, one day before my 22nd birthday. At that time, I had spent my 19th 20th and 21st birthdays in Vietnam. I had great assignments: six months TDY to SOG MACV, a year and a half at Davis Station, and the remainder with DODSPECREP. Like my Air Force brother, I brought home a beautiful young girl who I have been married to for 43 years.

I did it for $1.25 a year
By Jerry Frankenburger

I had been working as a lumberjack, and the snow got too deep to work in the woods and we ran out of timber at the mill, so I was laid off until the weather broke. I was hanging out in a pool hall with my buddy when the guy who owned a shoe store came in. He suggested that the two of us enlist in the service.

We said, "What's in it for us" and he said, "Five bucks if you go in."

So we drove to Lock Haven, Pennsylvania to the recruiter's office. On the way we decided to go into the Marines. However, the Marine recruiter was not in and so we talked to the Army recruiter and signed up. We went back to the poolroom and collected our five bucks.

The next morning we were on our way to Wilkes-Barre to be inducted. There I met Bobby Delver, the ASA recruiter. He gave me a sales pitch and asked if I would want to be a linguist and then went on with the pitch of how I would become the next James Bond or more like Matt Helm since Matt's an American. That sold me and off I went on an ASA tour. So the moral of my story is, I signed away four years of my life for a buck and a quarter a year. Go figure.

I was a Mercenary
By Lee Hendley

My story may break down to being a mercenary. I joined the Air Force at age 17 in 1956. After being in the Air Force for 14 years, and reaching the exalted rank of E-5 Staff Sergeant, I decided to make my break. I had been recruited, while in the Air Force, by the ASA equivalent, the Air Force Security Service. I was a Signal Intercept Maintenance Sgt.

In order to improve myself and to make more money than I could as an Air Force NCO, I applied for an Army program to become a Warrant Officer. Four months later I was discharged from the Air Force and sworn in at Goodfellow Air Force Base, Texas by an Army Captain named Hale. Thirty five days later I on-processed in at the 509th RR Group in the Republic of Vietnam! I was in the ASA! I was on-processed to the 224th Aviation Battalion and thence to the 138th Aviation Company at Phu Bai in early June, 1970.

After Vietnam I went on to the 326th Operations Company at Flak Kaserne in Augsburg, Federal Republic of Germany. After three years with the 326th I went to Ft. Devens as the Operations Officer for the 33S School, and retired on 30 June, 1976. My mercenary intent was satisfied. My retired pay as an Army CW2 is a hell of a lot better than it would've been as an Air Force Staff Sergeant.

Car guy turns Spy
By Skip Saurman

I graduated from high school in 1969 from the area vocational technical school where I was an A+ automotive student. My automotive instructor just happened to be an ASA alum and let loose with a story every now and then. Being a somewhat insecure teenager, I turned down a premier job at the local Cadillac dealership to join Uncle Sam's Home for Lost Boys - better known then as the US Army. Did I mention that my draft number was two?

I decided that I wanted to be in the Army Engineers as a heavy equipment mechanic. After taking the physical and extensive battery of tests, some important looking guy comes up to me and takes me into his office. Since your scores were so high, would you like to join the ASA? Of course, he talked about the civilian trench coat, concealed weapons, worldwide travel except Vietnam, of course, and all the other cloak and dagger BS. Well, I already knew about the ASA, or at least I thought I did.

As my class was finishing up 05D20 Special Identification Techniques Operator and 05D30 Special Identification Techniques Analyst classes a paper was passed around with a whole lot of duty stations listed. You got to pick your first, second, and third choice. We all looked at each other and said the last three classes had all gone to Vietnam so where do you think they're going to send us? Why not just check the box? We did, and they did. Every one of us went to Vietnam, except for one guy who somehow managed to end up in Hawaii. Go figure. Well, that's my story, and I'm sticking to it.

I Bought the Three Legged Race Horse
By James 'Barney' Reynolds

After finishing Electronic Technical School, I went to work in East Tennessee for Magnavox, which changed my draft status from student to 1A. Three months later I was told to report for my physical in Nashville. Two others and I rode the Greyhound bus to Nashville and had to stay overnight at the Noel Hotel.

One guy thought if he got drunk enough on beer, he would fail his physical. The next morning while standing in line he knocked over his specimen cup all over someone's paperwork. The Sergeant grabbed his papers and marked passed without any further exam. I was told I had passed and it would be about ten days before I would be drafted.

I went to check on Air Force and Navy and was told they were full. The Army recruiter said that I could sign up for three years in Nike missile repair in Huntsville, Alabama which was only 60 miles away from my home. The only problem he said was that if I worked on Nike missiles, I would also work on Hawk missiles and they were in Vietnam. But if I went to ASA for four years, I could get the best electronics school, be super-secret and the best thing - NO ASA in Vietnam! That was not a hard choice. I bought the three legged race horse.

After Fort Gordon Signal School and 33G, DF and ECM at Devens, 11 out of 14 of us went to Vietnam. Looking back, my only regrets are some dumb decisions I made in Vietnam. ASA gave this Tennessee country boy an opportunity to travel, make lifelong friends in Germany, work and be associated with so many great people. I'm glad I bought that horse! It was a good ride!

No Marching, Running, Digging, KP or Washing Tanks

By Lon Ludwig

After two years at a pretty good college in upstate New York, years I would really like to forget, the Dean of Students suggested I leave his college and consider the military. The Air Force ROTC professor suggested I seriously consider the Army. What the hell, those classes, the few I went to, were interfering with beer and lacrosse anyhow.

In early August, 1961, I went to Troy, New York and enlisted. I took the physical, passed simple tests including the Morse code test and since I got good scores, I had the inevitable interview with the ASA recruiter. He was an over-aged SFC getting one last punch in his ticket before retirement. He explained ASA to me not in terms of Vietnam, but in terms of the lack of marching, running, digging, KP and washing tanks.

On September 11, 1961, I raised my hand and was off to Fort Dix for Basic Training. I went to Fort Devens and became a 058. I made a stop at the Oakland Army Terminal on the way to Davis Station. The couple of weeks at White Birch convinced my Trick Chief that I really wasn't kidding when I told him that I wasn't very good at copying code. By mid-September, I was on my way to Da Nang. We had a good crew in Da Nang. Four months later we packed it all up and moved to Phu Bai. We lived in the buildings that have often been referred to as 'The Old French Barracks' which were brand-new in January, 1962.

Because of my Dang Second Cousin
By Ivan Riggle

I graduated from high school in June, 1965. I was working as a forester for six months when I got my draft notice. My family did not have enough money to send me to college so I could get a deferment. I had a second cousin who was in ASA. He talked me into four years to avoid the draft. Does that make me a draft dodger?

The recruiter said there was no ASA in Vietnam. So what if I have to spend four years wearing civilian clothes, eluding spies that are trying to pry secret information from my sealed lips. I could certainly resist their hot young bodies and reveal nothing that would endanger the USA! So, I signed up. Then I went to Ft. Devens, and the Direction Finding School. The next thing I knew I was getting shot at manning our perimeter during the 1968 Tet Offensive.

Daaammm! Do you think the recruiter lied to me?

Master Sergeant Told Me I'd be Working on Secret Missions

By Lucky Rupp

In the spring of my senior year a group from the local National Guard outfit, the 104th Armored Cavalry, came to the school recruiting seniors to join. They took us out to the local Armory and gave us rides in an M4 tank; took us through a wooded field and ran over trees and everything. That was it! I was going into Armor. I wanted to be a machine gunner in a tank.

I went to the induction center in September, 1962 having just turned 18 and enlisted. After taking tests a Master Sergeant interviewed me and asked if I would consider anything else than Armor. My test scores were high enough to qualify for anything but a cook or radio repairman because I am colorblind.

I said, "No, I want to be in a tank." Then he suggested ASA.

I said, "What's that?"

He said, "I can't tell you, it's classified." He told me I'd have to get a Top-Secret Clearance and I'd be working on a lot of secret missions.

So, (the dumb ass that I was) I said, "Sure, sign me up." My first choice though was a tank.

Couldn't get MI in the Marines or Air Force
By Robert Flanagan

In early 1960 I was living in Sacramento, California, having moved there from my Mississippi home in search of work in one of the aircraft industry plants. I served seven years in the Marines in the infantry, artillery, and eventually in aviation electronics. I wanted to transfer to military intelligence in some form, but the Corps said they spent too much money training me in electronics; I'd never get there. When my enlistment was up, I appealed to the re-enlistment office, but they were adamant. So I left the Corps.

After some 15 months pursuing non-existent job opportunities, I was ready for military service again. I checked with the Marines: sure, you can come back as a Sergeant with all 35 months time-in-grade to make E-5, but you'll still be a 6641, a radar tech. The Air Force would take me, but they only wanted me in a relevant radar tech MOS and would consider nothing else. I didn't talk to the Navy; I'd done Navy bases and ships, and I knew I didn't look good in bell bottoms. So I went to the dreaded Army, so derided during my Marine service. As a former Marine, with high battery scores and in good physical condition, they offered me 'anything we have,' according to the Sergeant First Class recruiter.

I said I wanted military intelligence. The recruiter was straight brown-boot Army, and didn't know from MI. When he asked just what I sought, I described something near to his meager knowledge of CIC counterintelligence, and what he explained, sounded good to me: snooping after spies, wearing a cloak, carrying a rusty penknife.

I said, "Yes."

Sacramento promptly sent me to Oakland on a bus for testing and physical, and to meet a board for the CIC. Got tested and probed,

16

but was told I'd have to return to Sacramento and wait the convening of a board.

In the meantime, I had no job. I had a wife, and a 15-month-old baby boy, but no job. I was anxious to get enlisted, get some pay started, and conveyed this attitude to the recruiter. He said he would do anything he could do to help.

And in a surprise move, in three days he called to tell me, "Bob, you're in luck. I know you wanted CIC, but all I'm hearing is that the board may only meet once a month and it could be weeks for you. It just so happened that a recruit I had lined up for an ASA slot, due to leave for Basic in the next few days, was involved in a traffic accident and has some broken stuff. He's out. So I have an open ASA slot, available right now. You got everything done and could go as soon as tomorrow or when you're ready."

My reply: "What's an ASA?"

"Well, it's another one of those MI groups, sort of like CIC, except you don't have to meet a board."

He told me I would go to further training in the States after Basic, and I made the choice to take it. To this day, I don't believe the recruiter was shanghaiing me; I don't think he had a clue as to what/who ASA was, what or how they did it, or anything related to it.

I didn't have to take Basic at all, either. I took the graduating infantry recruit test, passed it with flying colors, and sat around in the Casual Company for three weeks, awaiting orders for Fort Devens, where, with all the doors open to me there, I held out for 058 School. Well, no one ever said I was smart in all these shenanigans.

Chapter 2

The Early Years 1961-1965

The Army Security Agency arrived in Vietnam in May, 1961, at the earlier order of President John F. Kennedy. The South Vietnamese Army was having a great deal of difficulty locating the Viet Cong to fight them. The Viet Cong chose the time and place to fight and then disappeared. Within six months after arriving in Vietnam the ASA group had located major Viet Cong commands throughout Vietnam and surrounding countries. The stories here are from that early time period. Early ASA surroundings were rustic military quarters in tents with dirt floors. These quarters were common to many ASA units as the war progressed.

Davis Station had permanent structures that can be best described as 'corn cribs' after the storage building in many Mid Western states. They were basically wooden buildings with rain slats on the side walls, wooden floors and a slate roof. Walls were screens to keep the bugs out. At the end of the war the North Vietnamese used Davis Station as a headquarters and called the buildings primitive. They were good enough for ASA troops and much better than tents during the war.

Off the Plane and into Saigon
By Gary Spivey

It was 4 July, 1964, my first day in Vietnam. I had scarcely checked in at Davis Station when some friends whom I had met at ASA school at Fort Devens, and who had arrived before me, asked me to come to town with them. 'Town' was Saigon, the Pearl of the Orient. As the taxi made its way through the wide boulevard lined with tropical trees and congested with a battalion of bicycles and every other form of transportation, I could see why it was called that. To my small-town eyes, it was beautiful and exotic.

I had been briefed on the danger, of course. The terrorists were always blowing up something, most recently a movie theater frequented by GIs. But, like every one of our age, my companions and I felt invulnerable. We soon were to find out that we weren't. Within the year, twelve Americans would be killed when a Claymore mine exploded at a popular floating restaurant, and one of my barracks mates would be injured. The terrorists blended with the local population. They could be anybody, including our taxi driver.

Our destination was Tu Do Street, which stretched a mile or so from the twin-spired Notre Dame Cathedral on the northwest to the broad Saigon River, an ocean port, on the southeast. It was the site of several first class hotels, cafés, shops, movie theaters and, bars that catered to lonely GIs.

After changing money on the black market at the Indian bookstore, where the exchange rate was much better than the never used official rate, we entered a side street and walked into a narrow hole-in-the-wall with a long bar in front and a few tables in the back. Ceiling fans turned lazily overhead, providing a small measure of relief from the steamy heat of the rainy season. Behind the bar, talking with customers on bar stools were a dozen or so of the loveliest young women that I had ever seen.

One of my brothers saw me catch my breath. He explained that this was a respectable bar, not a front for a brothel like some bars near the base. The bar girls were nice girls who offered pleasant conversation but nothing else.

He led me to the bar and introduced me to one of the girls, who offered me a handshake, which was more touching of the flesh than traditional Vietnamese culture would allow. She was demure in her silken *ao dai*, the traditional Vietnamese wide-legged pants covered by a long sleeved tunic split along its sides. Her glossy black hair hung loosely to her waist.

I talked with her and nursed a *Ba Moui Ba* beer as she sipped a 'Saigon whiskey,' the weak shot-glass size tea that customers were expected to buy for the girls in exchange for their company. She taught me how to pronounce her name and asked me about my work in the Army. I gave her the standard lie.

She spoke English fairly well, sprinkled with some common French words ('beaucoup') and GI slang ('same-same' for the same as). She had trouble pronouncing some English words, especially those ending with s or z sounds. The word Vietnamese became *Vietnamee*.

Easy to talk with, she told me that she lived with her mother and other family members in Saigon while her father served in the Army in the outlying provinces. She hoped to find work in the office of an American company once her English had improved sufficiently. I told her about myself and my plans to study to become a lawyer once I left the service. '*Ong trang-su*' (Mr. Lawyer) she called me, with a hint of tease.

Too soon, my friends told me that we have a lot more to see and that it was time to move on.

Although I could not have known it at the time, I was destined to spend the next three years in Vietnam. The days that were to come would bring a rush of new experiences and new memories. The memory of that first day has survived through it all, and over all the years that have followed, and returns every Independence Day.

James Thomas Davis and Christmas of 1961

By Gary Spivey

Christmas of 1961 was a carefree time for me. Home from college for the holidays, I was seeing Christmas through the enchanted eyes of my three-year-old brother, the product of my mother's remarriage after eight years of widowhood. Even with college expenses, I had extra money in my pocket from a well-paying summer job to buy special presents for the little guy and other family members.

School was going well as I recovered from a sophomore slump, and my grade point average and enthusiasm for my studies were growing in tandem. A Yankees fan from childhood, I was still basking in the afterglow of the Mantle - Maris's home run race and the Yankees' World Series victory. My social life was as complete as I wanted at the time. In short, life was good

I knew little about Vietnam. If prodded, I probably could have told you that the French had lost Indochina at Dien Bien Phu. And I knew that the country of Vietnam had been divided like Korea, with the communist North and a free South. From Reader's Digest, I had heard about Dr. Tom Dooley and how he had helped many Northerners escape to the South, becoming known as something of a savior and a saint in the process.

But I didn't just know that American servicemen were in South Vietnam, assisting the new government. Or that just three days before Christmas a young Tennessee soldier named James Thomas Davis had become, as the President would later describe him, 'the first American to fall in defense of our freedom in Vietnam.' Knowing nothing of these events, I could not have imagined that I too was destined to serve in Vietnam in the same unit as the one in which Tom Davis had served, or that Tom Davis would become a part of my life forever.

After completing basic military training, Tom had been selected to join the Army Security Agency, a top secret organization that picked its recruits from high scorers on a battery of aptitude tests. The military arm of the civilian National Security Agency, the ASA's mission was to intercept and analyze the enemy telecommunications and to protect our own telecommunications from being intercepted by the enemy.

Tom had been trained at the ASA School in Fort Devens, Massachusetts, as a Radio Direction Finding Intercept Operator. Radio Direction Finding (RDF) (which turned out to be my military specialty too) was one of several communications intelligence weapons in the ASA arsenal. Tom's job was to listen for enemy radio transmission as he traversed the countryside in a specially equipped ¾ ton truck. When he picked up the signal, he would plot a line on a map from his location in the direction from which the signal originated. Another team working the same target nearby would plot a second line, and where the two lines intersected would show the location of the enemy transmitter.

Tom's unit, the 3rd Radio Research Unit (3rd RRU), had been dispatched to Vietnam in May, 1961, by President Kennedy in one of America's first acts of commitment to the support of South Vietnam, against the Vietcong communist insurgency supported by North Vietnam. President Kennedy had deployed the ASA to Vietnam in keeping with his inaugural promise to "bear any burden, meet any hardship, support any friend, and oppose any foe." Our resolve was being tested, he said "and Vietnam is the place."

Adopting the motto, 'first in, last out,' the unit settled into a compound next to the runway of Tan Son Nhut Air Base on the northwestern perimeter of Saigon. A converted airline hangar on the runway served as the operations center for the unit.

Tom was proud to be there and to carry on a family tradition of military service. "I don't feel too badly about having to be here," he wrote to his father, a World War II veteran "when I think of all the potential good it will have for this country." The presence of the Army Security Agency in Vietnam was a secret. The 3rd RRU was a cover name for the 82nd USASA Special Operations Unit, and the soldiers of the unit wore no ASA insignia. ASA troops reported to an ASA officer, not to the regular Army Chain of Command, and local commanders were not even allowed inside ASA facilities.

On the morning of Friday, December 22, 1961, Tom set out for his final mission. He was riding in the shotgun seat of the truck, next to his Vietnamese driver. Nine other Army of the Republic of Vietnam troops - RDF signalmen and a small security detail - were in the back. As they proceeded west on a provincial highway outside Duc Hoa, about ten miles northwest of Saigon, their eyes scoured their surroundings. Enemy activity in the area had been increasing and another RDF team had only narrowly escaped a recent ambush attempt.

Tom could not have known, and none of us knew until much later, that the communist military command in the area had ordered strong action against the RDF teams because of their success in disrupting guerrilla operations.

We can only speculate about what thoughts were in Tom's mind that morning. Christmas is a hard time for a soldier to be away from home, and Tom must have missed his family, especially with an infant daughter experiencing Christmas without him. Surely he thought about his little sister, who was celebrating her birthday that same day. The true meaning of Christmas almost certainly was on his mind since, as a buddy recalled, Tom was often seen with a Bible in his hands.

Shortly before noon, a remote-controlled landmine detonated under the tailgate of the truck. The troops in the back were assaulted by

Vietcong guerrillas with rifle and machine gun fire and hand grenades as they attempted to escape the vehicle, which had come to rest in a culvert at the side of the road.

Tom kept his wits, scrambling from the cab. He hurled his satchel, containing his secret communications codes, into a rice paddy to prevent the codes from falling into the hands of the enemy. He pulled his injured driver into the culvert where the driver concealed himself in the water beneath the truck.

Tom ran up the gravel road, turning and firing his M-1 carbine as he went, and in an effort to draw enemy fire to himself and away from his driver and the other team members. At a position about 50 feet in front of the vehicle, he was hit by a bullet that pierced his skull, lacerating his brain and killing him instantly. Only the driver survived, and from him we know of Tom's valor.

The body of the first American to die in combat in Vietnam was recovered more than an hour later in the first mission flown by a newly arrived American helicopter unit.

Two weeks later, the 3rd RRU compound was given the name Davis Station. I served there through three Christmases, beginning in 1964. Through it all, a portrait of Tom Davis stared down on my comrades and me from its place of honor, reminding us of our mortality - a reminder that was painfully reinforced one night in April, 1966, when a mortar and rocket attack on Davis Station took the life of another of our brothers.

Many Christmas seasons have come and gone since that event in 1961. Like thousands of others, I went to Vietnam, did my duty and returned home safely. While not without its sorrows, life has continued to be good to me. The Christmas enchantment that I saw in the eyes of my little brother in 1961, I now have seen in the eyes of my own sons and grandson.

Among life's many blessings have been the friendships forged in Vietnam and the comradeship with those who served there. And I'm especially grateful that I have come to know the family of James Thomas Davis. They have welcomed me into their home, and shared many memories with me and stood with me at Tom's grave. For them, as for me, the love of God and country is more than a slogan.

Through the Davis family, I have come to know Tom as well. I have walked the streets of his hometown, have seen the site of the family drugstore where he worked as a boy, the hills where he hiked and hunted, and the football stadium named in his honor by the school where he won his letter as a defensive halfback and was crowned the Harvest King. I've seen the family home where he grew up and where he lay in state in January, 1962.

Despite the passing of the years, Tom Davis remains forever young in our hearts, just as we remain young in our memories - forever the boys of Davis Station. May God's love bless Tom Davis and all the boys at Davis Station, his loved ones and ours, at this Christmas time – and always.

The Early Years
By Thomas B. Rowe

It was early 1961 and I was a senior in high school. The new President, John F. Kennedy, was making his inaugural speech which set forth the tenets of what would encompass his presidency:

"Let every nation know, whether it wishes us well or ill, that we shall pay any price, bear any burden, meet any hardship, support any friend, oppose any foe to assure the survival and success of liberty. This much we pledge - and more."

While a junior in high school, I joined the US Naval Reserve, as my older brother had done before me. Our dad was in the Navy during World War II and we were following the tradition. After the Bay of Pigs fiasco, I decided that President Kennedy was going to get us into a war soon, so, I joined the Army to get out of the Naval Reserve.

I had an established active duty date and would have to be in the Army 60 days before that date. That meant I would have to leave high school early. The principal of the school said I would get my diploma anyway because I was joining the military. I enlisted and had a career option choice for the Army Security Agency. After Basic Training, I was off to Fort Devens, Massachusetts, for advanced training. I went through a number of communications intelligence procedures and obtained a Top-Secret Crypto clearance.

As we learned later, a group of U. S. Army personnel had arrived in Vietnam in civilian clothing in a clandestine operation to set up an intelligence gathering operation. No one, not even the men's families, knew of this operation.

At the end of our training, I received orders for Korea. Then on December 22, 1961, there was an announcement that an American soldier, Specialist 4 James Thomas Davis, had been killed in Vietnam. The Army notified three of us we would be going on a classified assignment and we could not tell anyone where we were going.

We were given a one-week leave and sent home for Christmas. The secrecy orders notwithstanding, I told my parents and then went to see my grandfather, John Pearce Rowe, who was on his deathbed. I told him about my great adventure. I'm so happy I did because he died shortly thereafter.

We were issued official passports that stated, *'The bearer is abroad on an official assignment of the United States government.'* This was heady stuff for a 19-year-old who a few months earlier was a high school student. We were taken to a large clothing store and allowed to spend $200 on civilian clothing. This may not seem like much now but I bought four suits, a dozen white shirts, numerous ties and other clothing.

We arrived at Tan Son Nhut Air Base just outside of Saigon on January 13, 1962, wearing suits and ties. It was so hot most of us took off our jackets and ties before we reached the bottom of the stairs coming off the plane. Military trucks immediately took us to a secure area where we found we were not going to be housed in hotels like the earlier personnel but in tents without floors with just four showerheads for 200 men. The cooks were military, and we, the lower ranking personnel, had to clean up after the cooks. It really broke our spirits for this clandestine assignment when it was declassified and we were ordered into uniform.

Called the Paris of the Orient or the Pearl of the Orient, Saigon was beautiful then - with stately old trees more than a hundred feet high lining the large boulevards. The city was clean, neat, and well kept. During the rainy season, it rained every afternoon between 1:30 and 2:30 PM and all the shops closed for siesta. They stayed closed for a couple of hours and would reopen until 8 or 9 PM along with the bars and restaurants.

A friend of mine rented an apartment near the main gate of Tan Son Nhut for $20 a month. It had two bedrooms with a living room and a kitchen. A beer in a bar cost a dime and imported American beers were 20 cents. After working in the hangar all day, a five-mile taxi ride into Saigon cost about a dime. I could go to Saigon, have a good meal in a nice French restaurant, hit several bars, and return to the tent with a dirt floor, and spend less than five dollars. When I was reassigned to Vietnam four years later, the ride to Saigon cost that much alone.

The city was alive with French culture, fine dining and an active nightlife. Then along came Mme. Ngu, the wife of the Minister of Security and the sister-in-law of the president of Vietnam. She was the surrogate first lady of the country. She engineered the passage of morality laws. No Vietnamese woman was allowed to walk down the street with a foreigner; closing times were put on the bars, restaurants and nightclubs; rock 'n roll music was banned along with dancing. These laws were aimed directly at us. They were mostly ignored but they did cause some problems for us and the women we knew.

I started a friendship with security guards Bobby Scott Ashmore, Linus Bledsoe and Charlie Pulliam. One night we were out drinking. I had to go back to Tan Son Nhut to work later that day and needed some sleep and to sober up. Pulliam remained in Saigon and went to an eight story hotel with the restaurant on the top floor. He mistakenly got off on the seventh floor. The elevator had a collapsing grate work, sort of like the gates we now used to prevent babies from falling down stairs. Pulliam realized he had gotten off on the wrong floor and, as he stuck his head through the grate to look down, the elevator came down and decapitated him. This was my first, but not the last, loss of a dear friend in Vietnam.

I remained there until December, 1962, and then took a transfer to Okinawa. Less than a year later, JFK was assassinated in Dallas. At the time of his death, there were about 16,000 American servicemen in Vietnam. I was sent back to Vietnam in August, 1966, and remained there until January, 1968. A third tour started in January, 1969, and ended in October, 1970, totaling four years in Vietnam. By the time I finally left, costs had skyrocketed, and the once beautiful city was literally a war zone. It was dirty, noisy and dangerous. By then more than 52,000 American had died there, including six of my friends.

October, 1962

By Ken Hoggard

One Sunday evening, October 21, 1962, I managed to sneak back into Fort Devens despite increased security. I had no idea what that increased security was all about, and I was leaving the next morning, the 22nd, for San Francisco on my way to Vietnam. The entire 058 class of about 14 was all on our way to Vietnam. We arrived at Oakland Army Base, stowed our gear and were given a pass. Our orders were to be back by midnight because they told us we were shipping out the next day by a charter airline.

Most of us took off for Fisherman's Wharf. We were a mixed crew of guys ranging in age from 18 years nine months (me) to some guys in their mid-20s. I was a hick from St. Louis, Missouri, not very worldly, so I was excited to visit the landmark area that I had heard about. The New York Giants had moved there in 1958. We wandered around a bit and then we stopped at this restaurant for a meal. It was a fancy place as I recall but we were early so it wasn't too crowded and we all sat together.

As I sat looking at the menu not understanding half of the things on it, the waitress came around and asked us if we wanted a cocktail. Unfortunately, she came to me first. I quickly glanced at the menu and ordered the first cocktail I saw. Unfortunately, it was an oyster cocktail. Boy was I surprised! Others ordered beers and a Rob Roy, I remember. When the cocktails were delivered I sat there staring at this cocktail glass full of snotty looking crap that turned out to be oysters! Not wanting anyone else to know how dumb my choice was, I managed to choke them down. It was not a very good start to the evening.

After the meal we went over to some bar which I don't remember the name of, but it was pretty large and they were willing to serve me beer, so things were looking up. There was a lot of buzz about President Kennedy making a speech and it was coming on the TV in the bar.

We were there a couple of hours and some guys talked to us about who we were and what we were doing. And of course, we didn't let on about who we were or where we were going or what we did. They later identified themselves as some government folks who were checking on military personnel. I'm not sure if they were military or not. We had a few beers and went back to base uneventfully. I'm pretty sure Soldati, Hodge, and Simkins were among the group but don't recall the names of the others.

Next morning we were off to the airport and got on a beautiful DC-6 four engine prop operated by Riddle Airlines and left for Hawaii. That flight took a while and after refueling in Hawaii, we took off for Wake Island, then Guam, then onto the Philippines, and eventually landed in Saigon. I remember calculating that it took 46 hours from the time we left San Francisco until we stepped off the plane at Tan Son Nhut. Having left October 23, 1962, and flying for nearly two days, and crossing the International Date Line, we arrived on October 25, 1962.

No time was wasted as there were a lot of guys who were getting short and they needed replacements so we went to work the next day. It was then I discovered that I knew nothing about code! They sat me down to train with somebody copying a Viet Cong radio. It sounded like he was under water beating on an oil drum from inside. If it wasn't for Glen Freerksen I would have probably wound up as a cook because I really was lost. Eventually, I started to get the hang of it and the rest as they say is history!

Twenty - six months later I arrived back in San Francisco on New Year's Eve, 1964 and went to my first topless bar, but that is another story.

The Classified Beer Run

By Dave Siegfried

It was in the fall of 1962 and I had been at the 9th ASA Field Station on Clark Air Base in the Philippines since the middle of January. It was the very early days in Vietnam and Tom Davis had just been killed in Vietnam right before I got to the Philippines. It was then that I found out that there was a courier plane that circumnavigated the globe each day picking up and dropping off diplomatic packages for the government.

I was the Morning Report Clerk at the time. The Sergeant Major from Operations was talking to the First Sergeant about something he needed to be done. It seems that the guys we had sent TDY to Phu Bai to help get the operation started there were getting antsy. There were, as I remember, 15-20 people, mostly PFC's and E-4's with a few NCOs and a Lieutenant or two in Viet Nam. They had been promised that they wouldn't have to stay long but it seems like things weren't going well and they were going to be there over Christmas.

Anyway, there was a promise made to get each guy a case of San Miguel beer. Nobody seemed to think it was a problem. The First Sergeant said something like, "Siegfried, here's the money; you take care of getting the beer and we will see that it gets there."

It didn't seem like there was going to be much of an issue; I went out and bought a case of beer for each guy and had it packed up on a skid and then everything started going off track. It seems we couldn't just stick it on an airplane and send it to Phu Bai since everything, name, location, etc., about the mission was classified. Besides that, there was the usual suspicion about Air Force guys stealing the booze.

Well, the Sergeant Major and the First Sergeant got together with an E-6 or E-7 Criminal Investigation Division (CID) or MI guy; I'm not sure what he did. He wore a uniform around our unit but he and his clerk had diplomatic passports that I kept in the safe and a big civilian clothing allowance. Anyway, I think he was the guy who came up with that idea to send the beer as a diplomatic package.

So that's what we did. We packed it up better, concealed the address, put a guard on it, and made out the necessary diplomatic paperwork and sent it on its way. I know that it went on the flight because I was the last guard before the plane picked it up and we got a message back that not a bottle was broken.

Phu Bai, the Early Days

By Bruce York

We got to Phu Bai in June, 1963; there were seven of us, all fresh out of Fort Devens, brand-new 058's, or NUGS as we were known to the other guys. Our first impression was that we were now at the end of the world. Phu Bai was still mostly under construction and it was hot, dirty and dusty. The seven of us were assigned to sleep in a six man tent as the barracks were not yet ready for us. The tents were small for seven or eight guys so we had to climb over each other.

Another thing we noticed while we were in the tents was that there was a bunch of ARVN troops running around in the valley behind us. We were not sure what was going on but they were all carrying their weapons and looking very serious. We were advised that they were ARVN basic trainees practicing squad maneuvers and stuff.

After a few days we were allowed to move into the new barracks, which were later called The Old French Barracks, by newer ASA guys around 1968. There was no air conditioning, only ceiling fans and screens on the windows with wooden shutters. We were soon assigned to a working Trick and went to work. The Operations building was not yet finished so we were working out of the old communication vans. Of course, there was no air conditioning and so if it was 100° outside, it was at least 120° inside with all electronic gear and a few fans to blow the hot air around; we learned to sweat very well. That was the main reason that at Phu Bai the work uniform was only a T-shirt and your pants. Soon we were listening to the Viet Cong and North Vietnamese targets and passing on our work to the NSA for analysis.

We had a little theater when I first got to Phu Bai that was a sheet hung between two metal poles that we could run old movies on. We had old shipping crates and wire spool reels to sit on and watch the same movies over and over again. We would trade movies with units from Da Nang whenever we could and the skies were clear enough to fly.

Another thing of interest at Phu Bai in the early days was the night fire that would go on around us. On the back side of Phu Bai was a big valley where the ARVN had several ammo dumps dug into the hillside. Every now and then the VC would try to get into these ammo bunkers and the whole valley would light up with tracer fire. We would sit and watch the fireworks from a back door.

Another item of interest was that on the south side of the unit was an ARVN firebase with 155 howitzers which the ARVN would crank up and fire onto the Ho Chi Minh trail whenever they detected traffic on the trail. Of course the 155 can make a hell of a big noise and shake the ground pretty well. One night about 3 AM they turned that 155 north and fired a round right over our barracks roof. Well, at 3 AM that puppy blew us all out of our racks and I was sure we were taking rocket fire or something. Guys were jumping out of the racks grabbing weapons, helmets and looking for cover. I'm sure I came about 5 feet out of my bunk. As it turned out, other than shaking the walls and roof and scaring the hell out of us, it was only the ARVN shooting down the road at another conflict.

My barracks was about ten feet from the EM club, and my bunk was right near the main window of the EM club, so every night we would listen to the ASA drunks drinking into the early morning hours singing such great songs as Him, Him, Fuck Him; this would go on until about 2 AM. At last we would hear the bartender call last call for alcohol, and we could finally get some sleep.

Back in that day, we didn't have a basketball court but we could walk down to the MAAG Phu Bai, which was about a mile or so down the road, and use their basketball court. The MAAG guys were advisers to the ARVN troops in the area, and they had a very nice court so we would get a bunch of guys and walk down to the court to play for a couple hours. One day after our game we were coming back to our compound to take a shower and get cleaned up only to find out there was no water at Phu Bai. It seems that the guy who was in charge of the water station at Phu Bai got a Dear John letter from his wife or girlfriend, and went nuts and took an ax to the water station and chopped many of the water pipes.

Well, it took several days to get the water station parts from Da Nang and get us back up and running. So we had a couple sweaty and stinky days waiting to get a shower. The last we heard of the water station guy was that he was in handcuffs and taken to Da Nang for court-martial.

One nice thing during the early days at 3rd RRU Det J was that we could go to town most any time we were not working. We did have to be back at 6 PM because the roads were closed at night. The City of Hue was about 7 miles from Phu Bai and had a nice river running through it.

In the traditional way of the ASA we had to establish ourselves at a couple of bars. There were two main bars for us; the nice one was called the Fresh Bar, where the nice girls were, and the infamous Green Door Bar where the hookers worked. In the Green Door Bar was a gal named Mumbles. She was a French and Viet mix with a speech problem, so whenever new guys came to town we would try to send them to see Mumbles at the Green Door. They had some very interesting stories to pass on back at the base. Later I found out that Hue was put OFF-LIMITS, and nobody could go and see Mumbles. Of course, all of Hue and that area was a major battlefield during the Tet Offensive and many people were killed.

Well, my time at Phu Bai ended in August, 1964, about ten days after the Gulf of Tonkin incident. I was working that night when all hell broke loose in the Ops building, with officers and NCOs running all over the place. But my time was up and I was too short to care. I was off to the 14th ASA Field Station in Japan where life was, oh, so sweet.

Just Another Day
By Harlan Olson

This morning while taking a shower, I started to reminisce about my youth and my thoughts carried me to early 1964 at the 3rd RRU. I remember dressing in civvies and standing at the front gate outside Davis Station and waiting for the dong cart to come by for ride to the main gate of Tan Son Nhut Air Base and then hailing a taxi for a ride to downtown Saigon. What I didn't remember was going to the orderly room and getting a pass. Were we supposed to?

I then thought about the times CJ, Bennie Byrd, Steve Siebel and I would go downtown, and CJ dragging us from bar to bar, introducing us to all sorts of sin. Anyhow, we ended up at the Bristol Bar where this young lady took a fancy to me. I know she liked me because she kept asking me to buy her tea and then later she asked me to walk her home.

Early the next morning, she woke me up saying there was something bad going on. There were low-flying Sky Raiders flying overhead. We could also hear gunfire off in the distance. She motioned me to come quickly and led me outside to the street and motioned for a taxi. She spoke to the driver in Vietnamese for a minute or two. He didn't say much, only nodded his head. I remember wishing I could understand what was being said. She handed him a 500 P note and off we went, but we weren't on the normal routes back to Tan Son Nhut that I had become familiar with.

I'm thinking I'm in big trouble. How am I going to get back on base? Get back on base! How do I know this guy isn't taking me over the Bien Hoa Bridge? That was forbidden territory. Am I going to die?

After some time, he pulled up to the perimeter fence of Tan Son Nhut, but on the far side of Davis Station; I could see hangers and other buildings and he was pointing to a hole in the fence. He was motioning me with his arm outstretched, palm down and the forefingers flicking towards the hole. He wanted me to hurry.

I jumped out of the taxi and scrambled through the hole in the fence and walked maybe 50 yards or so and was out in the open where I could get my bearings. There's the control tower and I spotted the helicopter pad and the back fence to Davis Station, but it was a good half to three quarters of a mile away. I hoped the door in the fence was unlocked; if I could get through the fence, my hooch was right there.

Oh crap! I thought to myself. I'm in so much trouble! CJ, why the heck did you leave me in town?

I had to cross a runway to get there; I thought sure the tower folks were going to spot me and they would call the MPs and my ass would be grass. What the hell! I started walking expecting half a dozen MP jeeps to come racing out to nab me. I made it halfway, I was in plain sight of the tower, and I could see people moving around behind the glass, but no MP activity, YET! So I pressed on and made it to the door in the fence. I turned the handle and it opened! I then went to the back door to my hooch, no one was there. I quickly changed into my fatigues.

Now what? I took a deep breath and stepped out the front door. I saw some guys milling around near the front gate outside the EM club, all in uniform. I walked over and joined the group; it appeared I wasn't missed. WHEW!

So for the next couple hours we continued to watch the RVN fighters make diving passes at various things. I didn't see any bombs dropped or their guns fired.

It was just another day in the Republic of Vietnam.

Torii Station to Vietnam

By Robert Miller

I entered the Army on October 31, 1963, in St. Louis, Missouri. I was sent to Fort Leonard Wood, Missouri for Basic Training. In February, 1964, I was sent to Fort Gordon, Georgia for a communications school. I learned how to set up different encryption machines, how to set up a communication network, and how to type thirty five words a minute.

In the summer of 1963 I'd taken flying lessons and wanted to pursue a career in flying. In fact I took my last flying lesson at Fort Gordon. That was the day I flew backwards. I went to the local Army flying club at Fort Gordon and asked to take a flying lesson. I thought I was good as I had all of 30 or so hours flying time and had flown solo.

It was a windy Sunday someplace near Augusta, Georgia. The instructor told me to head into the wind and to stall the Piper Cub. I headed into the wind and pulled back on the stick and waited for the Piper Cub to stall but nothing happened. I started to lose altitude, and nothing on the horizon started to change. After a short time the instructor asked me why was I not stalling the airplane and my comment was, "I'm trying!"

Then I looked out the window and saw the land going backwards from the direction that I was heading. I have no idea what my thoughts were at the time or what I said to the instructor but it was the last flight I had as a student pilot.

After graduation from the US Army Southeastern Signal School in the summer of 1964, I took off for Travis Air Force Base, California, for a flight to Okinawa. I landed at Kadena Air Force Base on Okinawa.

I was stationed at Torii Station - a small post that overlooked the main airbase and was on a gently sloping hill. Torii Station was a small post with probably no more than 1500 to 2000 personnel; but it was important. Located there was the Joint Sobe Processing Center (JSPC) which was a clearinghouse for all SIGINT and ELINT intelligence collected in the Pacific. There was also a CIA group located there that did many of the analytical functions of turning raw data into useful intelligence for decision-makers. The post was primarily staffed by Army personnel, but there were also Air Force, Navy and Marines stationed there as this was the regional processing center for the Pacific Theater.

The first time I walked into the Communications Center at JSPC was an experience I shall never forget. There were over 100 teletype machines running; and they made quite a lot of noise. There were also bells and buzzers continuously going off and they did not stop until a quality control operator turned them off. There was a special gong for a critic communication and I assure you that you didn't miss a gong. This was by far the most pressure-packed place I have ever been in. The night after the first day in the Communications Center everyone wakes up with nightmares. I don't know why, but everyone does.

The Communications Center at JSPC in 1964 was an interesting place to be as you were able to see a war start to unfold. In August, we had the Desoto Patrols off North Vietnam. Then there were the Blue Springs Missions which were unmanned reconnaissance drone flights over China. This was such a hush-hush operation that the messages for the planning of these flights were encrypted before they came into the Communications Center, a very unusual procedure.

It was during one of the Blue Springs missions that the drone was shot down. This created a mass of critic and flash traffic between JSPC and Washington. I was working the map unit on the send aisle on this day when I noticed that some of the messages were going to some of our allies - the British, Australians, and someone else as I recollect. I took three or four of these messages up to the Sergeant-in-Charge. Under the circumstances speed was critical and they did not have time to encrypt the messages before they came to the Communications Center. The Sergeant was very pleased to stop the messages before they went out to our allies and spilled the beans.

In October, 1964, I was working in the back room of the Communications Center and I had to count all the message groups that the CIA was using to talk on-line with Washington. It was during this time that China was getting ready to set off their first nuclear bomb and much of this on-line traffic dealt with that subject. Our intelligence was so good that we actually knew 24 hours in advance as to when the Chinese would set off their first nuclear bomb. The key reason for this was that we had weather flights between the Philippines and Okinawa on a regular basis. We thus knew when the winds aloft would be favorable for blowing in the 'right' direction (towards Russia in this case) for China to detonate the bomb.

Nineteen sixty five was another busy year at JSPC. Major events included: the sapper attacks on Pleiku Airfield and Camp Holloway, the bombing of the US barracks at Qui Nhon in Central Vietnam, the start of Operation Rolling Thunder and the bombing missions over North Vietnam, the ARC LIGHT Operations - B-52 missions over South Vietnam and Laos. In March or April a Lieutenant Colonel Odiker came to the Comm. Center and was talking on-line with Washington about the transfer of the 173rd Airborne Brigade to Vietnam, which took place in May.

It was also during 1965 that the Comm. Center shut down to nothing but operational immediate, flash, lateral critic and critic traffic as we had four or five incidents happen that day. A Russian freighter rammed a submerged US submarine near Haiphong harbor. The Chinese sent a squadron of fighters towards Da Nang from Hainan Island and there were some other incidents. I think we had five critics and an untold number of flash messages that had the military and the CIA in crisis mode.

In October, 1965, I left Okinawa for Fort Bragg, North Carolina. It was there that I found out my next duty station would be Vietnam. The next four months were hectic as we were getting all the equipment ready for shipment, and going through training for deployment to a war zone. Some of this training was with Special Forces. We spent a week in the field with them.

Around the first of March, 1966, we took an American Airlines flight from Fort Bragg to Oakland, California, and then a bus to Oakland Naval yards where we embarked on the USS Upshar for Vietnam. The ship stopped in Hawaii, Japan, and Okinawa before arriving at Qui Nhon, Vietnam. The next day we sailed down to Cam Rahn Bay. We unloaded, and took a convoy to Nha Trang about 25 miles up the coast.

After several days I volunteered for a special mission and ended up at First Field Force Headquarters working in an air-conditioned van at the Grand Hotel's compound. In the latter part of May, I was sent to Pleiku Temporary Duty Station for two weeks. I escorted a communications van up and was supposed to open a special Communications Center during Operation Hawthorn. It never became necessary to open the Communications Center.

During this time I learned how to keep track of enemy units. We utilized airborne radio direction finding planes which triangulated on a radio transmitter and then if the enemy unit warranted it, an artillery mission or an airstrike was called in on the unit.

After two weeks I returned to Nha Trang and had more insight on how the war was being fought. One night at the Comm. Center I started talking with an acquaintance in the compound and found out he was monitoring all the phone calls in and out of First Field Force Headquarters. They were trying to find out how the Viet Cong were able to know when B-52 raids would take place and any other intelligence that may be escaping our lips. As it turned out, a lot of people did not use good communication security on our side; as I understand this continued to be a problem throughout the war.

In October I was sent back to Pleiku on a permanent change of station. The 4th Infantry Division had just arrived and the Pleiku Radio Research Station had a major infusion of personnel. It was now the major intercept and direction finding station in the II Corps area.

About January 18, 1967, I began to feel weak and sick. I went on sick call and spent the next week in the hospital. I didn't get any better and was sent to the evacuation hospital at Pleiku Air Base. After a day or two of tests I was diagnosed with the hepatic liver abscess. I was operated on that night.

Over the next few months I made hospital stops at Qui Nhon, Clark Air Base in the Philippines, Camp Drake, a small post outside of Tokyo and then on Good Friday, 1967, I took a C-141 medivac to Walter Reed Hospital in Washington, D.C. After tests at Walter Reed I was given a 30 day convalescent leave. I went back to Walter Reed where more tests were run and after a week or two, I took another 30 day leave.

My next assignment was to Vint Hill Farms Station. This is where I spent the last couple of months of my enlistment.

On October 30, 1967, I mustered out of the Army and returned to my home in Central Illinois.

Survivor Guilt

By Ron Holt

My brother-in-law, John, and I were best friends through most of grammar school and all of high school. After graduation from high school, John went to work for the telephone company and continued his education part-time. I went to work for the US Army.

John became engaged to Diane, a girl he knew in high school. While I was on leave after my first tour in Vietnam, I dated and later married Diane's younger sister, Peg. About midway through my second tour in Vietnam, John and Diane were married, and John promptly received his draft notice from Uncle Sam.

After Basic Training and AIT, John found himself a grunt in the Infantry and, shortly thereafter, a grunt in the 1st Infantry Division in Vietnam. While serving in Vietnam, he received a Purple Heart and the Combat Infantry Badge.

John, like most combat veterans, never speaks much about his experiences in Vietnam. But, some 43 years later, during an email exchange, John let down his guard somewhat and briefly mention that he personally knew several of the names on The Wall, and that his best friend in the 1st Infantry Division was KIA.

I told John that although I served two tours in Vietnam, I know that I was not exposed to any of the danger, or fear, or horror that he may have experienced. Even though many or all the places I was at; the 3rd RRU in Saigon, the 8th RRU in Phu Bai, Nha Trang, Dak To, Tuy Hoa, Pleiku, Kontum, and Phan Rang, were attacked at one time or another; I was never there when it happened. I was never in combat and as far as I know, the closest I ever came to being killed or wounded was when Viet Cong terrorists blew up a bar a block away from the one I was sitting in on Nguyen Hue Street in Saigon.

Neither do I have any symptoms of the presumptive diseases associated with Agent Orange. I'm also aware that many of my ASA brothers lost their lives like Arthur Glover and Donald Taylor or were wounded like Dan Bonfield was during my first tour in Vietnam.

In addition, I told John that because of the fact that I was always in a support unit, I sometimes feel somewhat guilty, questioning whether I should refer to myself as a Vietnam Veteran, and think that I might possibly be thought of by people who served in combat as a REMF, a Rear Echelon M*****F*****.

John's reply, with his usual subtle wit, was, "You know, just because you're placed in a situation where you could possibly be killed or wounded, doesn't necessarily mean that you have to take advantage of the opportunity. You served in Vietnam, and that makes you a Vietnam Veteran."

I guess I knew that all along. But somehow it made me feel better to hear it from somebody who had been there in a combat capacity.

We all gave something of our lives there, and many gave their lives. I suppose, in the backs of our minds, we were always aware that death or injury was a possibility for any of us, anywhere. You didn't dwell on it and you just never knew who, or when, or where it could happen.

The Frying Pan

By Dick Amick

I had a neighbor at Devens that I used to ride with - he on a Harley, me on a lowly Honda. When I met him he was with the 10th Special Forces Group and he did not drink - a rarity. However, at one time he had liked this liquid refreshment a bit too much to please his full-blooded Cherokee spouse. He blew all his money in the bars, or on women he met there. His wife said he was one of those folks that were not pleasant to be around when he was drunk.

He came home one night totally plastered. His wife decided that she'd had enough and when he passed out in bed she pulled the bottom sheet up around him and sewed him in it. She then took a good old cast-iron frying pan and tenderized his body from head to toe. I guess the first whack knocked him out as he never moved while she worked him over. She undid the sheet, spread it out over the bed, crawled beside him and went to sleep. The next morning he woke up so sore he had to ask her to help him stand. He asked her what in the hell happened. She said she had no idea, he'd come home drunk, as usual, and beat to shit. That was the last time he went drinking - gave it up cold turkey.

When I knew him it had been several years since he had had a drink and never did when we rode together. It was several years after we met them that his wife told my wife the story about that night. My wife did not tell me until after they had rotated to Germany I never ran into him again and doubt if he has any idea what happened to him that night.

The Inspection
By Wayne Robertson

It was the summer of 1963 at Fort Carson. Our ASA unit was assigned in the support of the 5th Mechanized Division. Fort Carson was home to the 1st and 3rd Brigades, and the 2nd Brigade was located at Fort Devens. America was deeply involved in the Cold War and the 5th Division was one of America's STRIKE outfits, meaning it was supposed to be highly mobile and capable of being anywhere in the world and operational within 48 - 72 hours. Man, was that ever a joke; I would have been willing to bet that they couldn't find the whole division in that length of time.

Our company sized unit, being assigned to a Mechanized Division, was also mechanized, meaning we had armored personnel carriers (APC's). Our radios, mills, tape recorders and DF equipment were all neatly packaged in a rack that rolled into the back of the APC. The rack was made portable so it could be taken out of the tracked vehicle so the APC could be used for its primary purpose if the need arose.

That summer the powers that be decided, correctly, that we were not capable of being combat operational anywhere, much less anywhere in the world in any kind of reasonable time. They also decided incorrectly, that the way to make us combat ready and mobile was to have an Inspector General's inspection. Of course, you know what that means; many practice IG inspections. We spent literally days getting ready for 'junk on the bunk' inspections. You know the kind, where your hankies have to all be folded just right, your undies, and the proper number of them, all laid out just so, the bunk made with the top blanket so tight you could bounce a quarter off it. Yeah, all the important combat stuff. Such was stateside duty.

We also had practice inspections of our operational equipment. On one of these equipment inspections they were inspecting our APC's. Our vehicle had a crew that consisted of a driver, vehicle commander, and two equipment operators. The driver and the vehicle commander doubled up as Ops as well. We even had a .50 caliber machine gun mounted on top. No bullets, but we had to keep the damn gun cleaned and oiled anyway.

On our APC, I was designated as the driver as well as the one designated to maintain the equipment. On this particular practice inspection we had all our APCs lined up in two rows. They were nose to nose and the back of the vehicle was facing out with its tailgate down so the operation's rack could easily be inspected. They only had the driver and the vehicle commander standing by because we were not fully manned and I don't think any of the crews were full.

The inspection began with the CO, a Captain, and the Executive Officer, a butter bar second Lieutenant, followed by one of the Staff Sergeants. These were the inspecting party. We were about third or fourth in the line and as we stood at parade rest on either side of the lowered tailgate, we could hear how the inspections were going. They were picking us apart. Nitpicking at every little thing. They found a thermos one of the Ops had stupidly left behind the radio rack in the APC next to us and reamed the vehicle commander's ass for about ten minutes. They told him if he wanted to keep the thermos to paint it OD and number it.

Our turn was next. The Captain, and the party, moved over in front of us and we snapped to attention. The Captain started in the back while the Lieutenant started looking over the driver's compartment, engine compartment and the vehicle commander's station. Miraculously they could not seem to find anything to gig us on. We had worked very hard trying to get everything as it should be. They both finished looking over our vehicle at the same time and were standing in front of it. For some reason the Lieutenant stooped down and looked under the vehicle. He stood up and directed himself to the vehicle commander, who was a Sp 4, and said, 'Specialist what is that black oily stuff under this vehicle?"

The Sp 4 replied, "I don't know Sir. May the Specialist look under the vehicle?"

"By all means," replied the Lieutenant.

The Sp 4 dropped down and looked briefly then stood back up and said, "The BRT is leaking, Sir."

The Lieutenant had a look on his face that clearly said that he didn't have a clue what a BRT was. He stammered a little and said, "Well Specialist, we can't have BRT's leaking, now can we?"

"No Sir," replied the Sp 4.

"See that the BRT is fixed immediately," the Lieutenant exclaimed loudly all the while looking very proud of himself and feeling very sure he had put that this Sp 4 in his place.

"Yes Sir," replied the Sp 4.

The inspection party returned to the rear of the vehicle and the Sp 4 fell into his position, came to attention and saluted the officers as they proceeded to the next APC. After they had moved out of earshot I whispered to the Sp 4, "Hey, Lawson, what the hell is a BRT?"

He looked at me and replied, "Big Round Thing."

Speaking Of the Green Side Up
By Al Lewis

In the fall of 1963 at Phu Bai, the CO, Captain Muir, as I recall, told the First Sergeant, affectionately known as 'Snuffy Smith' that he wanted grass around the orderly room. Specialist 4 Ralph Adams, Vietnamese lingie extraordinaire, and lately of NSA fame, at least with those of us who served with him in Vietnam, was tasked with securing a deuce and a half, a shotgun rider - PFC Al Lewis of second Trick and of 058 fame, half a dozen local nationals, and then they motored off to Hue City to find, cut, load, and return and lay the said grass sod.

We drove to Hue, into the Citadel and found someone to sell us sod. We put the local nationals to work cutting and loading the sod and we went off to have a cool drink while we watched them work. At the '33' cart, we encountered two very young ladies and bought our cool drinks. Soon Ralph was suppressing giggles and rather badly it seems, because the girls got suspicious. They didn't know that Ralph spoke their language yet.

I pestered Ralph until he told me what they were saying. The girls were wondering what I ate that made me so fat - I was 165 pounds and 5'8" and was also wondering about Ralph. They had never seen a Black American. There were explanations tendered by Ralph. The girls were impressed, I think. Once they found out Ralph was fluent in Vietnamese, the fun began but ended rather quickly. Unlike most of us that were 19 or so years of age, Ralph was not in the market for his own personal hooch mate, no matter what her qualifications might have been.

With the deuce loaded, we headed for Det J of the 3rd RRU, located next to Highway 1 just west of the old French landing strip. Upon passing through the village marketplace, I advised Ralph that a very large water buffalo had just tossed its very young handler and was making *di di mau* right behind the truck, scattering local nationals all over Highway 1 and making me and our local nationals very nervous. Ralph dropped the deuce one gear lower and put the pedal to the metal. We arrived at the 3rd in record time and the water buffalo got tired of chasing us after about a quarter-mile.

The sod was duly laid, and hand watered for several days or maybe a week or so. Of course it died. Being a dumb hillbilly from West Virginia I kind of guessed that sod didn't grow worth a shit in beach sand, but Captain Muir never asked my opinion. The good Captain had other ossifer qualities, however.

Captain Muir instituted 'in ranks rifle inspections', and 'junk on the bunk' every Saturday morning and it wasn't long until PT three times a week began for those of us with too much time on our hands; that was everyone below the rank of E-6.

Needless to say, Captain Muir, as far as I know, was the only ASA CO in Vietnam to precipitate a full-fledged, 24 hour NIL HEARD in Operations by the 058's, as well as, the 056's - just one of those fluke atmospheric inversions, I guess.

The NCOIC, the OIC and various and sundry other types suspected something else must have been the cause of the lack of copy. The Executive Officer read Article 91 or 92 'Mutiny and Sedition' to each incoming shift; had me worried but not much.

Exactly 48 hours after the NIL HEARD, a Lt. Col. and a Chief Sergeant Major from the 3rd RRU at Tan Son Nhut magically appeared and subsequent to reading a modified riot act to the assembled multitude of enlisted men - everyone who worked in Ops - listened to his speech and he said - *a la* George Patton - "Now which one of you sons of bitches is gonna tell me what the fuck is going on?"

DEAD SILENCE - then Sp 4 Ed Clark of 058 fame, and now retired fire chief in Kent, Ohio, stood and told the man exactly what was happening, chapter and verse. That day Ops went back to normal; PT stopped, junk on the bunk stopped and in ranks rifle inspection stopped. Sandbags continued, but we understood the sanity of well-built bunkers, and before the week passed - Captain Muir went bye-bye, never to be seen again.

How Ken Hoggard Saved Al Lewis' Stripe

By Al Lewis

One fine day, Al Lewis decided to go to town. Al knew he was up for guard duty, but he went to town anyway. Later that evening in town, Jim Pellasear bumped into Al and told him he was in deep shit for missing guard mount. Al went straight back to Davis Station about 10 PM, and then went to work at White Birch on Mids.

The next morning the First Sergeant requested a meeting with Al, who, finding time in his schedule, met with the First Sergeant. Al was informed by Top that the CO wanted to see Al if he was available. Fortunately, Al was free at the moment and went into the CO's office. After saluting and reporting formalities, the Captain read to Al a story out of the UCMJ. The title of the story was Article 15. The Captain went on to inform him that he was about to be a PFC again, and did Al have anything to say for himself before the hammer fell?

Al, being of the top 10% and having met Old Hawg Hal, when Hal was a piglet, began to think and talk at the same time - not the best strategy. Al's story was that he had checked the guard roster at noon the previous day, and the roster did not have his name on it. It wasn't exactly true, but since the Captain didn't follow Al around and since the company clerk was habitually late posting rosters, it sounded plausible.

Al assured the Captain that he knew the penalty for failure to repair and certainly wouldn't deliberately risk a stripe just to go into sin city, Saigon. And finally, when Al did learn that he was supposed to be on guard duty, he had a crucial decision to make. Did he report to White Birch to cover the Mids-mission where there was no replacement available, or did he find the Sergeant of the guard and report for guard, where there was a guard who was already covering Al's post.

Al chose to do the top 10% thing; Hal would have been proud. Al covered the Mids-mission. The VC never sleeps as we all know. Al said to the Captain, "I thought the mission was most important, Sir."

The Captain flinched. He closed the big book and offered a deal to Al. The offer was to walk eight hours of guard duty around Davis Station that very evening and that would suffice. Of course there was one little catch the Captain said and told the following to Al.

The previous evening, probably about EM club closing time, some dirty, low down enlisted scum, obviously not of the top 10 per cent had used the fine ground pile of gravel, which was being used to cover the Company street prior to re-tarring, and written in very large letters FTA on the Captain's beloved street.

As we all know, FTA stands for Fun, Travel and Adventure in the ASA. But somehow the Captain didn't appreciate the sentiment. Al was informed that if FTA or any other message should appear in the Company street during the time Al was on guard duty that night, the deal was off and Al would be a PFC again.

Leaving the Captain's office, Al's next trip was to find another of the top 10 per cent and inform him that since Al's stripe was on the line, he would appreciate if the other top 10 per-center would keep his drunken ass in the EM club and then go straight to his bunk or anywhere but the Company street that evening. Hoggard expressed concern for Al's stripe and assured him that he would pass the word on Al's behalf. He expressed dismay that 'I would think that he had had anything to do with the previous evening's happening but was sure he knew who was guilty and would have a word with him.'

Al uttered his thanks, questioning Ken's parentage under his breath, and went off to get it together for guard duty. Al's pal, the top 10 per-center, Hoggard, was as good as his word. To this day I am grateful to Ken for helping me not earn PFC a second time. Thanks Ken!

A New Guy's Indoctrination at Phu Bai
By Steve Polesnak

I have to thank one of our favorite lingies, a Chinese Mandarin Voice Intercept Operator, for reminding me of these true stories, which made the new guys in all ASA units, feel at home. They were called new guys 'NUG's', and NUG was usually preceded with a seven letter word starting with 'F'. This story is the best description of what I believe occurred in my old memory, which is 39 years after the event.

As we landed on the Tan Son Nhut, Republic of Vietnam Airport in Saigon, it became apparent that this was going to be a long, long year. As we left the plane and walked into the terminal, we all could see that the humidity, heat, and local sites would greatly influence what we thought about Vietnam. All of the soldiers loaded onto the ground transportation, and we proceeded to the orderly room. We then saw our billets - chicken coops. This chicken coop had chicken wire and wood slats and open air ventilation system. It did not protect us from the hot sun. I just figured that someday I was going to take advantage of volunteering to get out of this crappy place called Saigon.

After one and a half months at the unit I found out at a meeting that they needed twenty 058 Morse Interceptor's, the slang name was Hawg soldiers, to go to a vacation resort in northern South Vietnam. The detachment, referred to in military documents as Detachment J, 3rd Radio Research Unit was located only 6-8 km southeast of Hue. If you traveled 30 or more miles north you would arrive at the southernmost border of North Vietnam. We called Phu Bai the Land of Enchantment. Yes, and I was to be enchanted for 10½ more months.

We disembarked the C-123 onto the Phu Bai airport and looked around. My personal thought was *what a friggin wasteland*. The airport was a reinforced dirt pad. It had a large tin garage for aircraft, and a small building used for Operations. We loaded into our transportation, crossed over Highway 1, and entered into a one half by one half mile square, temporary, ASA intelligence listening installation. As we hopped off the truck and looked in all directions, I said to myself *what have I gotten myself into?* I was in constant turmoil in Saigon with the heat, living conditions and seeing sewage material floating down the street. But at least Saigon was civilization with milkshakes and hamburgers at the USO. *God, what did I give up? Why did I volunteer? You stupid friggin NUG! ASA wasn't even supposed to be in Vietnam.*

So I went about the process of clearing in, setting up my area in the tent, and going over and having a drink at the EM club. This was where all the trouble started. While I was sitting at the bar, the slovenly and bad smelling GI's were talking and making sure I was listening. I was being pulled into their web. So one of the guys introduced himself, and I told him my name was Stephen. He befriended me and started to talk about the area and what was happening and not happening. He gave me a special tip that only old guys knew. They turned on the hot water in the shower next to the EM club at 1700 hours each day. Of course they repeated the time in civilian time - 5 PM.

He would let me borrow a cake of soap, since a small PX had nothing in stock. Remember we were at least 2½ to 3 hours flying time to Detachment J, Phu Bai, from Saigon.

These guys were professionals at screwing with the NUG's. They had the experience. So early in the evening of my first day I was hot, tired, dirty, I wanted a hot shower. So I made excuses to everyone to get to the showers prior to 5 PM. So I turned on the shower and waited for the hot water.

Unbeknownst to me the ARVN battery always had a practice or real fire mission normally each day at 1700 hours just to remind Charlie living in the vicinity of Virginia Hill, Hill 180, that we had big guns. The 105 mm artillery pieces on post started their mission, and the power in the building went off and on, the shower shook in its foundations, and at least one or two windows broke, and the doors were shaken off their brackets. Someone in the EM club, which was adjacent to the showers yelled, INCOMING.

I scurried out the door adjacent to the EM club like a wet rat and hit the dirt stark naked. Those friggin guys in the EM club were just laughing so hard. I quickly wrapped something around me, and being tall in stature, I walked over to the EM club window without using a box to stand on and I told them explicitly I would get even with every one of you 'Som' Bitches' if it takes until I leave Phu Bai.

After a week or so I cooled down enough to laugh at the friendly joke they had at my expense. I never totally forgave them for their actions because I found out they did it to as many people as they could find who were as gullible as I was. It was the camaraderie and the getting to know the men and the soldiers of all ASA units around the world. Little did I know that the hot water boiler didn't work before I arrived and would not work for at least six months after I arrived at Det J.

After I settled down and decided not to be pissed at the guys, I had to start working on what type of indoctrination I would do for the next new guy who came to Phu Bai. This was a true tradition of the old people screwing with the new people arriving at the unit. I really became a professional at indoctrinating the NUG's for many, many years.

Play with Fire and Get Burnt
By Steve Polesnak

In the latter part of 1964 we had many people being assigned to Phu Bai. After the Gulf of Tonkin incident and other encounters with the VC, Detachment J, 3rd RRU, started to increase in the number of collectors to man the positions. Everyone knows how the Hawgs, Morse Intercept Operators were. They worked hard, and played hard, drank hard and always had something mischievous up their sleeves to make a day interesting.

One of the newer operators came to Phu Bai from Bangkok. Ken was an experienced operator and full of bull shit, all the time playing jokes or shocking you by something he would say. He made the day go fast. And of course, I used to pull jokes on him all the time because he sat in the position in front of me.

We arrived at work before 6 AM in the morning because the first enemy schedule of the day started at this time; not one minute before nor one minute after. We zeroed our watch each day with the schedule because net control at this time of the day told everyone what their schedule was to be and whether he had traffic for the outstations. You didn't screw off because the schedules could last from 30 seconds to a minute. Everybody on the eight positions just waited to see what the big guy was going to do.

Well, net control on this day came up right on time, and I had my splits on and ready to go. He started tuning, and his stations started to answer him. *I am A outstation and I have traffic*, then *I am B outstation and have traffic*, and so on. Well, at this point in time, Ken was screwing around with something in the front of my position.

I just went on directing what should be done and which operator should take what schedule or traffic on the outstation. Lo and behold, black smoke started to rise and fire started to show above my mill. I almost freaked out. Smoke was billowing towards the roof since the six ply fan fold paper had carbon, which was highly volatile when on fire. I yelled to Rick, Ken, and Sonny to go ahead and get the damn fire extinguisher and get this paper fire put out. They accepted that task and started to put out the fire.

Just then the door of the new Operations building opened and our Operations Officer walked into the room, trailed by a believe MSG Drohan, Ops Sergeant at the time. I said to myself *oh shit; you and your guys manning these racks are in trouble again.*

The Ops Officer and Ops Sergeant didn't understand what had happened. The Ops Officer immediately said, "What is going on here."

Thinking quickly, I was still standing above the mill on my position with my headsets on, I turned to the Ops Officer and said, "Sorry Sir, some of my ashes from my cigarette must've fallen into the box of 'six ply fan fold paper' and it caught on fire."

Geez, I thought all our asses were really in trouble. Well he accepted my answer and left and told everyone to get this mess cleaned up in the bay.

After the Ops officer left, I looked at Ken said, "You rotten $$#&&, you are definitely on my shit list, and if you do any stupid shit like that again there are going to be some consequences."

Well you had to know Ken; he just looked at me, smiled, and said, "Yeah paybacks are hell. So we are now even," or some words to that effect.

Ken never did that trick again, and we became good friends. He went back to Bangkok. Ken is still alive and kicking somewhere in the South.

Now you all know what the 'Hawgs' did on one day in the Land of Enchantment trying to make their day interesting while the VC were traveling the trails and wanting to surprise us as they passed by Hue, Republic of Vietnam.

Two Old Ladies, a Pig and a Sack of Rice
By Jim Pierce

About midnight one night in May, 1964, I was returning to the Saigon apartment in Da Cau that I shared with CJ, when I was cut off by a deuce and a half full of ARVN soldiers. The only choice I had was to lay my motorcycle down under the wheels of the deuce and a half or cut across four lanes of oncoming traffic. I made it across three of them before being broadsided by a motorized rickshaw going about 35 miles an hour. The motorized rickshaw contained the driver, a big sack of rice, two old women and a large hog on their way to market.

I never felt the impact. The next thing I knew I was laying on the sidewalk looking for my glasses. I had a tingling sensation from my big toe to the top of my head - like when you hit your funny bone. I tried to stand up and a piece of bone came through my leg. That's when I knew I was in trouble.

A large crowd of Vietnamese people were gathering around me in the accident. The driver of the motorized rickshaw seemed to be okay. One of the old women was on the ground but seemed to be okay. The other old woman, with the help of several Vietnamese people, was trying to catch the hog.

A Vietnamese man waved down a taxi and helped me into it. I gave the driver 50 piastres and told him to take me to the Saigon Naval Hospital. Instead of taking me to the Saigon Naval Hospital, the taxi driver took me to a French Missionary Aide Station on the outskirts of Saigon. The nuns at the aid station, with the help of the taxi driver, got me out of the taxi and onto a small operating table in the aide station. The problem with this was that the table was too small and my head hung off one side and my legs hung off the other side. During this whole ordeal no one spoke English, so I was not sure what was going on. All I could remember is that my whole body had this tingling sensation, like when you hit your funny bone.

About noon the next day the MPs located me. They asked me what I was doing here. They said that they had been looking for me all night. They said that the area we were in was not secure and they needed to get me to the Saigon Naval Hospital as soon as possible. That sounded fine with me. We had to wait another half hour for an ambulance to transport me to the Saigon Naval Hospital.

When I arrived at the Saigon Naval Hospital they took me to the emergency room and started to cut away my clothing. The naval doctor looked at my leg and told the nurse he would have to work on it right away. He told her to give me a shot of morphine for the pain. About this time, as they were cutting away my clothing, the doctor found my ASA Worldwide Badge under my T-shirt. He looked at me and said, "Are you with the 3rd RRU?

I said "Yes."

He turned to the nurse and said, "STOP! Do not give him any medication." The doctor turned to me and said we are not allowed to give you any medication until an officer from the 3rd RRU debriefs you.

The doctors went into a huddle and decided that they could not wait. The one doctor came back to me and said that they needed to do some work on my leg right away, that they could not wait for an officer from my unit to show up to debrief me. They strapped me down tight on the operating table and had several people hold me. Then they began to work on my leg. It took the straps and all the people they had around the table to keep me on the table. We all learned some new language before they were done.

It took two days for the 3ʳᵈ RRU to find an officer to debrief me. When he finally showed up, all he did was ask me to place my hand on a Bible and swear that I would not say anything while under the influence of drugs. My legs hurt like hell and I was willing to swear to anything to get some painkiller. As soon as I was debriefed the nurse mainlined Demerol into my arm. It felt great, just like my whole body was sliding into a tub of warm water.

This leads to the story of how my buddy CJ brought both of my Vietnamese girlfriends into the Saigon Naval Hospital, at the same time, to visit me. The Saigon Naval Hospital was supposed to be a secure area. I'm not sure how he got them in there, but he did. But that's a story for another time.

Here Come the Monkeys
By Wendell Davis

It all started on January 7, 1963, when I arrived in Saigon with the 303rd ASA Battalion. The temperature was 120° with 100% humidity. I then weighed a whopping 204 pounds. A wee bit heavy and this overweight condition caused me difficulty in breathing.

Having been fired upon during our landing caused all of us to be somewhat reluctant to leave our plane. After gathering our belongings we were escorted in a camouflaged bus to Davis Station. Many days went by and homesickness prevailed. In February we decided to have a mascot for our company. This was a monkey named Sam.

At first I remained ambivalent toward the hairy creature but after holding him for a few minutes he became enamored. A friend in need is a friend indeed. One day after work, Sam and I were exchanging pleasantries being together, when Sam decided he would have my Marlboro cigarettes. I, in turn, was determined that he would not! In the pursuit of taking and returning the pack to me many, many times brought on a very negative encounter which unfortunately ended with Sam biting me! Needless to say, this caused a great deal of anger in me and as I as a result I threw the fucking monkey or should I say, hurled the fucking monkey against the slotted barracks so hard that, I, indeed thought he was dead!

After a few minutes I noticed some movement and he arose looking directly in my eyes and said something to me in his own language! I went to grab him again but to no avail. He escaped my clutches and ran into the dense, dark, deep jungle. Thank God Sam was gone.

A few minutes later, maybe longer, I heard monkeys screaming and doing mayhem in the jungle. Soon I saw many monkeys coming out of the dense forest led by Sam, heading for my, and I repeat, my barracks. I sensed something was wrong so I ran into my sleeping quarters, which was held together with wooden slats, screens and tiled roofs and I locked the door. Within seconds, thirty or more monkeys were trying to get in.

At this point, I saw Sam, red-eyed and full of anger with his only solution - to get revenge. Having no weapon available and being totally alone, I hid under my blanket for what seemed to be hours. Finally the scratching, screeching and banging stopped. I peered out from under my blanket on my bed to see that the sons of bitches were gone.

Oh well, that's life. I gathered myself together and with a few dollars, left my barracks for the NCO club for a few shots. About halfway there I heard screeching monkeys again and they were on the warpath with their goal to KILL me. I ran to the nearest shelter which was a truck and I escaped into the driver's seat, rolled up the windows and waited as the battalion of monkeys completely encased the truck frame trying to get to me! No matter what they attempted they were unable to reach me. Thank God for army vehicles! By the way, it was a deuce and a half.

Finally giving up, the creatures leapt from the iron frame vehicle and left. At this point I was uncertain of what to do. I didn't, however, leave the truck immediately. Being somewhat frightened I scoped the surrounding area for the fucking beasts. None appeared at least in my field of vision so I said: "What the hell. I really need a drink."

So I unlocked the door and stepped down only to be greeted by Sam and his comrades. Those fucking, red-eyed killers were after me again. I ran like a rabbit to the Commanding Officer's billet. I ran in and locked the door behind me. The Commanding Officer said: "Why are you here?"

I began to explain the occurrences to him. He looked at me with total disbelief and said: "I know you want to get out of Vietnam but this story is ridiculous!"

He asked me to leave but I begged him to come with me because Sam and his comrades were waiting outside. With trepidation and looking somewhat baffled he consented and went with me outside. Guess what? No Sam and no comrades. He looked at me and said: "Well son, good try, but please don't bother me again."

He left me alone and returned to his quarters. As soon as his door slammed, out came Sam followed by those little cannibalistic fuckers seeking revenge and OUT TO GET ME! Fortunately, I was able to save myself by escaping through the Commander's door, only to be greeted by: "What the hell are you doing back here?"

I grabbed his arm and pulled him to the window. Sam and his fellow slayers were still there waiting. My Commanding Officer was stunned! Only by a moment's notice was I vindicated because Sam remained too long where he could be seen.

What happened next after this remains a SECRET and only those who have heard this remarkable TRUE story know!

Chapter 3
The Middle 60s

In Vietnam the mid-sixties was a period of transition both in the government of South Vietnam and in the military commitment of the United States. The United States started this transition with its approval of the coup to overthrow President Ngo Dinh Diem in November, 1963. A series of coups and unstable governments followed. Many ARVN generals were involved in the intrigue that followed and none were as strong as Diem had been.

On the US side the Vietnam War became our war. That meant that increasing numbers of Americans bore the brunt of battle. Likewise, the war burden fell to our allies; the Australians, the Koreans and to other nations that felt the need to battle communism in a place other than their own country.

After 1965, the United States committed hundreds of thousands of combat and support troops to the war. ASA increased its units in support of the combat units. ASA personnel found the need to go with these units into remote areas of Vietnam and were exposed to all the hazards of war along with those units. Our ASA counterpart in the Australian Army, the 547th Signal Troop, experienced similar risks and losses.

The Greater Gift

By Gary D. Spivey

It was my birthday, my third birthday in Vietnam, after having twice extended my tour. The Special Identification Techniques or SIT, Section Chief pulled me aside and told me that he was sending me TDY to Con Son, an island in the South China Sea off the southern end of Vietnam about 150 miles south of Saigon, where we had one of our listening posts. I protested, pointing out the amount of work we had to do, but the Chief wouldn't relent. "The war will still be here when you get back," he insisted.

My stay at Con Son would be for a week. I'd go down one Wednesday and come back the next. That's how often the Air Force C-123 made the round-trip from Saigon's Tan Son Nhut Air Base to resupply our detachment. Almost everything we needed had to be brought in, since there wasn't much of a local economy. The main business of the island was the prison. Since the days of the French, criminals of one stripe or another had been incarcerated there. Now it was where the Republic of Vietnam locked up its Viet Cong prisoners.

On the morning of my departure, I crawled into the cargo bay of the big-bellied transport and strapped myself into a seat on one of the benches that lined the hull. My traveling companions were some ARVN soldiers in red airborne berets and about a dozen Vietnamese civilians - military dependents, I figured - carrying what looked like all their worldly goods, including live chickens. They scrutinized me pretty well. A Gulliver among the Lilliputians; I guess I looked as alien to them as they did to me.

I was met on the landing strip by the Staff Sergeant-in-charge of the Detachment. Actually, it was an ARVN facility, so he was technically just an Adviser. But, in reality, our headquarters in Saigon was calling the shots, and our man was in charge.

He wasn't glad to see me. I don't know what the Chief had told him, but he knew that the official reason for my visit was a pretense and that I was really there for R & R, rest and recuperation, the Chief's idea of a birthday present. My reception was no better when he introduced me to the guys that he shared a villa with, but their disposition mellowed when I contributed several bottles of Chivas Regal™ - which was ridiculously cheap at the PX - to their liquor cabinet.

The guys at the villa were British. They said that they operated a communications relay station for ships at sea. I figured that the British mission, like mine, was classified, so I didn't pry.

The ranking ARVN soldier at our detachment was a Staff Sergeant, the same rank as his American advisor. He spoke pretty good English and was the only person I had met on Con Son who seemed genuinely happy about my visit. Or maybe it was just the American cigarettes that I freely shared. After the two sergeants showed me around, I was free to begin my real mission: relaxing in the sun.

It was a tropical paradise! I'm sure the prisoners didn't think of it in those terms. It was Devil's Island to them. But when this kid from the Midwest saw that endless expanse of golden sand beach at the edge of a tropical rain forest, I thought that I had died and gone to heaven. The beach was in the shape of a crescent that framed an inlet and stretched a good 5 miles from end-to-end. The water of the inlet was a robin's eggshell blue capped by a gentle frothy white surf, turning to a deeper blue as the ocean stretched out into the horizon. And I was all alone. I spent the rest of the afternoon exploring my domain and didn't see another soul.

I liked the solitude. Rather than stay in the villa with the Brits and the Sergeant, I jumped at the offer to stay in the beach house. It was a white stucco affair with a spacious bedroom, American plumbing, and an eating area that opened into a stone patio filled with tropical greenery and aromatic flowering plants.

It came with the services of a house girl who had been hastily recruited by the house girl at the villa. She looked like she was about 12 years old, but then I always underestimated Vietnamese ages.

This house girl was good. I saw that she had pressed and hung up all the clothes that I had stuffed into my duffel bag, including my dress tans, the summer khakis that I was instructed to bring for no apparent reason. Be prepared, the Chief had explained. And she offered me a cold *Ba Moui Ba,* the local brew that I had developed a taste for.

She even found an ointment and insisted on applying it to the soles of my feet, which were sliced up from walking on coral at the water's edge. I hadn't even noticed the cuts until later, but I learned my lesson well: coral is sharp. Also, she pointed out that I was turning red on my back, where I couldn't reach with the lotion, and from then on she made sure that I was thoroughly protected.

I was up early the next morning to catch the sunrise. I felt none the worse for having stayed up pretty late with the Brits socializing over the Chivas. Actually, I had a heck of a time understanding half of what they were saying, given their accents and the effects of the scotch. But I did learn a lot about the island, including the fact that the villa was on the site of what, in an earlier war, had been a Japanese coast watcher's hut. I could see why, given the panoramic view. With binoculars, you could almost make out some of the smaller outlying islands in the archipelago. And if you turned the binoculars toward the land, you could see pillboxes from that earlier war cut into the side of the mountains.

I also learned that, even though I thought I was alone on the beach, there were curious eyes everywhere. Those were the eyes of the Viet Cong prisoners who had earned trustee status and were pretty much free to roam the island.

I entered the water and discovered that I could swim out a good distance before it was over my head. The shallow water probably explained the old Chinese junk that had been abandoned at the mouth of the inlet, tilted at a 45° angle with its keel partially buried in the sand. I made a point to investigate it later.

Swimming and sunning myself, I spent my first full day in Shangri-La. I skipped breakfast and would have passed on lunch had my house girl not pressed me to take some fruit. That afternoon, I pulled my beach blanket into the shade of the palm tree at the fringe of the beach and tried to read a Hemingway novel about some misguided fool fighting for the communists in the Spanish Civil War.

For the next few days, I lived the life of a beach bum. I didn't shave. I sunbathed, swam and read my Hemingway. Occasionally, I had to duck inside to escape a monsoon, but they were brief. Nothing except the monkey chattering in the nearby trees and something - *a wild boar?* - rustling in the woods disturbed my solitude.

Midway through my stay on Con Son, the ARVN Sergeant invited me to ride into town with him on the following day. "Shave, and wear your best uniform," he instructed. "The boss wants to meet you."

"The boss?" I questioned.

"You'll see," he said.

Over dinner, the guys at the villa were just as mysterious. "Grin and bear it," they advised.

So the next morning, smooth-cheeked, spiffy in my dress tans and freshly spit-shined by my house girl, I climbed into the shotgun seat of an ARVN Jeep and set out for 'the town'.

I was glad that I hadn't eaten breakfast, for I surely would have lost it on that ride. My maniac escort zipped along a twisting, narrow road cut into the side of a mountain with no guard rails between the road and the steep drop-off to the ocean below. In the event that there had been any oncoming traffic, I'm sure that I would have died on Con Son. Seeing a bird of prey circling overhead didn't help. My driver, however, just laughed at my expression of horror.

We passed the guard towers surrounding the sturdy walls of the prison. It was a massive complex, with several different prison compounds. Within the cellblocks, I learned, were long rows of sunken concrete cages, about 8' x 5', each containing several prisoners. The ceilings of the cages were barred, like tiger cages, as they were known. The cages for incorrigible's had no roofs, exposing the prisoners to the extremes of temperature and the elements, including the brutal sun and violent monsoons. It was harsh, but I had no pity for them. They were terrorists, not soldiers. If this was what happened to the bastards who blew up my buddies and innocent civilians back in Saigon that was just fine with me.

We arrived shaken but safely at our destination, a small town that seemed largely uninhabited, with no markets, storefronts, or other signs of activity other than some fishing boats tied up at a pier. The Sergeant drove into an area of small houses, really little more than shacks, and invited me into his home. I entered a large dirt-floored room with only a few pieces of furniture and was offered the only available chair. A gecko hung on the ceiling, defying gravity as it patiently waited its next meal. Scampering behind a curtain into an adjoining room, my host returned with a glass of water and a tablet that he dropped into the glass to create some kind of a carbonated fruit-flavored drink, a 'fizz-pop' if you will.

Then, from behind the curtain the family began to emerge. How many members, I can't say, but a lot. They were of all ages, from babies carried on the hips of older girls to venerable elders. I felt awkward sitting in the only chair as the others stood or squatted on mats on the floor, and I was embarrassed to have a drink in hand while they had nothing, but I sensed that I should just accept their hospitality without protesting.

Not knowing that I was to be a guest, I had come empty-handed. But at least I could share a pack of cigarettes and some gum, which was accepted all around with great delight. Soon, some of the children began to approach me. They would come forward, giggle, and run back. Eventually, a brave one would run up, touch my arm - the hair seemed to be a source of amusement - and scamper away to be scolded by the adults.

Finally, one of the boys came near and handed me a small picture book that showed various objects in their English names. So I gave them an English lesson, pronouncing the words and inviting them to repeat. The shyness of the children evaporated as they squirmed to get closer to me. Even the adults joined in the lesson. I basked in their friendship until my host indicated that it was time to go see the boss.

We walked across a sun-drenched esplanade to meet an ARVN officer who was the Commandant of the prison and, I gathered, a sort of military governor of the island. He was admiring the ocean view in the company of an aristocratic-looking middle-aged couple, a Frenchman and his Vietnamese wife. She was stunning in long billowy white pants and a flowered long sleeved silk shirt. Her hair, made up in the beehive style of the day, showed no signs of grey. The sight of her caused my heart to race, and I hoped that my newly acquired tan concealed my flushed face. The ARVN Sergeant presented me to the Commandant who, in turn, introduced me to the

French couple. The Sergeant was dismissed and told that a driver would return me to the villa.

I learned that the French couple were old friends of the Commandant, dating back to the French war. They were visiting him on the island, having arrived by boat from the coastal city of Vung Tau, or Cape St. Jacques, as they called it. They even called Con Son by a different name - Poulo Condore, which the French, through some play on words, translated as 'Chicken Island.' A pretty ironic name, I thought, remembering the chickens on the airplane coming down.

The difference in our ranks didn't seem to matter to the Commandant. He treated me like an honored guest and he invited me to join him and the French couple. That wasn't the only time that superior officers went out of their way to be nice to me. Maybe they were just nice people. Or maybe it was the mystique of 'RRU', as we were known. They were never quite so sure who they were dealing with. That we had a secret identity, usually assumed to be the CIA, was something of an open secret.

The sharp scent of the salt water blended agreeably with the perfume of the abundant frangipani as we sat on a terrace overlooking the ocean and sipped champagne. My mind drifted back to the ARVN Sergeant's family just across the road, but a world apart. I smiled to myself as I admired the champagne, recalling the bubbles of my earlier fizz-pop, and knew which, as birthday presents go, was the greater gift.

Tet Message
By John Klawitter

It was over 40 years ago; if I remember correctly, my MOS was 065, which I think meant I was a crypto/linguist, a lingie for short. It was late January, 1965, a week or two before Tet New Year, a big holiday celebration back then in South Vietnam. I was stationed at the White Shack on Tan Son Nhut Airbase, located at the West End of Saigon proper. The White Shack was a white-washed cement, a one story cinderblock building, with a burn-bag incinerator on one side surrounded by a high cyclone fence topped with razor wire. The windows were painted with thick white paint, and there was a terrible handmade poster on one wall depicting a bleary GI talking to a bar girl. A ship was sinking in the background and the obvious slogan, 'Loose Lips Sink Ships!' I was on swing shift and it was late and I was hoping to get to the Hong Kong Bar and then to the villa on Trung Minh Giang Street that I rented with six or seven other non-coms from the 3rd RRU.

I was hustling through the usual batch of covert one-liners: *Han muon ammo.* (Han needs bullets) *Dai nai toi sem hai nguoi my day quoc xam luoc.* (I saw 2 Invader-gangster Americans today) I was about to close up shop for the night when I ran across an entire paragraph. This was odd enough to not slip under the pile for tomorrow. Covert messages are necessarily short because the senders do not want to get triangulated. Anything over one hasty sentence like 'Killed two invader-gangster colonialists with a bouncing Betty' had to be something unusual. So I put away my plans for the evening and pulled out my Hoa's Viet-English dictionary.

Dear comrades and true Vietnam sympathizers. We stand united in our mighty efforts against the colonialist Invaders and the Imperial pig soldiers from over the sea. However, this year, in accord with the well-being of the united people of Vietnam in their heroic struggle against the puppet government and the lackey troops of the false dictatorship of South Vietnam, we are declaring a truce for the week of the Tet festivities, to begin the evening before Tet and to run a full seven days. Stand firm, comrades. Victory is assured.

Well, that was news to me. Here it was a few days left until Tet and I knew there would be no Tet uprising this year! Manpower could be shifted, outposts resupplied with less fear of enemy activity, and maybe even lives saved! I typed up my translation with trembling fingers and added the special TOP SECRET CODEWORD on the top. I would tell you the codeword, but knowing the military, I doubt it has been declassified nearly a half a century later. Anyway, I ripped the paper out of the typewriter and ran down the hallway looking for the officer on duty.

But it was late in the shift and the Lieutenant had left the White Shack in the hands of the Sergeant on duty.

"I've got a hot one to go to the States!" I told him.

"Yeah, and I got a mother who wanted me to be a priest," he said, picking his teeth as he looked up at me from the remains of a buffalo burger on his desk. If you have ever experienced water buffalo meat, you can sympathize; you know he needed a toothpick.

"No, Sarge, honest! This is special!" I'd stamped my translation with the highest priority CODEWORD. That meant it was supposed to go out through a system that coded it and jumped it from ship to ship across the Pacific and through special landline circuits across the States directly back to the Puzzle Palace at Fort Meade in Maryland. It could be back at Meade, halfway around the world, in minutes, a very big deal back in 1965. Could be, but wouldn't be. My translation

80

was dumped in a sack with the rest of the one-liners. It would be back at Meade in three days.

Swing shift was over and we were an hour or so into the night shift. I had missed the bus back to the barracks, so I decided to hoof it, a little less than a mile down the runway. I was scuffing my feet, looking down as I walked along the tarmac, disgusted with life in general, and with the Army ways in particular. *How the hell did they expect us to win the war?*

I glanced up and was stunned to see a glorious but entirely alien night sky. It was a clear late winter night, and the Southern Cross hung gloriously above the horizon. I'll never forget that night, the night I came to realize we were not going to win the war. A few months later, when the White Snake came around with his re-up package loaded with bennies, I quietly but firmly turned him down. "But these are hard stripes," he yelled, as if I didn't understand Army.

Over the decades since, I wondered if anybody who cared was on duty three years later, the night the comrades called for the bloody Tet uprising.

My Bud

By George 'Tam' Tamalavich

Pete and I grew up together during a time when an older person from the neighborhood took care of the younger guy. Pete was my guardian angel who took me to and from school. We hung around together, in the park and in the pool hall. Just buds. Pete went into the Army and a few years later I did also. We met a few times while in the Army and I always looked up to him as with the eyes of a kid having an older person bring him to school. To me Pete was the older brother I never had. There are no words that can express the feelings I have and had for Pete.

For many years I've been unable to express the common bond we brothers have in losing a friend. While at the reunion at Angelfire I started to have closure about a lot of things from my past. The first time I went to the memorial I was all tears. My knees trembled and my legs became so wobbly I had to hold onto the skids of the chopper. I remembered the sounds of Vietnam like it was yesterday.

The following is an abbreviated synopsis from an after-action report from the Internet that gives a more complete history of the events of the day Peter went missing.

Russell Peter Bott was attached to Detachment B - 52 Delta, Special Forces Group, First Special Forces. November, 1966, he was second-in-command of a reconnaissance team on a reconnaissance mission in Laos. Shortly after being inserted the team was ambushed by elements of the 325B NVA Division. Over the next two days a running gun battle ensued as the team moved to the Northeast, attempting to break contact. Later on the second day, Pete Bott made radio contact with forward control aircraft and reported he was down to one grenade and one magazine of ammunition. He also stated that several of the Vietnamese team members were dead or wounded, and that Willie Stark, the team leader, had sustained wounds to his chest and leg but was still alive. Staff Sergeant Bott requested an immediate emergency extraction. At the same time Sergeant Bott ordered the surviving strikers to escape and evade. He was staying with Sergeant First Class Stark. He would destroy the radio since he believed capture was imminent.

An attempt was made by a number of helicopters to extract Sergeant Bott and Sergeant Stark and in the process a helicopter was shot down and crashed into a village with all crew presumed dead. Two of the Vietnamese strikers eventually made their way back to American forces. The escaping strikers heard no shots emanating from the American's location as they continued to evade NVA troops. However, both of the survivors reported clearly hearing North Vietnamese soldiers yell, "Here you are. We been looking for you. Tie his hands. We will take him this way."

Sometime afterwards it was reported that Peter Bott was seen with his arms tied behind his back being led through a village three days after being captured. No further sightings were reported and both Willie Stark and Pete Bott are reported as Missing in Action.

They and members of the flight crew who were killed in the crash were among nearly 600 Americans who disappeared in Laos. Many of these men were known to be alive on the ground. The Laotians admitting holding 'tens of tens' of American prisoners of war, but these men were never negotiated for either by direct negotiations between our countries or through the Paris Peace Accords that ended the war in Vietnam since Laos was not a party to that agreement.

Back home in Worcester, Massachusetts we tried to name a park after Russell Peter Bott in the area where we grow up as kids. For some reason the whole park would not be renamed after him but the bathhouse was.

SSGT Easy and RF Energy
By Ken Jones

As with every job in the Army, there are always prescribed procedures for doing everything. Generally, these are published in a document known as Standard Operating Procedures or SOP. Each section within ASA Operations had such a document, and while it was intended to be a guide, some people assumed it to be gospel, to be followed without exception. One such individual arrived on the scene at Phu Bai and assumed duties as 'Trick Chief.' A Trick Chief is the person in charge on a work shift. This story is about one such Staff Sergeant at Phu Bai.

For the purposes of this story his name will be Staff Sergeant Easy, a man who was to become my nemesis for the remainder of my stay in Vietnam. Staff Sergeant Easy was a 'legend in his own mind.' He had read the section SOP, and could quote it as justification for chastising the DF operators for almost any infraction.

Anyone who has spent time in the military has met a Staff Sergeant Easy. He is the guy who never needs a haircut, always has starched fatigues and spit-shined boots, even in a combat zone, and while he may not be the most knowledgeable person in his particular specialty, he is the one with the rank, so that makes him the authority.

Our operation consisted of two positions where we sent and received Morse code; the Flash position and the Report position. The Flash position was a broadcast position, and when the operator was not sending information, the frequency was kept clear through the use of a channel marker. This was a motor driven device that sent the letter D every six seconds as prescribed by the SOP. It was a responsibility of the flash operator to turn on the channel marker as soon as he completed sending a mission, and Staff Sergeant Easy - a scholar of the SOP - made sure either the operator was sending with the Morse key, or the channel marker was on. He had been known to turn the channel marker on in the middle of a flash mission if the flash operator stopped sending for more than a few seconds.

Unlike other operational specialties, Duffy's or Direction Finding Operators, were required to maintain their transmitters and antennas, and in order to maintain communications with outstations, we often had to install new antennas directionally oriented to provide the strongest signal to the outstation. We used BC-610 and T-368 model transmitters that were set to transmit at 300 Watts. The transmitters were in a Quonset shed outside the Operations building.

During a day shift, I was given the task of helping Sergeant Bass put up another antenna that was better oriented to transmit the flashes to our more distant outstations. After erecting the antenna, we ran a coaxial cable into the transmitter hut. Due to the long warm-up time of the T-368, we were going to just swap the antenna cables with the transmitter powered up. As long as the transmitter was not actually sending anything, there would be no problem and it would be perfectly safe. I called into the Operations building and asked the flash operator to turn off the channel marker and not send anything until I called him back, so I could remove the coaxial cable from the transmitter and connect the coaxial cable from the new antenna. I watched the power meter on the transmitter, and when it stopped moving - indicating it was not transmitting anything - I removed the coax cable from the transmitter.

The next thing I remembered, I was picking myself up off the floor across the Quonset from the transmitter. Sergeant Bass was asking me if I was all right. Other than being a little disoriented, I seemed okay, and I asked Sergeant Bass what happened. He told me the transmitter had been keyed when I removed the coax, and I had taken 300 Watts of RF energy. He called inside again, got the channel marker turned off, and we completed the change of antennas.

We went back to operations, and I went up to the flash operator and asked him why he turned the channel marker back on. Staff Sergeant Easy came up and said, "I turned it on because it is not to be left off if we're not sending flashes."

Without thinking, I punched Staff Sergeant Easy and screamed: "You son-of-a-bitch, you could have killed me."

He held his jaw said: 'Specialist, I'll have your stripes for that." Just then, SFC Sutton, the NCOIC came up and asked for an explanation of what was going on. I explained to him what had happened.

After the explanation, SFC said: "Jones, take the rest of the day off, and think about holding your temper. Staff Sergeant Easy, come into my office; I want to talk to you."

I took the rest of the day off, and shortly after, Sergeant Bass took over the Trick and Staff Sergeant Easy was moved to straight days where he no longer was in charge of the shift workers. He continued to be a bother to most everyone in the section, and continued to monitor the Flash and Report nets for OPSEC violations. Staff Sergeant Easy did learn one thing, though, RF Energy can get you hurt.

Bugs

By James Methvin

During my time at the 330th RRC, September, 1966, through June, 1967, I had the opportunity to observe many entomological specimens found in that region of Southeast Asia. While working Mids in the Operations compound, the bored operators would search for the most fearsome looking bugs that flew around a large, bright light outside Operations. We would put them in an empty box and watch them battle it out.

Another chance I had to study an entomological specimen was when I felt the call of nature. I was again working Mids and when the call came, I answered, grabbing a roll of toilet paper and made my way out to our one-hole latrine. The latrine had a modesty screen facing the Operations area. I was sitting there contemplating the South East Asian night when I heard a whizzing sound and a thump. At first I thought it was an errant round from somewhere. But then I looked to my right, mind you I was still seated, and there was the biggest and ugliest rhinoceros beetle staggering around on the latrine. I finished up what I was doing and left the beetle to his own devices.

However, the most amazing specimen I observed was in the 330th NCO/EM club. A bunch of us were enjoying the club, playing cards and getting smashed. Tom Gilley, a Hawg, was catching little bugs and just popping them in his mouth for a buck a pop. He gobbled down three or four of the little ones. Someone said that he would bet Tom that he wouldn't eat any bug they found for him. Tom agreed and two or three of the patrons went out on a bug search. About $60 MPC was placed on the table. After 15 or 20 minutes they returned with big grins on their faces. Between the thumb and forefinger of one of the bug searchers was the biggest moth I have ever seen.

They put the moth down on the table in front of Tom, who regarded it with interest. Everyone around him was snickering and mumbling: "We've got him now!"

Tom picked up the moth, looked at it and popped it in his mouth, chewed all a bit and then pulled a leg out of his mouth saying: "Tastes a bit like orange peel." A couple of the patrons made a fast exit and the sounds of retching could be heard from outside. And that, my friends, ain't no shit.

TAREX Participation in

Operation Cedar Falls

By Glen Caldwell

Each of us brings back memories of our tours in Vietnam, some funny, some sad and some tragic. One I remember the clearest, now 45 years later, was one of my primary contributions as the TAREX NCO assigned to the 303rd Radio Research Battalion, which was stationed at Long Binh. There the 303rd was tactically subordinate to Headquarters II Field Force, also at Long Binh, but under the operational control of the 509th Radio Research Group, Saigon. TAREX stands for Target Exploitation.

My duties as TAREX NCO was to brief military intelligence units at all commands, brigade and above, on the proper handling and processing of captured signal information, to include code signals operating procedures, captured enemy signal personnel, as well as captured signal equipment used by the Viet Cong and the North Vietnamese Army. Upon identification it was designated HANDLE VIA SPECIAL CHANNELS ONLY. When I was notified of possible information of value, I was flown or driven to the site of collection and if the information was of significant value, I would courier it to our TAREX unit, located at J2 MACV in Cholon, by the quickest means possible.

In January, 1967, I was tasked to deploy with the 337th Radio Research Company, which was located with the forward element of the Division to participate in Operation Cedar Falls. After arriving at Brigade Forward, a Sp 6 Vietnamese linguist and I took up residence with the other members of the 337th RRU. We took up routine military duties that, for us, was reviewing documents at the MI

Collection Point where all captured documents and material were processed.

I can clearly remember that on the second day we were awakened by the ground being shaking violently. It turned out to be an extended ARC LIGHT B-52 strike which had targeted known enemy concentrations a few miles from us.

The next morning about 0600 I was awakened by my Sp 6 partner who was very excited and showed me a book and several pads of paper with a series of numbers on each page. He recognized this as some sort of codebook and encryption material to go with it. He was told that it had been captured by an Australian ambush patrol that had camped next to a trail. During the night, the patrol fired on an enemy soldier coming along the path. At first light, the body was searched and the documents found.

I immediately briefed the Captain who was the CO of the 337th. He asked me what I wanted to do with it. I requested to see the 1st Infantry Division Intelligence Officer and immediately briefed him that this was presumed high-level intelligence and should be taken to TAREX in Saigon as soon as possible.

He agreed and immediately assigned his personal two-seater, a light observation helicopter called a Loach, to ferry me to Saigon ASAP. I remember that flight clearly. I loaded myself, all my combat gear and a bag full of documents into a very small helicopter. The pilot, who seemed to be a young Warrant Officer who looked to be in his teens, outfitted me with headphones and a mike and instructed me how to communicate with him. He started off immediately at a fast clip down what he told me was Highway 13. The pucker factor was a bit high. He was flying so low to the road that Vietnamese bicyclists were driving off the road into rice paddies to get out of his way. Further in the trip he climbed for altitude and my guess is we were probably between 5000 to 8000 feet high.

As we came into Tan Son Nhut Air Base he asked me, "Sarge have you ever auto-gyrated before?"

Auto-gyration is when the pilot cuts all power and the blade on the helicopter reverses. It provides a very fast descent, and sort of feels like you're dropping in a very fast elevator. The Warrant explained that we needed to do this to approach the airfield as it had commercial flights and we needed to get out of the flight paths.

We landed about noon without incident and were met by two individuals from TAREX in a Jeep and I turned over the documents. Basically, my job was completed. But I did hear later an interesting story as to what happened later.

The TAREX Team at J2 were experts and immediately identified the documents as a personal notebook of a VC cryptographer with encode and decode instructions, a complete encode and decode book, and numerous reused one time encryption pages for a high level code that was identified as being used by Central Office of Vietnam (COSVN) Military Intelligence Element of Region IV.

Later that afternoon, when the CO of the TAREX Detachment started to brief Brigadier General McChristian, J2 MACV, on the value of the capture, the General was said to have stood up and shouted "Captain, don't you bull shit me! I wait for weeks for important intelligence to get here. There is no way possible that these documents were captured this morning."

Unshaken, the Captain showed General McChristian the capture tag showing the date, time and coordinates of the capture that same morning.

I learned of this later, and was surprised when I received a Letter of Commendation from Col. John J. McFadden, CO of the 509th Group for the timely handling of intelligence. Later that year after reassignment to Frankfurt, Germany, I got called to the Office of the

Commander of USASA Europe at my new assignment and in the presence of my wife, was presented the Bronze Star by the Commanding General.

Wiretap
By Glen Caldwell

While deployed with the 1st Infantry Division Forward as TAREX NCO, during Operation Cedar Falls, I was called in by the CO of the 337th RRU and asked if I knew anything about placing a wiretap on a wire found during a combat operation in the field. I told the Captain that I had zero experience and zero training with the procedures for tapping wires. He took me to see the G2 intelligence colonel of the 1st Infantry Division, who asked me what I thought should be done to gather intercept from a wire found in the major Search and Destroy operation that was being conducted. Although I told him I had no experience, I was tasked to take a Sp 4 Vietnamese linguist with a tape recorder and wire clips. We were put on board a Huey and flown to the site of the wire.

The area we landed in was a patch of ground recently cleared and surrounded by jungle canopy. I was taken to a colonel who briefed me that earlier a tank had run over a multi-line communication cable and severed it and that when an ARVN soldier took a field phone and attached it to one end of the severed cable, he heard a VC voice, obviously enemy. After he spoke, the VC immediately went silent. The colonel wanted to know what could be done with the wire. I reasoned that if one end knew we had captured the wire, it would immediately try to alert the other end of the wire of the status. I told the colonel that I thought we should tap the wire end that had not been compromised.

To cover the fact that we were working on the wire, the colonel assigned an infantry platoon to go with us and we followed the wire several hundred yards into the jungle along a well-worn path next to the wire. As we set up our position I told the Lieutenant that, based on intelligence reports that I had read, if the VC suspected anything unusual was happening to the wire, they would send out a scout patrol to check it out. Based on this, the Lieutenant sent an ambush patrol to cover the path several hundred feet forward of our tap position. The linguist hooked up his leads into the wire and turned on the recorder. He immediately heard a voice calling, "This is XXXX, this is XXXX, come in, come in." He told me the voice sounded desperate. As he listened, a helicopter went overhead. The Specialist said, "Damn he must be close, I just heard that helicopter through the wire."

Knowing this was important, I asked the Lieutenant for an escort to go back to tell the colonel the situation. Several infantrymen and I quickly set off to brief the colonel. I had gone about 20 feet when I heard the rat-tat-tat of an M-60 machine gun, and a hand grenade went off. I thought, *oh shit, the Sp 4 that I'm responsible for might be in trouble.*

I briefed the colonel, and later the patrol and my Sp 4 returned safely, dragging with them the body of a dead VC whose papers identified him as belonging to a security regiment of a major VC Headquarters. The switchboard was captured later in the operation, with the name XXXX over one of the phone plugs. I came to realize that by hooking up the tape recorder, we lit up a light on the VC switchboard as if someone were trying to contact him. We didn't get much from the intercept other than the cover name XXXX.

It must have caused a bit of a stink at the 509th Group, because about a week later I was called into a debriefing by a Major and a Captain to go over the details. I think there was some concern that two ASA troops with Top-Secret clearances were that close to enemy action, but it did add a wire tapper story to my collection of war stories.

Soviet Military Liaison Mission
Visits Camp King
By Glen Caldwell

After an interesting and productive assignment as TAREX NCO in Vietnam, I was given my choice assignment to TAREX ASA Europe, Det. B, which was at Camp King, Oberursel, Germany. Camp King was the Headquarters of the 18th Military Intelligence Battalion. I was part of a three-man ASA detachment assigned to debrief refugees and defectors from the Eastern Bloc on communications. It was a plush assignment; civilian clothes, separate rations, and no military duties. I was living in base housing which was a three minute walk from where I worked.

To make this story understood, I must first tell you about the Soviet Military Liaison Mission (SMLM). After the end of World War II, each of the occupying powers, US, France, Great Britain, and Russia, divided Germany into occupied sectors. Further, as a condition of the Potsdam Agreement, each of these countries was allowed to have a limited number of legally recognized spies (Military Liaison Missions). These Missions were only allowed to travel in clearly marked vehicles with special license plates. Since the Soviet SMLM was spying on US forces in the US sector, each soldier in the US forces was briefed on what to do when one of these vehicles was seen and given a card with instructions on how to report a sighting.

On Sunday morning, 18 August, 1968, I awoke early and decided to go off post to the nearest German bakery to get some German rolls. For those of you that have had these, you know that with butter and marmalade, nothing tastes better. Anyway, I got the rolls and was returning to Camp King.

As I pulled up to the gate, I found that I was behind SMLM number three. I observed that there were three people in the car. They were in Russian uniforms, and one was taking pictures through the gate. Posted on the fence in large letters was a sign: THIS IS A RESTRICTED AREA - NO ENTRY BY UNAUTHORIZED PERSONNEL. This was posted in English, German and Russian. As I pulled up behind them in my car they stayed for a minute and then sped up the hill towards the Taunus Mountains. I immediately went to the gate guard and had him call the Staff Duty Officer, since this was early Sunday morning and the post was asleep; mine was the only vehicle I saw moving on the post. As I was walking to the gate guard, SMLM number three returned from up the hill and proceeded to take more photos. I had this reported to the Staff Duty Officer

Now this would not normally be an interesting story, except for the fact that this was 18 August, 1968, and on the morning of 20 August, the Soviets invaded Czechoslovakia. It was clear to me later that the SMLM was checking US alert status prior to the invasion, and it was clear to them we were not preparing for anything!

At War with the B-52
By Mike Conaghan

Mike Conaghan served in Vietnam with the 547th Signal Troop of the Australian Army. He was the first combat airborne DF operator in the Australian Army. His work paralleled the work of ASA ARDF (Airborne Radio Direction Finding) units in Vietnam. Mike lives in Queensland, Australia with his wife, Denise.

It was August, 1967, and after some three weeks of 'in air' training with the new ARDF equipment, we had finally been declared operational. To reach the status, we had done a familiarization with the equipment on the ground and then gone airborne. In those times, convincing the hierarchy of our experience and skills was somewhat of a problem. No one had ever heard of 'electronic warfare' irrespective of the fact that the unit had been involved in it since the beginning of World War II.

The Task Force Commander held to the principle that none of the information we supplied be taken into account until it could be proven. Over the three weeks of 'in air' training, SAS patrols were sent in to verify our information and with their confirmations, Command then started to place some credence in our reports.

Sometime around the beginning of September, I had been flying a mission up around the Nui May Tao Mountains. The mission had been relatively successful, in that a couple of new fixes had been made and I had given the pilot the word to head home to Nui Dat. We headed towards the Courtenay Rubber Plantation, where we would bank left and fly back to Nui Dat to the south. About five minutes into our return trip, I was searching around the radio spectrum and came across a station that I recognized, both by its

97

sound and by the operator's fist. Lo and behold, it was one of our primary targets that had been quiet for some time. It was believed that he had been out of the province for retraining/regrouping.

I immediately reported his activity to my own HQ and then asked the pilot to do a run to the West and, depending on the results, we would do another to the South.

About three or four minutes into the run my own HQ came on-air and asked for my current location. Being rather busy at the time, operating the equipment and trying to counter the turbulence that we were going through, I quickly gave them a coded grid and carried on with my duties.

HQ came back and with what sounded like a voice in panic, told me to get out, quick. Leave the area immediately. Well, I wasn't being heroic, in fact, I don't know to this day why I reacted the way I did, no, nothing like that, I just wanted to get a good fix and really prove that we had the 'bull by the horns' so to speak. I called them back again and said, "Say again, you're breaking up," you know, one of those old tricks that you often saw in the movies. This I repeated, and then decided to just ignore the interruption.

At that stage, the pilot said to me, "Take a look out the window - I think we might be in trouble."

With that, I did look and suddenly saw that everything below us was being totally wiped out. I didn't realize what was doing it at that stage, but then decided that something was seriously wrong. It was then that I realized what all the turbulence was about. As we were only flying at around 1500 feet, we were copping all the updrafts from the explosions.

I suggested to the pilot that he get a finish point for me real quick and then we would get out; after all, I had sufficient good cuts on the target to get a good fix. Within two minutes we were out of there and heading for home. I called my HQ back and reported our ETA at Nui Dat and asked for transport to pick me up.

Well now - WE had a reception committee waiting for us when we taxied out to the hangar. There was the Commanding Officer from the Aviation Flight but worst of all, there was my own Officer Commanding, and he looked just about ready to explode.

"What's all the shit - Say again, you're breaking up" and then he blurted, or should that be spluttered out, "Do you realize you two just flew through the middle of a B-52 strike?"

I really got reamed on the way back to base, and I believe the pilot spent 45 minutes standing at attention in front of his CO, trying to explain.

Irrespective of all that transpired, I did get a great fix; in fact, I would say that the target was within 50 meters of where I placed him. This was later confirmed by Special Air Services as they had been watching an area they suspected of being prepared for someone's arrival.

Once the Task Force Commander had the information in his hands, the Task Force was placed on 'Stand To' and remained there for several hours until it was deemed that nothing untoward was likely to happen.

By the way, I did get a congratulatory call from the Task Force Commander on the job I had done. I don't know if he ever had been made aware of what we had flown through to get the fix though.

A Good Friend
By Mike Conaghan

Friends, in many instances, are hard to come by, and the loss of a good friend can really be devastating. In August, 1967, I had just been given a new task within the Troop, that of being the first ARDF Operator to take on the role under combat conditions. I guess it was a moment of some pride to have been selected, but little did I realize how the job was going to come back to haunt me later in life.

After many years, there are some occasions that come to memory but the primary one being that of the loss of a good friend really hurts the most.

Over the ten months that I flew ARDF, I had built up a very good working relationship with my chief pilot, George. This relationship had also turned into us becoming good friends. George was a Commanding Officer of the Australian Army's Independent Reconnaissance Squadron, based at Nui Dat in Phuoc Tuy Province in Vietnam. He was a couple of years younger than me but we had the ability to talk about many things. Home, family, where we lived and so on, were regular topics of conversation.

We, in our working environment, had been through many things, some of them life-threatening and others just something we could laugh about. We had flown through the middle of a B-52 strike; we had returned to base several times with bullet holes through the wings of the aircraft. We had the odd battle of trying to get around artillery action and we had been involved in some pretty hairy landings and takeoffs from very small strips. I guess they were all scary situations, but at the time, we just took them as being part of the job. Results of our operations were usually first class and it wasn't very often that we aborted a mission due to some problem arising.

Prior to my returning to Australia in early May, 1968, George had invited me to have breakfast with him on the day I was to leave. Unusual to have an NCO dining in the Officer's Mess but we managed to get through it without any interference. During the meal, we also discussed George's return to Australia, which was only three or four weeks away. We agreed that he would phone me as soon as he returned home and once he settled down, we would meet at the local hotel for a meal and a few beers, just to talk about old times. From there - it was onto the C-127 and out of Nui Dat, heading for Saigon in my return flight home on Qantas.

About three weeks after arriving home, I picked up my morning newspaper and there - on the front page - George had been shot down and killed. He had been flying escort on a Squadron of Leopard Tanks when he was fired on by a group of Provincial Forces and shot down. Witnesses said that George had actually been burnt to death. Provincial Forces - I thought they had been on our side. Witnesses said that these people were all standing back and laughing and joking about what they had done.

Hurt - Angry - Upset would all be as nothing as to how I felt that day. I was virtually inconsolable. I cried and I wouldn't talk to anyone, not even my wife.

I carried this hurt for many years and even now on occasion, something triggers the memory and I once again feel the hurt. I have learned though how to control my feelings, but always, George will remain one good friend that I had made under war conditions, and then lost under the same conditions.

Vale George

Never Volunteer

By Lee Bishop aka Lee Taylor

My first experience with personal recognition in the Army occurred in Basic Training: Soldier of the Cycle. That opportunity taught me a lot about volunteering information.

Our temporary squad Sergeant was, believe it or not, Sergeant Sergeant; I had two black friends whose last names were Sermon and Preacher; and there was another black guy, very obnoxious, from New York City named Ricketts. Sermon and Preacher always enjoyed it when Ricketts teed me off to a point where I had to pop him a couple of times to get him back into a proper behavior mode.

Now I was not an ideal soldier, but I qualified for expert at the shooting range, put on 30 pounds of muscle in those eight weeks, could perform on an obstacle course, and was blessed with a good mind such that I could memorize all the stuff they gave us. On the other hand, I wasn't very good at avoiding trouble.

One of the challenges in Basic Training was that each day was a major physical workout. Being a sound sleeper, I really slept soundly after a day of Basic. This particular night, being close to the end of our training cycle and graduation, I was awakened at two in the morning to handle my guard duties. I know that the guy before me had done his job properly, because when I awoke up the next morning I had one sock on and the other side partially on. Oops! I figured I was in big trouble.

Sure enough here comes Sergeant Sergeant who starts screaming in my face, "You've done it now, Taylor! We're all in trouble because of you; you're a real ass."

I was already aggravated, and I'd had enough, at least for the moment, so I popped him a good one right in the solar plexus. Preacher and Sermon were laughing their butts off.

Later that morning I was called to the First Sergeant's office. Knowing that I was truly screwed this time, I was desperately trying to figure out how I was going to avoid any more damage to myself than I'd already done. Honesty is the best policy; I'll go with honesty!

"Do you know why your platoon Sergeant, Sergeant Moore, sent you over here it, Taylor?"

"Yes, First Sergeant."

"You do?"

"Yes, First Sergeant."

"Really"

"Why don't you tell me why you're here, Private Taylor?"

"I fell asleep on fire guard duty, First Sergeant."

"You did?"

"Yes, First Sergeant."

"Get the hell out of my office, Taylor."

"Yes, First Sergeant."

As I walked back to my barracks, I'm figuring that really wasn't nearly as bad as I thought it was going to be. I fall asleep on guard duty which could, I guess, get me shot in a war zone, I pop an NCO, I get called to the First Sergeant's office, and all he does is get pissed off and tell me to leave. Maybe this Army thing isn't going to be so bad after all. My steps got lighter the closer I got to my barracks.

As I came through the door, Sergeant Moore grabbed me, big smile on his face, and asked, "How did it go, Taylor?"

Knowing for sure now that honesty is really the best policy but, I replied, "Great Sergeant Moore!"

"Well, Taylor, you been a fine recruit and you deserve that honor as much as any man I've trained."

"What honor, Sergeant Moore?"

"The First Sergeant made you Soldier of the Cycle, didn't he?"

So I ran it all down to him. He just said, "Taylor, you're a dumb ass!"

Then he turned on his heel, went into his room, and closed his door in less than a gentle fashion.

Well, after giving it some thought, I decided that while it's always nice to get a little positive recognition, I still got the best end of the bargain. I got a full night's sleep, I got to punch out a major aggravation in my life, and my friends, Sermon and Preacher, got to enjoy a little excitement.

But I also learned another thing. I could have skated entirely, I thought if I'd kept my wits and answered, "No, First Sergeant." But I volunteered information and that's what got me into a less desirable situation. After that, I neither volunteered information nor my precious self, especially in Vietnam.

Torture
By Lee Bishop

"So, NUG, would you like to see us interrogate a real VC?" asked Specialist Fifth Class Soprano. Having been in-country for nearly three months, I sort of thought the new guy appellation was less than appropriate, but my curiosity was definitely aroused.

"When and where?" I asked.

"Just come down to the CID tent this evening around sundown."

"Mind if I bring along my camera?"

"Make yourself happy."

I finished up my sandbagging duties and went looking for my friend and fellow linguist, Rooster, but was told that he'd left that morning with the 7/402 for an assignment in the boonies. Rooster and I had pretty much done everything together since meeting up after Basic Training. First there was the 36 weeks of training in Vietnamese, two weeks of combat training at Two Rock Ranch Station, then three weeks in Saigon acclimating ourselves to the people in the Southern dialect, then on to the First Brigade of the 101st Airborne Division, Phan Rang for jungle combat training, Operation Eagle's Bait out of Dak To, and now low-level voice intercept assignments in Operations out of Tuy Hoa on the coast.

As the sun began setting, I slogged through the hot sand over to the CID tent. I let myself in. Soprano was sitting in a lawn chair talking with some guy. He didn't bother to introduce me, so I just stood there waiting for them to finish. The other fellow, turned out his name was Smith, was holding a field telephone.

"Hey, NUG, go stand over here and be quiet. We've got us a real live VC who's been caught in an off-limits area for the fifth time. We want all the information we can get."

Another soldier came in escorting a middle-aged Vietnamese woman dressed in black. After reviewing the data tag hanging from her neck, Soprano and Smith put some wire nooses around her wrists.

"Don't say anything and don't do anything, NUG. This woman is married to a Vietcong and has been picking up and carrying supplies to him and his pals on more than one occasion. We want to know his unit designation, area of operations, command structure, and anything else we can get."

Without another word to me, or to the woman, Soprano turned, nodded his head to Smith, and Smith cranked the handle on the field telephone, pumping electricity through the woman's body. She jumped and shook like a puppet on strings. I numbly raised my camera and took a picture. The cranking stopped and Soprano began the interrogation.

The woman put her two hands together as though praying, looking at me and said in Vietnamese, "Please make them stop. I know nothing. The pain is too much."

I shrugged my shoulders and mumbled, "There is nothing I can do. Just tell them what they want to know, and you can leave this place."

Soprano lit up a cigarette, sat back in his lawn chair, nodded to Smith, and again she was shaking and grimacing in pain. I couldn't take it anymore and rushed out of the tent.

I went back and sat down on the gravesite that we used for partying. The grave was behind our tents at the base of the sand dune leading up to the Long Range Reconnaissance Patrol area. I just couldn't believe it. We're Americans, for crying out loud! We don't torture people. None of it sat well with me, nor would it ever.

I saw Soprano the next day. He asked, "Why did you run off? Right after you left she spilled her guts, and we got tons of good intelligence."

I thought, well, if it saves one American's life, maybe it's worth it. If it would save one GIs life, I would volunteer for the torture myself.

"Hey, man. About those pictures, I think you got me in one of them. Make sure you never show it to anyone."

I guess there's a reason the Army gave us those personality and aptitude tests when we enlisted. They obviously knew that human intelligence gathering was a field that I could not have handled. Electronic warfare was nerve-racking enough.

Beer

By Dennis Beerby

By the time we left Davis Station where we had processed in-country, we'd drunk up the entire supply of San Miguel™ beer at the EM Club. San Miguel's not a bad beer at all, and I fully deserved the massive hangover the next day. I almost lost it at breakfast when I put the first forkful of delicious egg and bacon between my lips. I gagged, I whimpered, my eyes watered, my hands and feet tangled, and the world grew dark. Those delicious looking eggs were duck eggs.

But as I said, we left soon after that historic run on Davis Station EM Club's beer supply and found ourselves, armed with only machetes and M-14's, in an overgrown area north of Saigon, near Bien Hoa and right next to a small village known as the 'Widows Village.' The machetes were for cutting down jungle, and the M-14's were for - well, you all know about that part.

Anyway, there we were, chopping down carnivorous shrubbery and slapping ants, filling sandbags and digging foxholes; deep ones too, with our entrenching tools, fighting the sand, dirt, insects, snakes, heat, and VC. The VC were smart enough to only to come out at night, when it was cool and we couldn't see them so readily.

At the end of the second week, when we had cleared enough ground, we set up three general purpose medium tents as a place for enlisted men to bunk. We set up two headquarters' tents, one for the officers and the other for the two ranking NCOs.

We guarded our perimeter for the first month. We set up two-hour shifts and everybody took a turn on guard duty almost every night.

One night after we'd been there about a week, just before we set up the tents, we were hit by a sapper platoon, probably from the 9th VC Regiment. There was lots of shooting, many grenades, back and forth. I fired a couple of magazines, just scoped out where the tracers were coming from, swung a few degrees to the right and pumped out rounds.

One guy, Roland Scherer, got hit with grenade shrapnel in the forehead. He wasn't hurt very bad, but Steve Fox and I took him to the medic tent where they removed the shrapnel and put a small Band-Aid over the wound. We went back to our foxholes and stayed awake the rest of the night. Ronald got a Purple Heart about three weeks later.

Anyway, we gradually got our camp together, as did all the units lucky enough to be part of the 2nd Brigade, First Infantry. One day, about three weeks after we left Davis Station, a Sp 4 came by our area driving a Jeep with a small trailer attached. He must've been from the newly arrived field PX, because he had a beer for every man in the detachment. Now it must be said that there was no ice, and no church keys, so upon finding this hot Schlitz™ in my hot little hands, and being the resourceful GI that I was, I reached for my dog tags.

Why, you ask, did I reach for my dog tags? Well GI, that's where I kept my P-38 can opener, hanging and clanging. So, using that small engineering marvel, I made two holes in the top of that hot beer and sucked it down. I never liked Schlitz, but let me tell you the truth! That was one of the best beers I ever drank. And that ain't no shit!

Chapter 4
1968

The year 1968 started with the Tet Offensive by the Viet Cong and the North Vietnamese Army in a countrywide attack. For many Americans this was a turning point for many reasons. It is for some Americans the only thing that matters about the Vietnam War. It was also a turning point for the military. The Viet Cong was destroyed as a fighting force and the North Vietnamese Army took on most of the fighting in South Vietnam. The US changed Presidents and General Abrams took command of all forces in Vietnam. The US and allied forces won the battle of Tet and the subsequent surge in fighting in May, 1968.

Captain John M. Casey was one of eight ASA soldiers killed in 1968. Casey's Hill is a story about him and the events of his death.

Communications Security (COMSEC) is one of the many ASA missions and the story of 'Joe' speaks of that mission but also gives an account of the death of a LRRP team. This story gives insight into the impact of the vicarious trauma that ASA soldiers experienced through their work.

Joe

By Dave Parks

Joe was COMSEC, serving his year in Vietnam with 856th RRD at roughly the same time as I. He hailed from Minnesota and would return there after two tours in Nam, the second of which apparently did him some long-term damage with PTSD. I never did find out what had happened once we had hooked up again some 28 years after Vietnam.

One day, in the spring of 1998, I received a letter from Joe, right out of the blue. He'd gotten my address from a letter of mine that was published in the 199th Light Infantry Association newsletter. I was thrilled; this was the first contact I had had from anyone in the old unit since leaving Nam. Joe remarked on a few of the things we experienced together over there, including eavesdropping on the 'rubbing out' of a Long Range Recon Patrol one night.

During our tour together we would sometimes end up on the same firebase in the field, Joe with his COMSEC van and me with my PRD-1 and partner. Sometimes too there would be other ASA types involved in these operations, lingies, and Morse Intercept Ops, for instance. Joe taught me the rudiments of COMSEC as I watched him monitor the 199th communication nets for security violations. Seems there was real job security in what he did; this 'Radio Cop' issued plenty of tickets. He would tape record the violations and write up a report accompanied with a 'ticket' to be 'acted' on by the next higher command.

Joe was doing an important job, a job that saved lives - you might even say he was saving people from themselves. This fact was brought home forcefully to me when Joe played tapes to me of incidents of the enemy manipulating American radio traffic to cause artillery or air strikes to be brought down on American troops. Once he played a tape of an enemy operator breaking into a net during a firefight, transmitting in perfect English, attempting to maneuver an American unit into an ambush.

Frankly, the Americans were often sloppy in the radio procedures. They failed to encipher their transmissions, especially those containing crucial information such as the coordinates of their locations, and they did not use 'challenge and reply' to authenticate a sender's information when it could mean their lives if they acted on false information. Americans gave away operations objectives by 'transmitting in the clear,' as it was known, giving out raw intelligence information that the other side could, and did, exploit to their advantage. One of the US Army's radio operators' major failings was not using the Army provided coding sheets to cloak the information they exchanged. They just blurted it out and hoped for the best, not realizing that the enemy was one sharp outfit and had them cold when they wanted to.

The violations ran the whole gamut and included every level of command. Joe's job was to plug the dike, stanch the flood of intelligence American radio operators were prone to give away and save them from themselves. For that he earned the title Buddy Fucker, for that is what the COMSEC branch of the US Army Security Agency was titled by those that received the 'tickets.'

Joe taught me some of his craft and I too traded craft with him. A couple of times I 'got up' a live VC during a radio transmission for him to hear. Once, against all regulations, I showed off for him by using his COMSEC vans CW transmitter to answer the call up of a VC target that I knew. It was a dumb thing to do, and I have "no excuse Sir!" It was a very short demo in any case - the COMSEC CW set's power output was probably 50 or a 100 times more than a VC set. The VC Op probably went silent, NIL MORE HEARD as we used to say. It's even possible that I blew the VC eardrums out, blasting him as I did with that COMSEC transmitter.

One of Joe's favorite pastimes was listening into the LRRP net. Generally it was pretty mundane, consisting of not much more than the LRRP team RTO briefly keying his handset (breaking squelch) twice every 30 minutes, signaling 'all okay' in reply to the LRRP net control's call for his Situation Report (Sitrep). The control would call each team in turn, saying something like "Silent Shadow One-Four, Sitrep, over." The Shadow One-Four RTO would then simply key his mike twice, meaning all was fine with the team. Sometimes this exchange would be even briefer, consisting of Control keying his mike once and the team keying theirs twice. If there was something to report, and these teams reported everything they heard or saw, then the RTO would whisper the information to Control. Such a report might be "Silent Shadow One-Four...break...single AK round fired, 550 yards, azimuth 240. Dogs barking 300 yards, azimuth 120...break...One-Four out." Control would key his mike to acknowledge receipt.

One thing about the LRRP net however, was that it got interesting when things went way off of mundane and exploded into pure life or death drama, such as a team getting discovered by the enemy. Teams were small, five or six heavily armed men. They were well supported with everything at hand, artillery, helicopter gunships, fast movers (jets), spooky gunships, and reaction teams of troops on stand-by to come and rescue them if needed. If a team was compromised they had a plan in place and it immediately went into action to escape. The result was often a running gunfight between the team and the pursuing enemy; the LRRP team left the area and ran for a PZ, Pick-up Zone, a landing area for the extraction choppers that were racing to rescue the team. The teams were good, expert at infiltrating enemy's territory, gathering intelligence and doing their best to get out without being seen, heard or suspected. It was a vicarious thrill to eavesdrop on their operations.

Through their radio transmissions you could put yourself with them and be in no personal danger. Picture yourself in there in the dark with the jungle funk in your nostrils; the jungle goes silent except for the footfalls of the enemy squad, or platoon, or company, or regiment passing behind you. You're expecting a bullet between the shoulder blades at any second…long, long seconds, seeming hours. You know your buddy is covering your 'six,' watching them pass, eyes averted, not daring to risk looking even one of the enemy in the face for fear of triggering their sixth sense. You've got your reaction planned if the shit hits the fan, you know which way you will roll, what part of the jungle you will fire into and the direction you will run if it comes to that. Sweat drops off the end of your nose and crashes into the dry leaves as your heart beats a high whine, loud as hell! Surely they can hear it. You've fingered the safety and fire selection switch on your weapon repeatedly, assuring that you are ready - knowing that you are not because you just don't want THIS. You want to open your mouth and take a deep breath but you would know from experience that your heart sound will loudly escape through your open mouth - and reveal you! Actually you know better, but you keep your mouth closed anyway. Or maybe it's all the other way with you and you welcome the contact, want it; because maybe that's who you are!

So, you see, one's imagination could safely run amok sitting in the COMSEC van and listening to the LRRP's do what they did in their corner of the war. Sometimes, off in the distance, one could hear and see the firefight, watching the gunships work out around the teams while they breathlessly adjusted fire and ran for their lives to the PZ. You hear the RTO or the team leader alternately whispering or screaming, cussing, requesting, insisting that help come quickly cause "THE FUCKERS ARE ALL AROUND US!" And you realize they must be judging by the AK fire plainly heard each time the team's radio transmits. No need to imagine now because for Joe and I the show was coming in live and in color, audio all the way up past desperate. Listening too and watching 'that', you would be about as close as you ever wanted to be to a running gunfight or on a LRRP team. At any rate, that's the way I felt.

Joe and I were listening one evening when an LRRP team lost the race. To tell the truth, I don't remember much past the high points of what Joe and I heard that evening. It happened fast; it was over in minutes except for LRRP Control calling and calling to the now silent team, his voice the loneliest sound I heard in all my time in Vietnam.

I happened to show up at the COMSEC van after having been relieved from PRD-1 duty that night. Joe immediately gestured for me to put on a pair of headsets as he patched them into the radios.

By the look on his face I knew it was something serious. A team had been discovered by an unknown number of NVA, Joe explained hurriedly, and they were now running for it, but each time they moved they ran into more NVA. We only had the radio transmissions; couldn't see or hear the firefight. Once my headsets were in place I heard the LRRP team leader running and firing as he tried to coordinate supporting fire. They had a couple of wounded and were trying to carry them. The weather was hampering the rescue and support effort; the clouds were almost on the deck and it was raining hard.

Silently, Joe and I listened as the team was run to ground and the NVA closed on their position in among some boulders. Each time the team leader transmitted, the flood of small arms fire could be heard, explosions, long strings of AK fire pointedly backing up the team leader's running commentary on what was happening. His voice had gone over to a sort of shaky warble suffused with a mixture of forced steadiness and contained fear. Anything you ever wanted to know about a firefight was in that voice. The team was putting up one hell of a fight, but the volume of NVA fire was increasing second by second.

The team leader couldn't be convinced to deploy a strobe light to mark their position; it would create a beacon for the NVA as it flashed through the low clouds, he screamed back when asked to do so by his six, the Lieutenant in charge of the LRRP platoon. It seemed perfectly obvious to us in the bleachers that the NVA knew precisely where they were. It was obvious to us that the team leader was losing it, losing his ability to lead, and to survive - but remember, he was there, Joe and I were not. Anything I say about the LRRP leader is not criticism or relevant. I only know what I heard that evening. It remains in my mind, however, that the team leader did lose it.

Within a few minutes there were two KIA on the team and all except one wounded; a grenade had found its mark. About then a screaming match developed between the team leader and a Major, probably the Brigade S-2; I never knew. The Major had come up on the net demanding that the team leader "pull his shit in order goddammit! We can't help you if you don't give us your location."

The team leader's response got strange as he went off on the Major in no uncertain terms, cursing him and reminding him that, "You fucking promised me you'd get us out, you mother fucker!"

It seemed that the two of them were picking up the thread of a private conversation they once had. It was plain to hear that the Major's concern was real, he wanted to help, he wanted to pull them out and was equally plain that the option was fading fast. The NVA were closing the door and maneuvering for the kill, a point not lost on the team leader.

Joe and I shared a quick glance and we heard the team leader's voice give into what could only be called barely controlled panic, "I hear the little bastard's! "THEY'RE COMING IN … FUCKING GOOKS ARE ALL AROUND US…"

AK fire, much closer now as the mike keyed off.

"Goddamn you, Major! You said you'd come to get us...GET THAT FUCKER, GET HIM!"

Sounds of an M-16 firing ... the transmission stops. Joe and I know what's going to happen now, the inevitable.

"AHHH SHIT, AH SHIT! YOU MOTHERFUCKER, GODDAMN YOU MAJOR, GODDAMN YOU...I'M HIT..."

The M-16 again, very loud AK fire; excited Asian voices... an AK burst, then silence.

And then the long string of unanswered calls from LRRP Control - until we both removed our headsets.

There was silence between us in the close confines of the van and in the red glow of the light from the radio dials; the sounds of us exiting, lighting cigarettes in the damp night, not saying a word for a long time.

My mind's eye was filled with images of NVA searching through the fresh blood of their victory - out there - in the rain.

Specialist Fifth Class Beale's
Plunge into History
By Dave Parks

For the moment let's leave SP 5 Frank Beale suspended in mid-air between a hovering Huey UH-1 and the ground. We will allow him to finish his plunge after exploring what led him there and relate why it was going to be so funny to see him complete the journey.

Frank was a nice guy and a buddy from my days in 05H20 School at Ft. Devens. He was from Boston. He and I had supped many a fine meal at his parent's table in Dorchester. It was a welcome break from Con-4, the Consolidated Mess Hall at Devens. He was a Tape Ape and that was part of the reason for his paying a visit to our PRD-1 site this day. He was delivering pin changes for our KY-8 radio, bringing us our mail, and getting away from the day-to-day boredom of Long Binh for a while.

Frank was a First Sergeant's dream soldier, in appearance anyway. His uniform was always sharp looking, boots gleaming and brass belt buckle shining. Today was no different; he looked like a brand spanking new Second Lieutenant on OCS graduation day. I had gone down to the chopper pad to meet him and escort him to our site. The site was on a Battalion-sized Fire Support Base.

As the chopper made its approach, the door gunner on the Huey leaned over to Frank and was earnestly shouting something in his ear. At one point the gunner paused, listening to his helmet headset, smiled, and leaned back in and continued with Frank. He pointed to the ground and Frank nodded and mouthed "OK." The chopper seemed to alter its approach slightly and began sliding sideways toward a spot at the lower end of the dirt pad, away from me. I looked over at the co-pilot who was grinning under his helmet visor and looking over his shoulder at the place Frank would exit. I knew immediately what was up but was helpless to do anything. Frank was poised on the skid and looking at the ground.

The door gunner's gloved hands turned thumbs up signaling go. Frank leapt and the gunner leaned out to watch. Frank had a canvas bag in one hand, his M-16 in the other and a bandolier of magazines strung across his chest.

Splat! He landed in almost two feet of soupy red mud, going down on all fours and throwing a spray of mud on his chest and chin. I was doing my best to hold back the laughter and was failing miserably. "That son-of-a-bitch gunner said it was too muddy to land the chopper but there was a dry spot I could jump on!" yelled Frank, murder in his eyes.

I knew better; they had pulled the same trick on a Major that morning, I had seen the officer being escorted to the Tactical Operations Center (TOC) covered in mud and mad as hell.

I wondered what was up with that scene, and now I knew.

Stand Down
By Dave Parks

Every 45 to 60 days the 199th Light Infantry Brigade, Red Catchers, as they styled themselves, would give up the chase and come roaring back to the 199th Brigade Main Base (BMB), at Frizzle - Jones at Long Binh for what was known officially as a Stand Down. A Stand Down was for refitting, resupply and a chance to get snot slinging drunk in relative safety.

Think about that - suddenly recalling a few thousand practicing young killers back off the Death Hunt and crowding them into a few acres of rocky red clay and allowing them all the booze and beer they could swill - a recipe for mayhem? You're goddamn right. A Stand Down was a wild thing, always. But all of that is beside my story, although it provides a useful background for what follows. Remember, a Stand Down is a wild time, crazy things happen, soldiers get hurt or killed celebrating not having been wounded or killed.

Captain US Army Millipede (name changed to protect the guilty of course) came to us fresh off six months of infantry duty. From the tip of his white side-walled head to the bottom of his spit-shined boots he was a Strac Troop! Spit-shined, starched, and squeaky clean outside and in, "Yes Sir! No Sir! Can do Sir! Follow me!" You know the type, the antithesis of us, the US Army Security Agency - military slackers in everything but the mission. Our jobs we performed with a passion, but aside from that, Happy Hour was always open in the ASA. The word that our new Company Commander was *infantry* shot through the 50 man 856th Radio Research Detachment like a prairie fire, and you might have thought you had heard *serial baby killer* instead of *infantry officer*. There was fear in the Detachment, change was in the air, and uncertainty replaced the enlisted man's affected *laissez-faire, laissez-passer* attitude.

The outgoing CO, a jolly sort, had understood it was important to keep the military bull shit to a minimum, and was liked for that. We'd laughed our butts off, of course, when he once caved-in a bunker with a Jeep in it - by insisting on having a tank dozer push earth onto the roof of our creation in order to 'reinforce it.' We were out about 20 miles west of Saigon in an area known to be 'Injun country', and digging in deep was the order of the day. We had spent a day and a half building our forward Ops bunker with heavy 8 x 8 timbers; we had then layered it over with Pierced Steel Planking (PSP) and were working at adding three layers of sandbags on top when the CO flew out to inspect. His idea was to dispense with sandbagging and cover the top with earth. At his 'suggestion' (you know how officers 'suggest' of course) we offered him fair warning. "It will crash in, Sir, all that extra weight."

But our warning was to no avail, "I am engineer trained," he replied.

When he turned to confab with the tank dozer commander, we troops scampered into the doomed bunker to drag out our personal gear. The tank dozer pushed red earth on top once, twice; the tank driver stopped and gave the Captain a raised eyebrow. The Captain gestured for him to proceed - a third time and CRASH! Naturally, we peons had had to dig out the damn Jeep and to rebuild the bunker; in other words, start all over.

The new CO, just as we had feared, soon began building a shining new ASA Detachment, pretty much the spirit of the ASA saying: 'Fuck the mission, clean the position!' Captain Millipede was making changes; administrative changes, procedure changes, changes to the Ops Compound and changes in the men's living quarters, beginning with the GI party that lasted into the evening - actually delaying Happy Hour! The changes to the Ops Compound, that half-acre of rocky dirt surrounded by a double apron of chain-link fence topped with razor wire, involved not only a GI party but, of course, sandbagging. No dusty old sandbags for the new CO; out with the old, in with the new!

In the course of things, change came as well for the members of the PRD-1 (Purd) teams who had missed the fun back at BMB. So far, we had missed all the fun for the simple reason that we were hardly ever at BMB. We generally only came during the Stand Down, for it was operationally necessary for us to be deployed on the same schedule as the infantry we supported. The PRD-1 teams deployed as two-man teams, three of them, and we spread out to cover the Brigade's Area of Operations (AO) as best we could.

Once you accepted that you worked in the middle of a war, and who didn't in Vietnam, a Purd team was pretty fair duty because you were pretty much left alone and didn't have to deal with the Regular Army very much. You and your team-mate set your own schedule, and all the two of you had to be concerned about was covering the mission; crack that nut and you were home free except for the minor detail of working around the clock in an environment tailor-made to kill you.

As we all know, when it comes to mind numbing enjoyment, you simply can't beat filling sandbags, and filling them seemed a Purd's team's constant task. Digging holes, filling bags, building a Purd bunker and a sleeping/fighting bunker. Tear it all down a few days later, empty the bags and fill the holes so Charlie can't use them. Pack up the bags with all the other stuff and move out to the next site. Fill the damn bags again, build, build, build, now quick, break it down again. Move. Do it all again in the 120° heat or the pouring rain - two weather choices to a customer. Work the mission and fill sandbags - two activity choices to a trooper.

Well, not quite true - you could fill your spare time by scrounging materials for bunkers or for heating those tiresome C-rations. Clean weapons several times a day and check gear and ammo. Go to the

water point and fill one 5 gallon can with water for drinking and
another for bathing, bring them back and set the bath one in the sun
to warm-up. Don't even think of keeping the other one cool. Run
messages of Purd results over to the Tactical Operations Center
(TOC), and while you are there try to get a feel for what the night
might bring - like an attack. Work the cranky ass, encrypted, voice
radio trading administration traffic, asking for supplies, mail or
whatever. Oh yeah - that KY-8 device could really eat your day if it
was not synced properly.

Check on the NUG, check on the NUG again - he's listening to
AFVN radio on the Purd again! Wash some fatigue pants and socks;
lay them in the sun to dry so you have some fresh ones after the
shower. Bake in the heat trying to grab a sweat-filled nap, or, during
the monsoon, find a dry place to sleep. Wake up and eat something
nasty out of a can before heading to the Purd site to relieve the NUG
for a few hours. Most likely he has done a half-ass job and is
confused - your fault of course - after all, wasn't it your job to train
him? All of this was the price of being left alone in the Army.

It didn't last of course, being left alone; there was a sort of curve ball
put into matters when the new CO widened his Reformation. He
visited the teams one-by-one, choppering in unannounced or, later,
doing some Eye in the Sky snooping. That flying around to spy on us
became a regular, very annoying, trick of his for a while.

We were supposed to be on the knobs 24 hours a day, work 12 on
and 12 off, seven days a week, but frankly that was not practical. For
one thing there was very little low-level enemy communication
happening once the sun got up, especially during the heat of mid-day.
As the sun raised so did the static hissing in our headsets and nary a
VC radio to DF. So we skewed the schedule to reflect that fact,
putting our efforts toward the more fruitful hunting times. We did so
too because Vietnam was so damned hot around mid-day, unbearably

hot. Most often there was no sun protection at the Purd except a poncho maybe, and that was hardly any protection at all.

But the Captain had in his mind that even if all we could hear was static, so be it - like other good little soldiers everywhere we would follow this Standard Operating Procedure to the letter. Naturally this mandate got us off on the right foot with the CO and we came to correct our ways. Like hell we did! We adapted, like all soldiers everywhere and developed countermeasures involving our being alerted via DF radio net when he left the BMB Ops Compound during the day.

A few weeks into Captain Millipede's Reformation came word from a 'reliable source' that plans were afoot to become more aggressive in the deployment of the PRD-1 teams. Word had it that his Grand Plan had been forwarded up the line to the 509th RRG, and, that the CO was to develop contacts with the ARVN and perhaps the Popular Forces (PF), so that the teams could co-locate with those sterling troops. Indeed, I believe the plan had been put into effect as my partner and I had ended up in a Special Forces camp: five Special Forces soldiers and loads of ARVN artillery trainees, some of whom were suspected to be VC. We spent a terrible night there during a perimeter probe.

Then too, one of our teams had recently been deployed to a small ARVN/PF stockade that was nothing more than a triangular shaped earthen berm with machine gun bunkers at the corners and filthy fighting holes with rickety tin roofs spaced along the bamboo spiked berm walls. I once delivered mail to our Purd team at the stockade, and I can report that it was cramped living and that the place smelled god-awful with general filth matching the smell perfectly. Believe me, those boys were very 'Nervous in the Service' and were questioning their deployment to such an unsecure base of operations. They didn't trust one soul in that camp, and were convinced that there was VC among the Popular Force types who were by far in the majority.

Specialist Five Fenster, the team leader and on his second tour, told me that there was one shifty looking slant eye that often lurked near the Purd site, close enough to hear the ditty bops. My visit was short, but the impression I left with was one of foreboding mixed with thankfulness that I was not where they were.

Along about this time there was a Stand Down, a welcome break. Back to BMB we went, anticipating a soft cot for a few days, luxurious showers, hot mess hall chow - and *cold beer!* Frosty beer, say it again, *taste it!* The guys in the barracks back at BMB kept it in little refrigerators - just leave a dime and take one. The 199th NCO club was just across the street from the barracks; the Long Branch Saloon, the EM club, was only a short walk from there. So, why not make the rounds, see what was happening and watch all the wild fun? Answer: YES!

After cleaning up and catching up on all the detachment news, mainly the Reformation and the recent GI parties, along with the dark fact of possible deployment to a crap hole like Fenster and his NUG had just left, I teamed up with a couple of the guys and headed out.

At the NCO club we drank and hashed over the events of the last deployment, told lies and generally had a fun time. After a couple of hours we walked up to the Long Branch to see the sights - just as we expected, it was a smoke-filled madhouse. We bellied up to the bar and ordered a few drinks each, the bartenders were busy and it was best to stock up when you managed to get the attention of one. You know, sometimes you and the booze meet just about perfectly and you feel you can't get drunk no matter how much you consume; and this was one of those times. The beer and the shots went down smooth and after hours of drinking, perhaps even closing the place, I don't remember, we ended up back at the barracks for a nightcap.

Throughout the evening one subject had center place - all the changes at the Det; the guys were not taking it well. As my drunk progressed and as sometimes happens in these matters, I became

126

more and more focused on one thought: *What if I and my crew ended up in a shithole like Fenster, or worse!* What was Captain Millipede up to?

Come the wee hours the Mids crew had departed for Ops and my buddy Frank and I were the only ones still up and talking. He was rambling on about the GI parties when an extremely brilliant thought came crashing in on me; it had to be brilliant, must be; Frank fairly leapt at 'The Plan!'

We had been low crawling for about 30 minutes, able to move only when the traffic cleared on the dirt road ahead. The field we were in was open with only an occasional clump of grass or a bit of a dip in the surface here and there. Ahead was the well-lit Ops Compound and in the middle right of the compound - our target. We were bent on gassing Captain US Army Millipede; our drunken brains knew he'd justly deserved it.

The plan was good and - simple. Crawl within range over the poorly lit field, pull the pins of our military issue CS gas grenades, rise, and throw them at Millipede's tent, then run like hell. There is another way to look at the plan - stupid! Here we were, crawling up on a highly secure area, guarded by very jumpy GI's, in the middle of a war zone. Not a problem; beer will lead the way.

The act itself was, indeed, simple. Frank had one great grenade, I gripped two, and we coordinated pulling pins and tossing them in tandem. As fast as possible I pulled the pin on my second grenade and threw it to the right of my first one, the Captain's sandbagged tent was bracketed and pop, pop, pop, the devices apparently worked as advertised.

But we only heard them as we were in full flight back to the barracks and when I cleared the field and got back among the buildings I stopped and looked to check the result because I was damn near puking from beer and adrenaline. I could see the gas cloud and hear yelling; success for us, panic for them. 'Them,' I say. You see, that moment, was the first time I realized that our little caper affected everyone in the Ops Compound. We had been so focused on the new CO that we had pretty much forgotten about the others who slept or worked there. I made it back to the barracks not long after Frank and that wise bird was already racked out. I took the hint, gave him a grin and a wink, and made it to my bunk and quickly undressed and slipped in.

It didn't take long.

There was sudden illumination as every light was flicked on and the First Sergeant yelling, angry and in full cry, "Everybody Up, Every swinging dick! Get up! Stand by your rack!"

Oh shit, THEY KNOW! This was my first thought. I was about to piss in my skivvies with the knowledge of what Frank and I had done and the fact that we were caught like the rats we were; and I was about to piss too from all that processed BEER that was backed up in my bladder. I had to piss! Too bad; maybe there would be a piss tube near the firing squad.

Actually, they didn't know, or maybe they didn't know for sure, or maybe - hell, I didn't know! My head hurt and those damn barracks lights hurt my eyes. But my heart knew and it was going wild and that didn't help what would soon be a massive hangover if I couldn't take some aspirin and piss. I knew by now that the hangover was going to be a beauty. They must have known something, or at least they had some idea - why else would they BE HERE.

Captain Millipede, the XO, Top, and a gaggle of lesser NCOs knew that SOMEONE IN THIS BARRACKS had scared the hell out of them. But my problem was I didn't know they didn't know for sure. Top lined up every swinging dick at attention and announced their mission: "To find the son-of-a-bitch that gassed Operations!" The guys were looking around, puzzled - you could almost see the 'WOW!' and 'NO SHIT!' cartoon balloons forming over their now alert heads. My problem was that I couldn't see Frank. He was down at the other end of the barracks on my side. I wished I could see him; might give me a clue about making a run for it.

"We are going to be here UNTIL SOMEONE STEPS FORWARD! I WANT the INDIVIDUAL who DID THIS!" Captain Millipede was speaking. He and Top were slowly walking up and down the aisle, and now and then the CO would pause and stare at someone; a muted conversation might ensue, he then moved on and I realized he was concentrating on the Purd's Ops. Slick, I think; we're the ones just out of the field, the wildcards in the group, and we Field Rats were most likely the only ones who had access to gas grenades! Eventually though, it became obvious to even a drunk such as I that he was getting nowhere fast. I began to relax as it dawned on me that Frank and I were the only ones who knew what had happened and we were damn sure not spilling the beans for a guaranteed trip to Long Binh jail.

Forty five minutes stretched into an hour and a half, and finally the game was over.

'They were just going through the motions,' I thought as I slipped off to sleep near dawn. 'They don't have a fucking clue.' And with that relaxing thought I arose and snatched a beer out of the nearest icebox, opened it with a snap of a church key and smiled.

And I was right. They didn't have a clue, never did; we got clean away…but they had their suspicions. Soon after, it was reported to the redeployed Purd teams that Captain US Millipede had ordered major renovations to a small bunker in the Ops Compound. He'd had it reinforced, re-sandbagged, coated with a layer of mortar, and equipped with various arms and accouterments from the detachment's small arms locker - and he had moved in!

We also heard that things had lightened up back at the 856th, where a kinder, gentler Reformation was afoot. Along with this news came the word that the 509th had nixed the good Captain's push for more aggressive deployment of the PRD-1 teams.

Now I'm not claiming that the insane gassing of our Fearless Leader contributed to the Counter Reformation soon in evidence, but it is odd that the event preceded such a reversal by not very much.

PS: I'd like to extend an apology to Captain Millipede and all the troops of the 856th that Frank and I terrorized that night. Sorry guys, it was *war*.

It's a Gas, Gas, Gas

By Dave Parks

B Company, 10th Battalion, Second Infantry, Basic Training, Ft. Jackson, South Carolina:

B Company's final exam in CBR (Chemical, Biological and Radiological) training would be to successfully survive the Chlorine chamber. Chlorine gas will kill you dead as a mackerel if you screw up, so before visiting that facility there was the CS gas chamber. CS is a riot gas and will incapacitate you pretty fast. It causes your face, and any exposed skin to feel as if it is burning off, your eyes to gush tears uncontrollably and, if inhaled, proceeds to attack the lungs and leave you coughing, if not puking. It's awful stuff.

The theory was that by experiencing the CS chamber it would give us a chance to practice our masking skills and develop the confidence to face the chlorine chamber. By masking I mean taking your gas mask out of its case and properly putting it on and clearing it so that there is no gas trapped in it when you take your first breath.

We entered the CS chamber a squad at a time with our masks on, then, at Sergeant Savage's command, we were to take them off, shout our Name, Rank and Serial Numbers in unison and replace the masks. Sergeant Savage was our company Drill Instructor. My squad entered and went through the drill. We were putting our masks back on when fun-loving Sergeant Savage, steps up and stops me.

"Private Parks, he shouts through his mask, "What is your first General Order?"

"Sergeant, my first General Order is to remain at my post and obey all orders of the Sergeant of the Guard." I choke it out. Don't hold me to that, but I haven't the foggiest notion what the first General Order really is 30 years later. By now I'm dying, burning all over and choking like mad!

Sergeant Savage continues with this fun; "Good, Private Parks, What is your third General Order?" I was unable to reply I was suffering so much.

"Get the hell out of here Parks." Sergeant Savage snaps. I did. I had no idea he liked me so much.

Okinawa, 51st SOC, early 1968:

It's time for re-qualifying in CBR, a re-hash of our Basic Training. There is a general purpose medium tent set up on the ball field near the gym that will serve as the gas chamber. Being in the ASA, the training Sergeants were giving us the 'short course' so as to not to cut too deep into our quality time at the EM club or, more importantly, theirs. We had to go through the gas chamber, however, to complete the course. After the verbal stuff we processed over to the tent affecting boredom and playing grab-ass.

I was a member of the first group to enter. Immediately upon entering I felt as if my skin was on fire. There were small round dishes with smoking pellets in them giving out the CS gas. It looked pretty dense, not like I remembered from Basic. The command to unmask was given and the instant we did, every one of us doubled over gasping and choking, every orifice absolutely on fire. I felt like I was about to die. A couple of smarter ones ran out of the tent. The Sergeant saw there was something dreadfully wrong and started shouting and shoving everyone to get out. No one had to be invited twice.

It turned out that there was about five times the concentration of gas that should have been in that tent. We were all sent to the aid station to get checked out. Just minor complaints after we aired out for a while.

Vietnam, 856th Radio Research Detachment, late 1968:

Some fire support bases are better than others. This one sucked because it was so small and so spooky. I had just returned from Kuala Lumpur, from an R&R carrying a gift bestowed on me by the sweet little lady I had spent my week with, though I didn't know that yet. I had been choppered into the base a couple of days before. The base had been created by simply pushing trees over with a tank dozer, and scraping cleared spots here and there. There were splintered stumps and trees lying every which way; pissed-off snakes were a danger there too. The base was only about 150 feet across. The hundred foot plus trees of the surrounding jungle started at the very edge of the perimeter.

The infantry that were detailed to provide security were a nervous lot, generating many false alerts and reports of movement out in the jungle. The evening prior to this one a trooper walking to fill his canteen had been shot and killed by a bunker guard. That fellow was about 20 feet from us when he went down. The guard never challenged him; the guard just fired three M-16 rounds into his back.

The enemy had attempted to mortar us earlier that evening, but their shells fell harmlessly in the jungle 50 yards out; bad aim, not usual for them.

We ASA Super-troops were bunkered down about 30 feet from the perimeter. The bunker line had recently been outfitted with the latest in Human Wave Stopper technology, a CS gas launcher gizmo that fired 24 gas grenades in a fan pattern. Every other bunker on the bunker line was outfitted with one of these neat-o things; I wanted one to play with. Soon after dark that evening I was startled nearly out of my skin by a volley of rapid explosions, close by! It was the gas grenade device at the nearest bunker firing off its load. A few seconds later the gas was rolling over the perimeter and engulfing the ASA bunker. Gassed again!

I knew it would be useless to look for my gas mask, its case was slung over my shoulder, full of M-79 rounds. The mask itself was stowed safely in my locker back at Long Binh. The infantry types had been playing around with their new toy and accidentally fired it. The wind was not in our favor.

The last time I was gassed was in Washington, DC, near the Washington Memorial, about a year after the jungle incident. I was happily watching a bunch of unwashed yahoos demonstrate against the war. When the grim-faced Riot Police launched a counter-attack from the parking lot of a nearby building, I got upwind fast after seeing that the so-called 'pigs' opening gambit included CS gas being fired at the crowd - old hat to me by then.

The Ancient Mariner

By Robert G. Knowles

It is an ancient Mariner,
And he stoppeth one of three.
'By thy long grey beard and glittering eye,
Now wherefore stopp'st thou me?
　　-　*Samuel Taylor Coleridge, 1798*

I learned more about war in 12 months in 1967 and 1968 than I ever could have in books or films or by sitting in a garrison for another 15 years. In my head, I had chased images of war across three continents over 25 years. Viewed at a distance, war is courage and glory and marching reviews, with military bands playing and regimental flags, with battle streamers dancing in the breeze.

After I beheld war's face one particular March morning in Vietnam, I fled screaming away into flash-backs and nightmares that haunted me for years. I tried to share that vision with all the folks who over the years asked me, "What was it like?"

They didn't understand an old soldier's desperate need for absolution to wash the blood from his trembling hands. War resolves nothing, and violence has a long memory. It isn't about cold statistics, or wins and losses on a cosmic chalkboard. In the often misquoted words of General Nathan Bedford Forrest, a Tennessean who became the premier Civil War Cavalry Commander, "war means fightin'," and fightin' means killin'." And dying. Forty-four years later, I can still recall at will the faces of the men I lost to war, and of the friends who died around me, long ago, on the plains of Vietnam.

A *caveat*. I was an Army intelligence, or Intel, officer, assigned to the US Army Security Agency. My encounters with the Vietnam War and the North Vietnamese Army weren't as 'up close and personal' as if I'd been an infantry platoon leader in a combat arms battalion. When war broke through to the personal level, it produced a few moments of terror and exhilaration, which helps to break up weeks or months of boredom. Strangely, occasional or intermittent brushes with death and danger proved harder to take than a regular diet of combat. They jarred my senses. Trained as an infantry officer, I was not given sufficient combat exposure to adapt to the schizophrenic rituals war demands. For example, I could not get used to running flat out, at a high adrenaline level, for days on end.

I saw only a few enemy soldiers, dead or alive, in Vietnam. However, I had frequent contact with them through their tactical military radio communications, which we were intercepting somewhere, every hour and every day of my Vietnam tour. Sometimes, I listened to actual recordings of voice messages, with the translator over my shoulder *gisting* the enemy soldier's comments. Most of the time, however, I was reading reports of translated radio messages, snatched by us from the airways over Vietnam after being sent in the dots and dashes of Morse code by enemy soldiers. Or I was examining translations of documents, field journals or maps, taken from dead or captured NVA combatants.

War and Rumors of War
By Robert G. Knowles

The first of a series of my limited-danger encounters with the enemy happened a few days after I arrived in Vietnam. The VC mortared the Presidential Palace grounds in Saigon, while I watched from a balcony of the Meyerkord Hotel a few blocks away.

After I reached my first duty assignment, on the slope of Dragon Mountain near Pleiku in the Central Highlands, the war drew steadily closer. January began amid increasing reports of North Vietnamese invaders who were moving to the South. The Vietnamese lunar New Year, or Tet, was approaching. On January 30, 1968, North Vietnamese commanders launched the Tet Offensive, a month-long period during which Charlie went for broke. Attacks were made across Vietnam in an effort to spark a popular uprising that would push the US out of what the North Vietnamese had always viewed as a civil war.

At first, North Vietnam's *politburo* called the offensive a costly failure. There was no uprising. The defeated attacks decimated Vietcong guerrillas in the South, forcing greater use of North Vietnamese regulars. That required increase conscription of youth in the North. North Vietnamese youths weren't any more eager than their American counterparts to leave their studies for war. However, the offensive's architect, North Vietnamese Defense Minister Vo Nguyen Giap, a former schoolteacher and military scholar, held a different view. Giap's book, *'People's War, People's Army,'* cites the writings of Chinese military genius Sun Tzu, who believed wars were fought, not on the battlefield, but in the mind of an opponent. The North Vietnamese won, and we lost, when American political leaders, including President Johnson, became convinced that they could not be defeated.

On March 31, 1968, six days after the attack on Camp Evans in which Captain Casey died, our President, Lyndon Johnson, announced in a prime-time television speech that he would not stand for re-election and would ask the North to begin a dialogue to end the war. We saw a tape of it a few days later. Since I was fighting the war at the time, and we apparently were preparing to invade North Vietnam, I could not understand what made my Commander-in-Chief, back in the World, come up with such a contrary view.

Years after the war, Marshall Giap agreed with an American Vietnam veteran that US forces won every engagement in the conflict.

"That is true," he told retired Army Colonel Harry Summers. "However, it is also irrelevant. Would you like some more tea?" He inquired.

It was clear to those of us there then, that at least in tactical terms, the Vietnam War was still winnable. It was winnable at the cost of additional American casualties, the 'butcher's bill' that decides an armed conflict. That cost was high. Maybe the President thought it would be too much for voters back home. We were killing ten VCs for every one American battle deaths.

But there were moments when my personal estimate of the war's value to our national interest wouldn't have allowed even one more dead American soldier. Presidents don't ask Lieutenants and Captains for their opinion about a war's worth. Perhaps they should, sometimes.

What do we owe the soldiers of today, sunburned youths in faded tan fatigues, coming back from the highways and deserts of hell in Iraq and Afghanistan? They're out there, fighting dust and disease, terror and bone-deep weariness, in places and towns most of us know only from Sunday school maps. They're starting to come home now. I meet them occasionally in class. Or I pass them on campus walkways. Seems to me, we owe them everything we have. We should at least give them a warm 'Welcome home!' greeting that Americans weren't quick enough to extend to their soldiers returning from Korea and Vietnam.

Do you want to know the price of freedom? Ask a returning desert warrior, while the cost, the lives of soldiers lost in battle from his or her unit, still is fresh on the veteran's mind.

Casey's Hill
By Robert G. Knowles

The devil came calling one March midnight in the Vietnam War. Hell followed close behind. I had been anticipating the encounter for 15 years, but had no real way of knowing what to expect. It took almost a decade for the nightmares that sprang from the incident to lose their grip, and for the madness that yawned before me in all its stark red horrors to begin to fade. Thirty eight years later, its mementos and the memories they invoke have the power to lift me straight up in bed in a cold night-sweat. Our brush with war that night cost me a third of the hearing in my left ear. Men died. Others were wounded. No one escaped it without being changed. In a few minutes, it felt like an eternity, something happened that brought us together as survivors, while at the same time, separated us from the rest of humankind.

The devil's calling card was a captured US 81 mm mortar shell, probably fired from a Chinese 82 mm mortar tube. It likely was delivered by gunners from the mortar company of the 22nd Rifle Regiment, People's Army of Vietnam. I dug the fin assembly out of the ground after the attack. It struck the ridge pole of the officers' tent in our crowded encampment and detonated at 12 minutes after midnight on Monday morning, March 25, 1968. The first shell was accompanied and followed by a steel torrent of more than 300 others. They marched with a giant crunching footstep across Camp

Evans, a former Marine Regimental Command Post about 15 km north of Hue and a kilometer west of South Vietnam's Highway 1.

Camp Evans was the forward, (or Jump) Command Post or Tactical Headquarters for the Army's First Cavalry Division Airmobile during Operation JEB STUART, soon to be changed to Operation PEGASUS: a helicopter assault to reopen main supply routes along Highway 9 to the Marine garrison besieged at Khe Sanh.

The attack that morning was not the first time North Vietnamese shells and rockets struck the camp after the Cav's helicopters touched down. It wouldn't be the last. Tents, trucks, jeeps, and helicopters were crowded together in a space too small to properly protect them from enemy assault. They caught fire and crumpled like spent cigarette packs or crushed soda cans under the impact of the barrage. Those among us who had gotten to cover kissed the ground against the inside of our sandbagged walls, our heads sunken turtle-like into our helmets and flak jackets. The black sky split often as round after round hammered us. A Warrant Officer crouching behind me in the roofless gun bunker suddenly slapped his face like he'd been mosquito-bit. He pulled a bloody hand away from the shrapnel wounds in his left cheek and neck.

The post office tent took a direct hit. Burning mail fell all around us like snowflakes, and then it was whipped up into a tall swirling column of white against the darkness. The shelling continued. Seconds passed like minutes, minutes seemed like hours, as the rain of North Vietnamese mortar shells swept over our tents and marched away uphill towards the Division Tactical Operating Center.

Not all of us had gotten out of the officer's tent before it was hit. We scrambled up from the bunker, still blinded by the light and deafened by the noise of the exploding shells. A waterfall sound persisted in our ears for days after the attack. A ringing sound started in my left ear that night. I have carried it with me for 38 years. It's an almost constant reminder of those few minutes of horror on a hilltop half a world, and a few lifetimes, away.

'Tennessee Volunteer'

Almost everyone liked Captain John Michael Casey. I remember him as a grinning, gangly, tow-headed, Tennessean. Mike stood about 5 feet-eleven in his jungle boots, which he shined, something none of the rest of us were inclined to try. His grey-green jungle fatigues started each day starched, with sharp creases. He proudly wore the 1st Cav patch, big as a man's hand, on the left shoulder of his fatigue jacket. Instead of depicting a black horse head and diagonal bar across the bright yellow shield, the patch was black on green. Although we were Army Intelligence, like me he wore the crossed wigwag flags of the Army Signal Corps branch on his left collar. On his right collar were the new parallel bars or 'railroad tracks' of a Captain, a *dia ui*. Signal Corps was part of our cover legend. The cloth insignia were sewn on our faded jungle fatigues in subdued black and green.

Casey was clean-shaven and wore gold-rimmed aviator glasses. I don't remember any barbers at Camp Evans. But Mike somehow managed to keep his blond hair in a crew cut, shorter than the rest of us.

Casey's helmet, uniform, web harness, and pistol belt were strictly regulation. No graffiti on the green cloth helmet cover. Flaps always buttoned and snapped. However, he carried a non-regulation six-round Smith & Wesson .357 Magnum revolver in an open-topped leather holster, in place of the standard issue .45 caliber semi-automatic pistol. Afterward, when I was packing his gear, I removed a souvenir cartridge from Casey's revolver. He had loaded it with silver-tip hollow nose bullets, and carved an 'x' on the nose of each one, to improve their stopping power.

Mike never got a minute older than he was at about 00:12 hours on Monday, March 25, 1968. Like other absent friends from the Vietnam War, he will always be 22 years old, while we, the survivors, grow older and greyer by the day. He had been a Captain for less than two months when he died.

Casey was from Sparta, Tennessee. He was proud of being a Tennessee volunteer, and flew the state flag on a six-foot staff stuck in the ground in front of the officers' tent. The flag was bright red with a blue round field in the center. There were three stars in the middle of the blue field.

I asked him, once, how to get a state flag. He told me to write to the Secretary of State of Georgia. After I assumed command, I wrote to Ben Fortson, the wheelchair-bound World War II veteran who had been Georgia Secretary of State most of my life. Old Ben kindly sent me a Georgia flag, which he said had been flown over the state capital. It was the 1956 flag, with the Confederate battle emblem set next to a blue field. Centered in the field was the state seal outlined in white. The letter with it commissioned me to fly the flag 'wherever it would do the most good.'

A month after Casey was killed, I left the First Cavalry Division for a new assignment at Phu Bai, south of Hue, about 30 miles below Camp Evans. I flew the stiff new Georgia flag on an 8 foot radio antenna over Alpha Company, Eighth Radio Research Field Station Command Post, a sandbagged bunker on Hill One, which actually was probably Hill 'Minus One.' Its elevation was below sea level on the Vietnam coastal plain. That proved to be important information when a typhoon wrecked our sandbag fortifications towards the end of August.

As the senior First Lieutenant, or *trung oi*, at Camp Evans, I was Assistant Operations Officer and Executive Officer of the forward unit of our ASA Company. Casey was the Operations Officer and Camp Commander. His cot was close to mine near the back wall of a tent that sometimes was home to a dozen officers. The 81 mm mortar shell that killed him that morning struck the tent ridge pole over his cot. It exploded on contact, showering officers who hadn't gotten to safety with white-hot, razor-sharp shards of steel. Casey was struck just above the heart while trying to get his flak jacket on. There was a lot of blood. Realizing first aid was futile; I baptized him, marking his forehead with a cross in his own blood, and gave him the last rites of the Episcopal Church.

The night before, Mike and I drove out to inspect a site we were planning to move the unit to, to get away from the mortars and rockets Charlie was throwing at the center of the camp each night. While he was refueling the Jeep, gasoline splashed in his face. Although he wiped it off with a green bandana, some of the gasoline got in his eyes. He rinsed them with water from his canteen, and we continued on our way. Near the site we planned to move to, Casey found a piece of plywood about the right size for a 'for sale' sign in a front lawn. He threw it in the back of the Jeep.

His plan was to trade a Navy Construction Battalion a pallet of beer in exchange for them digging a hole on the back side of the new site big enough to hold our tents and vehicles. I had brought the beer up from An Khe a week earlier. The pallet sat in the center of the officer's tent close to where the mortar shell exploded. The beer was Carling Black Label™ in cans and cases. Some of the cans were wrecked by the exploding shell. Afterwards, I traded the remaining beer with Seabees, and they dug the hole at the new site, which we named 'Casey's Hill.' We built sandbag walls around our new defensive position and moved in a few weeks after the attack. After that, the unit didn't suffer any more casualties while it was at Camp Evans. But it was forced to move out of the hole when the rains came.

A little later, the Cav's forward CP flew and rode away from Landing Zone (LZ) Evans to a new location near Saigon and the border with

Cambodia. The 371st forward element went along. The 'Casey's Hill' sign was thrown in a Jeep and taken down to the Cav's new IV Corps home. The fire never fell on Casey's Hill.

The Remington Raiders
By Robert G. Knowles

Among the special units assembled and disbanded in the dozen years the US was involved in its part of the 40-year Vietnam War, one of the strangest probably was an *ad hoc* Army detachment that named itself the 'Remington Raiders.' As second-in-command of the units from which the Raiders were drawn, which were attached to different Army infantry divisions, I had the misfortune to be both their creator and officer-in-charge. Raider contributions to the war effort probably will be determined by military historians to range somewhere between paltry and insignificant. The biggest expenditure for our operation was for gasoline. Only a few rounds of ammunition were fired, while the rusted steel bands sealing several crates of green, baseball size, hand grenades were never broken. However, between the start of the first mission on a November night in 1967, and the end of the third, and final, Raider's sortie on March 17, 1968, the three units, which were pulled together from two or three Army units - nobody, including me, is quite sure where some of the first Raiders came from - traveled over 1000 miles by road, sea and air. Jeeps, trucks and supply trailers were moved from fire bases at Pleiku and An Khe, in the Central Highlands of Vietnam, along dusty jungle roads through territory that came under heavy attack in the Tet Offensive of 1968. Neither a man nor a vehicle was lost in the effort. But the term 'irregular' doesn't begin to describe us.

The first raider mission developed with no warning and not much of a plan, which came to be regarded as our hallmark. One cool evening in late November, 1967, a disturbing message arrived at the Command Post of the 374th Radio Research Company, at Camp Enari, the well-fortified Dragon Mountain base of the 'Famous' Fourth Infantry Division. Delivered via *ding hua, Viet* - GI slang for field telephone, the message said a ton-and-a-quarter courier truck, bound from a brigade firebase to a unit on the other side of Pleiku City, had overturned in the road. The driver and a guard had been injured and transported via 'Dust Off' helicopter ambulance to the nearest Evac Hospital. Would we please send somebody to secure the area, and any classified material that might have been thrown out of the hut on the back of the truck?

I quickly pulled together a 'relief expedition', which almost as quickly named itself the Remington Raiders - for the typewriter, not the Tommy gun. The all-volunteer forces on the three raider missions were trained soldiers. But their training was as radio operators, clerks, cooks and motor pool mechanics. Their part of the war was being fought behind radio sets, desks and cook stoves, and they were bored. They hadn't had as much of a chance to participate in actual conflict. To a man, my raiders saw the first mission as a chance to emulate their heroes on 'Combat,' a popular TV program we watched at night, on small black and white TV sets, while sounds of real combat rattled in the distance. Most of us had not yet fired our rifles at anything more hostile than a pop-up target on the training range. But everybody in Vietnam carried a loaded rifle or pistol. Although reports of weapons accidents were increasing, the Army hadn't yet decided to take up and store the assortment of lethal hardware almost everybody carried in Vietnam.

By the time my eager crew was saddled up in jeeps and trucks, and roared out the main gate to find their war, they had grabbed and loaded a dozen M-16 rifles, a few M-14's, a couple of .45 caliber pistols, and a pile of bayonets and machetes.

Although my Jeep radio was full of static as we charged along, we weren't actually in contact with anybody. We also had neither a map nor compass, and possessed only a general notion of where to find the wrecked truck. And night was falling fast.

My daddy, a World War II veteran, always said the Good Lord looks out for idiots and soldiers. That could have helped explain why our four-vehicle column, fortunately, encountered a shortage of an important ingredient for a war: somebody to fight with. We at least looked like we knew what we were doing, if you didn't get too close. I located the wreck - abandoned in the middle of the road - and finished our assignment. I posted riflemen - actually, cooks and clerks toting unfamiliar M-16's - along either side of the darkened road, to cover our noisy reconnaissance. Night combat patrols usually try to keep from making unnecessary noise and light. They don't want to attract hostile attention. However, our flashlights and vehicle lights stabbed the dark in every direction, while we rounded up hundreds of pages of a classified computer printout that were unfolding in the wind, just beyond our grasp.

The raw, red, two-lane clay road ran up through a steep-sided gully. It looked as if it had been bulldozed out of a stream bed like the main road we'd traveled from Enari. It would be a great - that is, not so great for us - place for Charlie to spring an ambush.

But hair stirred beneath my sweat-soaked helmet band, as I glanced nervously at the dark triple-layer jungle that pressed against us from all sides. The Jeep radio and the night remained quiet. Perhaps, too quiet.

About five weeks later, the North Vietnamese Army's highly professional 32nd Rifle Regiment: three battalions, numbering almost 1000 soldiers, would emerge from the thick forests we passed through that night to attack Pleiku City. I later concluded Charlie must've been lying low during November, 1967, getting ready for the Tet or New Year, 1968 Offensive. The battle-tempered NVA soldiers hiding in those woods probably were greatly amused by our amateur efforts. However, there was no enemy contact that night and we got away without incident. But not, however, without a few complaints from our own commanders.

When we got back to Camp Enari, we learned that there had been a phone call from a sister unit. It was trying to locate a couple of my volunteers, who had not reported for their shifts as Morse code radio intercept operators. That's when I realized some of our soldiers who had joined us were not from my unit. They were not even from the Fourth Division! They had been visiting our camp, and hadn't told anyone who they were, because they wanted to get in on the excitement, such as it was.

I had served only a month in-country. The rubber soles of my green canvas jungle boots were still so stiff they made my feet sore. My big 'seven-shooter' pistol had never been fired. Its three pounds rode uncomfortably in a black holster on my hip. My new jungle fatigues marked me as a 'newbie.' They were still in an odd shade of olive green. Later, after being washed over rocks in streambeds, the color faded into a 'Namvets look'... that's a muddy grey.

I was also new to the ways of the Famous Fourth Infantry Division that had won its first battle star on Omaha Beach in the Normandy Invasion, in World War II. The four-stemmed, square shoulder patch of the Ivy Division had been worn on Army uniforms since the 1940's, when the Division was formed at Camp Gordon, near Augusta, Georgia, where I was born.

The enemy around Enari and Pleiku stayed quiet for a few more weeks, while I started learning how to be a real soldier. Their silence didn't last for long, however. And my Remington Raiders - hasty assemblies of clerks and cooks, radio operators and mechanics - rode out on at least two more occasions. One night in March, 1968, a week after the conclusion of the final raider mission, and a month into the biggest enemy offensive in the war, it all caught up with me.

But by that time, I wasn't Executive Officer of a company attached to the Ivy Division.

Instead, I was in the war Big Time, wearing the coveted First Cavalry Division shoulder patch, a green and black shield the size of a man's hand. I came home in November, 1968. The bright cavalry yellow First Team battle flag came home to Fort Hood, Texas, in June, 1971, after six years of war, the Army's First Air Assault Division for the Vietnam War that operated from helicopters. It was awarded more battle streamers and decorations in the conflict than any other Army combat command. After those first few months with the Famous Fourth, the war followed me around pretty closely. Still, there were occasions when Remington's Raiders were called for: No battle ribbons, no flags, and no glory - and also, thankfully, no casualties.

Just the satisfaction of knowing we'd made our own irregular, contributions to the war effort, despite the People's Army of Vietnam, and, often, despite the unwelcome attention of our own army.

Charlie and Mother
By Robert G. Knowles

We called enemy soldiers, including their radio operators, 'Charlie,' or 'Victor-Charlie.' In the military phonetic alphabet, the spoken word for 'V' is Victor and the spoken word for 'C' is 'Charlie.' VC was the acronym for *Viet Cong*. That's Vietnamese for Viet Communist. Charlie's radio operators were men and women about the same age as my soldiers. They sent their radio traffic slowly, with much profanity in their conversation, or chatter, between messages. I remember receiving a directive from the National Security Agency, in Fort Meade, Maryland, where our intercept reports eventually wound up. In typical NSA-speak, 'Mother' asked us to spoonerise the letters of the Viet swear-words, so that that 'fucking B-52's!' in enemy operator chatter became 'bucking F-52's!' in our intercept reports, before they were sent to Ft. Meade. It seems that NSA civilian analysts reading our intercepts were offended by the enemy's coarse language.

The 'Twix,' or Army telegram, from Mother was a source of amusement to my intercept operators. They could well imagine what it would be like to be an NVA radio operator, crouched under a mountain, when your headquarters was obliterated by a US Air Force B-52 bomber strike, called an ARC LIGHT. I remember a First Cavalry Division interrogation report of an NVA regimental officer, captured after such an airstrike. He stood before the Cav's intelligence officers in a shredded khaki uniform, still clutching the black telephone handset he had been talking to Hanoi through when the bombs hit. The broken connecting wire trailed behind him.

One moment, he said, he was in a command bunker near Khe Sanh, buried deep under a mountain. The next thing he knew, he was picking himself up from a trail on the surface, the uniform torn to ribbons, bleeding from the ears and nose from bomb concussion. His hundred soldier regimental headquarters had vanished. According to the report, that was all he could recall about his encounter with Mother's 'bucking F-52's.'

Cat's Paw 5-3-1

By Robert Flanagan

I'd come in-country in September, 1968, on orders for the 1st Radio Research Company, but was initially hijacked to S-3, 224th Aviation Battalion RR at Tan Son Nhut. On the first day of 1969, I was finally released to the Cam Rahn Bay unit, CRAZY CAT, or in NSA-speak, CEFLIEN LION (Sea-Flying Lion), a feline image in any connotation. My job as 051 (058/05H Warrant MOS) was mission controller on operational flights, and in addition, held a hefty bag of additional duties: Mission Crew Safety Officer, Mission Training Officer, Awards and Decorations Officer, and a couple more. This was my second attempt to win the war, following a tour in 1964 - 65 as 3rd RRU ARDF NCOIC, plus I'd done run-up time in White Birch as an A-slash.

Settling in at Cam Ranh Bay was a no-brainer. Our Army flight unit was wedged into the Naval Air Facility, awash on the much larger USAF base, all located on a scrubby peninsula edged with beautiful white sand beaches projecting into the South China Sea, and was one of the most secure ground facilities in-country. Security was the responsibility of the Korean White Horse Division, and they were devoted guards. We seldom got mortared, and even less often experienced rocket influx. And, except for the fact that the Naval Air Facility commander, a Navy *Captain Queeg* copy, operated his little plot of ground as an aircraft carrier (and we ASA-ers were relegated to below-deck standards), life was good.

But being secure on the ground and safe in the air are not necessarily inevitable dualities in the same war. The mission aircraft for the 1st RRC was the RP-2E Neptune, introduced in the Korean War era. The birds were acquired by ASA from the 'bone yard,' the airplane graveyard at Davis-Monthan Air Force Base in Tucson, Arizona, where they had been, and still regularly were being deposited when phased out of Navy use in favor of the new P-3 Orion. P-2s had seen service as 'Hurricane Hunters' for the Air Force and Coast Guard, in 'Nam' in the Navy's MARKET TIME costal, river and trail interdiction missions, and in many other diverse functions. The entire line of this model aircraft was tired. The six birds flown by the 1st RRC had been reclaimed from an inelegant ending, partly reconstituted, but not completely 'done over.' It was not uncommon that on any mission day, only one - sometimes fewer - aircraft would be mission ready, usually due to electrical or engine failure, but most often hydraulics. Far too many missions were aborted in-flight due to various system failures. Operator failure, a given, seldom entered the equation.

On 21 March, those of us on that day's manifest ate early chow, and drew our flight gear, groused through briefing, and ambled out across the blistering, white-hot concrete to board aircraft number 131531, a venerable old bird with an unenviable flight record. She also sported a Purple Heart painted on the fuselage, reflecting a 'wound' sustained from an exploding 37 mm anti-aircraft shell on Easter morning, eleven months before. The bird had just come out of maintenance, and the crew felt fairly confident we might complete the mission without abort, what with fresh engines and the windshield washer fluid topped off.

We launched, made our communication checks at Nha Trang on fly-by, and shimmied north on a track for Northern I Corps, the DMZ and the Ho Chi Minh trail. It was normally a two-hour drudge flight to get on station, just to begin the active mission of voice intercept of enemy communications for XXIV Corps and III MAF, usually a period of 8-9 hours. Upon mission completion, we'd make a night landing at Da Nang, drop the courier pouch of intercepts to a pilot/courier from the 8th RRFS at Phu Bai, refuel, and bumble down the coast to log a 13-14 hour mission. We carried a crew of 13: pilot, co-pilot, relief pilot, plane captain, a controller, communicator, five 98G's(Viet lingies), and two aft-station watches (who doubled on other duties, one of whom, as galley slave, prepared the late evening meal on board; the other was often a radio repairman or trade-off linguist). Sometimes we suffered 'straphangers' aboard, non-essential tourists seeking a thrill, cluttering up an already crowded and overly heavy aircraft.

On that day, somewhere north of Qui Nhon, but before reaching Da Nang where we would turn west on a new radial for our ops area, most of the Ops were already squealing up and down RF bands. I was poring over mission objectives on my clipboard when I felt a sudden, sharp jolt through the airframe. My immediate thought was: we've been hit! By AAA or missile I didn't know. At our altitude of 9,500 feet that was a workable scenario. But then the port watch keyed his intercom to tell the pilot that smoke was trailing from the port engine. The P-2 of 1st RRC were powered by two Wright R-3350 turbo-compound piston radial engines, complemented by two Westinghouse J-34 turbojets for added thrust in take-off/landing. The jets normally were not engaged during ordinary flight.

Shortly following the alert, the pilot, CW4 Glasgow, came up on the intercom to announce that we were aborting the mission; that we seem to have blown an engine, and he was feathering the port engine. He directed me to get all non-flight deck crew into ditching stations, but that we were okay; he was making a wide, slow turn to head back to Cam Ranh Bay. But in all our minds was that this soon after take-off, the bird was still nearly maximum load at 80,000 pounds, including some 13,000 pounds of aviation gas, a lot of weight for an aircraft with diminished power and control. A turn wide and slow might avoid us slipping into an uncontrolled attitude leading to unrecoverable flight failure. We non-pilots identified this condition as a CRASH.

The pilot started and brought on-line the jet engine on the port side to help replace power lost by a shutdown of the damaged engine. Looking out while in the turn, I spotted a thin stream of oil from the starboard engine; and as I was keying the intercom to report this new threat, the oil was joined by a heavy stream of smoke. Double independent engine failure - what were the odds of that? More to the point, what were the odds we'd survive a daily double?

The pilot, Glasgow, fortunately was not a rookie, but incomparably experienced. During World War II, he flew Corsairs for the Marines in the Pacific; as a reserve Major, he was recalled for Korea and flew Panther and Cougar jets. After the war, he'd returned again to farm in Nebraska; and when his wheat crop failed, he'd heard about the Army's Warrant Officer flight program, and he'd come on board. He wore master pilot wings, indicating at least 15 years behind the stick. We could have no better pilot containing this situation.

When Glasgow shut down the starboard engine and brought up the jet on that side-making us at this stage an all-jet platform - the aircraft became dangerously unstable in anything beyond straight-ahead flight. The pilot allowed the port prop to 'windmill' freely in the air to propel the generators to produce electrical power for communications and aircraft controls. The pilot, jumping through hoops, was demonstrating extraordinary skill and courage just keeping us in the air while telling the world on guard channel our plight.

"Mayday! Mayday! Cat's Paw five-three-one, emergency power loss. Mayday! Mayday! Five-three-one at base plus four thousand; coordinates..." He knew we couldn't make it back to Cam Ranh Bay and began a vigorous search for a runway sufficient to the long strip landing demands of a loaded P-2 - normally two miles.

Still in that slow turn, we sweated every increment of the maneuver. We could all feel the bird slipping off its stable track, and only a part of those feelings were psychologically induced panic: the P-2 truly was unstable and heavy. And without full power, the controls were sluggish. Glasgow later said he felt like he was driving a garbage truck through a high tide.

By this time, both J-34's were struggling to keep us aloft, and both reciprocating engines were trailing smoke and/or oil. Glasgow keyed the intercom and announced we were going into Thy Hoa, a fighter base a short way back along the coast. We'd been cleared for a straight-in emergency landing; that is, not required to go through the usual stack: downwind, base, and final phased approach. We only had one shot at it; there would be no go-around. Once that close to Mother Earth, we didn't have the power to climb out and make another circuit of the pattern.

During the course of urgency-driven landing prep, the co-pilot - a Major and a National Guard officer/pilot who'd opted to take his one-year active duty with the 1st RRC to fly the 'biggest birds in the Army inventory,' a thing that might look good on his records - attempted to gain control of the aircraft. He tried ordering the crew to bail out, not a thing close to your heart, as the parachutes we carried were most often useful as seat cushions, and it was suspected that if the D-ring was pulled on any or all of them, instead of a pilot chute pulled out by the airstream, a spiraling flight of well-fed moths would erupt into the sky. As with other mass hysteria, the Major was universally ignored.

The co-pilot kept insisting that as a Major he was in command; he was senior; he was god-like. But in-flight protocol, a 'plane commander' is designated preflight, not based on rank, but simple rotation of duties among various pilots. That day's manifest listed Keith Glasgow, CW4 , as the pilot and plane commander. But the Chief had to fight that panicky Major for the controls, and for some minutes, it seemed an unsure future. It was only supreme confidence in our pilot that prevented sure, uncontrolled panic on five-three-one.

The pilot called out for us to secure in ditching stations and that we were on final for an emergency landing and that it would be sudden and soon. From my starboard porthole-like window, small buildings, parked aircraft, a few palm trees, and vehicles came into view as we dropped down, touching down on two wheels and reversing thrust in the jets, we felt the tricycle front gear grab, wobble, and settle down and we were taxiing. Fast, *really* fast, but taxiing on the ground. Mesmerized by the panoply below, I never did make it to my ditching station, which was seated on the deck, propped against panels or equipment racks. With my headsets still on, I heard the tower instruct Cat's Paw 531 that the starboard reciprocating engine was in flames on touch-down.

No sooner had the bird been brought to a halt, still rocking on its axis and three wheels, when 13 bodies un-assed the aircraft and sprinted for the boonies. Air Police and emergency vehicles completely surrounded 531 within seconds, and blue, red, and green lights bathed the airstrip syncopated glare. I was the last out of the bomb bay doors; as controller my responsibility was to round up all classified mission materials and escort the mission bag everywhere. Keith Glasgow was last down the front wheel well access ladder exit. He walked a short distance away on the apron and stood, hands on hips, glaring at the stricken bird in disdain.

And suddenly, there we all were, a long way from home, our transport broke, and no bus tokens. I spotted a two-striper Air Policeman raising a Polaroid camera to take a shot of the bird and the crew milling about in the aftermath. I ordered him to hand over the picture: *Classified mission bird.* Beyond a few black and white shots showing damage to the engine someone took with a clandestine camera, the Polaroid was the only record we got of the incident. I still have it.

Following all the Air Force folderol - Glasgow filling out paperwork to justify USAF expenditure of the fire retardant, and callout of all those facilities - we walked across the strip carrying our weapons, bags, helmets and parachutes, locked in pucker mode, to a C-130, a sort of coastal taxi that made regular runs up and down the edge of the sea to all major ports of call. He'd been called, asked to wait for us, and flew us directly to Cam Ranh Bay, where we giggled through the most entertaining debrief we've ever experienced. Relief loosens a lot of inhibitions.

The aircraft, 531, sat on the Thy Hoa parking apron for several days, until spare engines could be flown up, changed out, tested, and approved; then it was flown home to Cam Ranh Bay and went back on the 'Active Board' for missions.

CW4 Keith W. Glasgow was awarded the Distinguished Flying Cross for his spectacular bit of pilot magic, and served out his time enduring the undying thanks of twelve grateful believers.

Take That You Dirty Rat

By Terry Hester

I arrived at Phu Bai at the 8th RRFS in the early part of October, 1968. Since I had a MOS 72B, after I was processed in through personnel, I was then assigned to the Communications Center. At this time I had almost 3 years in the Army Security Agency. I had been assigned to Comm. Centers in Korea and in Germany. The workload in both of my previous Comm. Centers was miniscule compared to what I would find when I first went to work at CRS - Phu Bai. The term CRS, indicated that Phu Bai was a relay station, in the very sophisticated, worldwide communications system. However, the term 'relay station' did not describe the vast amount of originated traffic that came out of the 8th RRFS Comm. Center. It was one very busy place, which meant that the personnel assigned there had to work, and work together well, to keep the place going.

When I first got to Phu Bai, the Comm. Center was pretty well staffed. There were actually enough people for three 8-hour shifts. However, this didn't last very long. I was assigned to the shift which had SSG Lloyd Moeller as the Trick Chief. He was, in my opinion, a good guy. He was on his second enlistment, so I thought he was career Army. However, as I was to find out later, he was not. Moeller was not an overbearing type of supervisor. He was a friendly, easy to talk to guy. In conversations with him, I found out that he was going to leave the Army at the end of his current enlistment. SSG Moeller told me that he had made arrangements for a job working on the trans-Alaska oil pipeline after leaving the Army. As I recall, arrangements for workers were being made then, as the pipeline had been approved, but the work would not start for another couple of years. Moeller was a kind a guy that working in remote Alaska on the pipeline would have been a piece of cake and right down his alley.

As I mentioned before, the volume of work at the Comm. Center at Phu Bai was such that everyone assigned there needed to work together to get the job done. SSG Moeller tried to assure that this was accomplished.

We had this one guy on our shift who was quite lacking in his commitment to do his job. I gladly don't remember his name now, but I would not even mention it if I did. I only remember that he was from somewhere in California. But, as I remember, his real problem was that he was forever ticked off at his decision to enlist in the ASA, rather than take his chances with the draft. Somewhere along the way, he decided to screw up everything that he was tasked to do. This was his way of letting the Army know how mad he was being a 72B in Phu Bai, Vietnam. I guess he thought that he could have had something better as a draftee.

Anyway, SSG Moeller was constantly on his case, trying to get him to shape up and help everyone else get the job done. This had obviously been going on since long before my arrival at Phu Bai.

One very busy day, as all days at Phu Bai were, SSG Moeller was expressing his consternation with this guy just screwing up some other easy task, when he turned around and walked over to our weapons rack, and took out an M-14 rifle. We kept a couple of rifles and ammo on hand at all times. He aimed the rifle at California and said something to the effect, "I am tired of your BS, and I'm going to put an end to it now."

Needless to say, everybody in the Comm. Center was watching, transfixed. He pulled the trigger and there was a 'pop' and California kind of wilted to the floor. He was kind of whimpering to SSG Moeller, something like, "What kind of idiot are you?"

SSG Moeller had taken a rifle round and pulled out the bullet, and poured out the powder charge. He had placed the casing still containing the primer into the chamber of the M-14, which made the pop that we all heard.

As I think back on this incident now, I really believe that this was not staged with any foreknowledge of California. I do think that this was something that SSG Moeller thought might convince California to get with the program. SSG Moeller left Phu Bai very shortly after that, and I don't remember that any disciplinary action was taken in regard to it. However, I would like to know if he made it to the Alaska pipeline, and if so, how that turned out.

Anyway, a while later, California went out one night with our nightly contingent to stand for perimeter guard, out by the ammo dump. Bunker assignments were given out, and California trudged on over to his bunker, still carrying his rifle and gear. Everybody freaked out when a lot of rifle fire began. California had walked into his bunker and saw a big rat inside, or so he said later. He emptied his entire 20 round magazine trying to kill that rat. To this day, I believe that to California, that rat was named SSG Moeller.

The Bunker

By Tino 'Chui' Banuelos

We had a body count when it was all over. Some of the guys even took pictures. It had taken about 15 minutes to kill them all. They were tough customers; only a few had been zapped with just one hit. Most of them had been pretty well chopped up but it wasn't that noticeable as they lay neatly lined up near the old bunker. We made sure that their tails were perfectly parallel. There were twelve rats altogether. They had been quick, but we had been quicker.

It was an amazing feat when you consider that we had not set out to kill rats. Our assignment was to tear down the old sandbags around the two CONEX boxes that made up the unit's bunker. We were to move the large steel boxes nearer to our hooches and replace the sandbags. It was not to be an easy task. Removing the old sandbags was simple enough but a three-quarter ton truck was needed to move the CONEX boxes. A large rope was secured around one of the boxes and the three-quarter ton began to drag it slowly. As the box moved just a few feet, a large rat bolted from a burrow underneath the box. Everyone began shouting and chasing the rat. Someone picked up a rock and threw it at the panicky rat. Instantly, without thinking, we all stooped to grab a handful of rocks as we gave chase. There was no escape for the rat. Our compound was ringed by a large wall. The rat ran frantically as we whooped and hollered and threw our rocks. One rock hit it on the back of the head, and that flipped it over. As it lay on its back, its feet were still moving as if ... were still running. We surrounded it and continued to pepper it with rocks until it was a bloody mess.

There was a moment when there was no sound. I could feel the sun burning the back of my neck and the perspiration rolling down my forehead. We all stood over it, out of breath, and stared at its lifeless body. Our chests were heaving from the chase and the excitement of the kill. Then someone started, "Let's see if there are any more!"

We ran back to the CONEX box and positioned ourselves around it so that we were ready, no matter which direction the next rat would run. The truck moved the box and again a rat began its frantic search for an escape. Each time we chased it as rocks rained down mercilessly. Sometimes two rats would run and there would be even more chaos as we ran shouting and running like crazy men. Finally there were no more rats. The fever pitch of excitement lasted quite a while.

That night in the EM Club there were laughs and drinks as the day's exploits were recounted. I still vividly remember that image of the twelve rats lined up with their tails so neatly arranged.

Phu Bai Target Practice
By Terry Hester

I arrived at the 8th RRFS at Phu Bai early in the month of October, 1968. I was a Specialist Four at the time. After getting checked in, I was given a bunk in a squad sized tent along with some other newly arrived personnel. I remember that the tent was located to the rear of the more permanent quarters. Thankfully, I didn't have to live in the tent for too awfully long, before room became available in the more permanent trailer type barracks.

Very soon after arriving at Phu Bai, I learned that the 24th Army Corps had recently assumed command of all military operations in the Phu Bai area. Prior to this time, the commanding presence in the Phu Bai area had been the 3rd Marines. With the arrival of the 24th Corps, things were going to change regarding the day-to-day lives of all personnel at Phu Bai. What with the Marines being Marines, they certainly felt they were the best of all things military. They gladly insisted upon providing all outside perimeter defense for the base at Phu Bai, which they did prior to the 24th Corps arrival.

My arrival in Phu Bai must have coincided with the takeover of the outside perimeter defense while the Marines were vacating the area. Since I was one of the newest enlisted men that had just arrived at the 8th RRFS, I began drawing frequent details of perimeter guard. It became very apparent to this Tennessee boy on the first night that I was sent out for perimeter guard, that our commanders had no real plan of action regarding securing our sector of the perimeter. My first night of guard duty consisted of myself and another guy with all of our combat gear, armed with our M-14's, with extra magazines, sent to guard the asphalt plant on the outer fringes of Phu Bai.

We took up our position in a ditch and alternated sleeping through the night. I remember lying in the ditch in front of the asphalt plant, looking out in front of me, thinking of hoards of VC coming here intent on stealing this asphalt plant; they'll have to get through us first. I only learned one thing; nights get very long and uncomfortable when you're lying in a ditch, waiting for the morning light. Morning finally came, and we returned to the 8th RRFS.

After a couple of days an Infantry type Captain came out to our sector; we were told that he was in charge of getting the defenses of our area back in good order. He had lots of field experience, having been in command of Infantry platoons in the past. I think that he came from Corps, probably at the request of the Commander of the 8th RRFS. As far as I was told by the other guys at the 8th, when the order came down that every unit at Phu Bai would pull perimeter guard, the 8th Commander tried to get all of us ASA personnel exempted. However, no one was exempted, per the Corps Commander.

The Captain made his living quarters in the CP tent on the perimeter. All 8th enlisted personnel from the rank of Specialist 5 and below began pulling guard every night. Also, each day for a couple of weeks, we had guys coming out to complete the repair of the whole line.

The Captain taught many of us how to set the claymores out in front of the bunkers, and how to put in the detonators, and how to wire them up. He showed most of us how to set up the M-60s, and how to stake them and interlock fields of fire with the adjoining bunkers.

He also made what he called barbed wire bombs to be placed out in front of the bunkers. In doing so, he took a spool of barbed wire and set it on fence posts about 36 to 42 inches off the ground. He packed the core of the spools with C-4 explosives, and then put in detonators. He told us that the barbed wire bombs were the absolute last line of defense. If they were detonated the whole spool of barbed wire would shred into hundreds of pieces and fly outwards 360° around, at about three or 4 feet off the ground. He told us to make damn sure if we had to set them off, to make sure everyone was down inside his bunker.

The Captain seemed to me to be a good guy. And God knows he sure taught us a great deal. Thank the Lord that the crap never hit the fan on the 8th RRFS sector, at least while I was there. However, I think that the good Captain perhaps became too friendly with a lot of us ASA guys.

I seem to remember cold beer, provided by the Captain for lots of guys at the end of some hot days after perimeter repair duty. I think that the Captain maybe became too impressed with the education level of lots of the guys from the 8th. I'm sure that he had never commanded guys with anywhere near the level of college that many ASA people had. Sometimes it became like college dorm room bull sessions when there was cold beer provided by the Captain in the CP tent. I think that fact may have led to his undoing later.

After getting the whole sector in A-1 shape, the Captain said one day that he had obtained two .50 caliber machine guns from somewhere. He said that we would put one in the first and last of our bunkers. After putting the first one in the last bunker on the right, he said he would allow some guys to fire off a few rounds. I know that I really wanted to get a chance to fire that *thunka-thunka* .50 caliber, but, I did not get to. I don't think the Captain knew where in the hell he was letting the first guy shoot that thing, because, since it was not staked, the guy walked it around too far to the right. He did not know that he was sending rounds through the roof of a Special Forces camp way down Highway 1.

To say that some holy-hell was raised after this incident is an understatement. Anyway, the two .50 calibers were taken away, and the Captain was gone after that. And this fiasco did nothing to get us 8th RRFS ASA personnel exempt from perimeter guard at Phu Bai. I spent many a night out there in the perimeter before I left Phu Bai, and many crazy things happened out there, but nothing any more crazy than our first days.

Chapter 5
1969

The war intensity of 1968 continued into 1969. The US dead was reported to be higher for 1969 than any other year but not for the ASA. The stories tell of ASA soldiers traveling around Vietnam and their exposure to fire from artillery, rockets and mortars. Wounds could be slight or deadly. Attacks could be few or many. Once again, the B-52 bombing runs played a significant role both for the enemy and US soldiers.

VC/NVA Movements

By Ken Luikart

It has always been my assessment that the North Vietnamese leadership ordered Vietcong-led infantry divisions to lead the attacks in the 1968 Tet Offensive. During this offensive, thousands of VC Infantry Division casualties weakened traditional VC units. The Viet Cong guerrilla fighter would be conscripted into a local VC Infantry Battalion. After several years of service, the guerrilla fighter could be promoted into a VC Division. This meant he would receive a higher rank, more pay, and more food for his family. After the 1968 Tet Offensive, VC divisions were backfilled with North Vietnamese Army Regulars.

During the nights of October 15, and November 15, 1968, I spent most of the night in a bunker while we suffered heavy rocket and mortar attacks on Bien Hoa Army and Air Force Base. On both of those dates, nationwide antiwar demonstrations occurred in the United States. This was so disturbing to those of us in Vietnam, that one of my buddies wrote a letter to several newspapers back in the States. In this letter he asked that the Stars & Stripes be changed to a 'field of red' (for the blood of American soldiers who died for freedom) with a very large yellow chicken in the center (representing the American people). The antiwar demonstrations were having a very significant effect on the fighting men in Vietnam.

After the Tet Offensive in 1968, the big question on all the experts' minds was, who was getting stronger, the enemy or us. The 1968 Tet led to the Paris Peace talks and a change of Administration in the White House, Nixon for Johnson; and a change of command in Vietnam. Gen. Creighton Abrams replaced Gen. William C Westmoreland. Nixon's advisers were asking him to take a hard line against the North Vietnamese Communists, while Nixon developed a strategy of 'Vietnamization' to extricate ourselves out of the country.

Meanwhile Gen. Abrams designed the strategy of attacking COSVN and NLF Headquarters trying to kill General Giap. General Giap was the North Vietnamese Commanding General. General Abrams wanted ground Bomb Damage Assessment to be conducted by the infantry immediately after B-52 strikes.

In 1969, the field infantry units continued to sweep, doing bomb damage assessments after B-52 attacks. This was a costly method of fighting a war. Nineteen sixty nine proved to be the bloodiest year of the war, even if it is the least talked about phase of the war. More than 200 Americans were killed each month during 1969. You must remember the men who had fought in World War II led us. Combat casualties were considered a price that had to be paid to close in on and kill the enemy. Moreover, antiwar demonstrations and speeches gave the enemy the opinion that most Americans were against the war. General Lewis W. Walt complained that the news media was not reporting the real war to viewers back home. The TV coverage was taking small remote daylight engagements and making a big deal out of them while most of the fighting was done at night. General Walt hit the nail on the head; television depictions of battles were skewed to make headlines rather than tell the truth about the engagements conducted by the grunts in Vietnam.

During 1969, and early 1970, our intelligence unit attempted to locate and kill General Giap in the COSVN area between the Fish Hook, the Dog's Face, and a bend in the river near An Loc. Our unit would study the COSVN movement patterns and attempt to predict their next move. Every week we developed a list of potential targets that were forwarded to II Field Force Commander. His staff would incorporate all the potential targeted areas and then choose the targets to be bombed. Within hours B-52s from Guam would be on their way to shake the jungle. I have seen B-52 strikes from less than ten miles away; it feels like an earthquake and the rumble sounds like thunder in the mountains. We were not successful in killing Giap but according to General Giap's own book, we came close more than once.

Interestingly, Nixon's advisers suggested some sort of selective bombing in North Vietnam. Targets chosen were stockpiles of ammunition, weapons and petroleum storage areas recently installed just north of the DMZ. In the South, more than 575 tactical air sorties, about a hundred more than usual, struck VC and NVA positions. B-52's carried out ten strikes against enemy base camps, weapons positions and storage areas supporting the three divisions attacking Long Binh and Bien Hoa. One of these attacks occurred near Bien Hoa in War Zone D and was quite visible from our location. The earth shook and the attack could be seen and heard more than 15 miles away.

During January and February, 1969, B-52's attacked VC and NVA strongholds with more than 2,000,000 pounds of bombs in the Parrot's Beak area near the Cambodian border. Some of these attacks were targets I had forwarded to II Field Force Commander as candidates for ARC LIGHT strikes. The areas were historically the 9th VC Division Area of Operations (AO) near the Parrot's Beak.

We also chose local targets to be attacked with H & I (Harass and Interdict) artillery. When we found a significant enemy unit that appeared to be stationary, we would write down the coordinates, and take them to the Tactical Operations Center. At the TOC we would verify that the enemy unit was located in a Free Fire Zone and that no friendly operations were in the area. Immediately after verification, the fire support bases would open up with their 8 inch guns or 175 mm howitzers. These guns could throw shells 16 miles at a target and hit the target with pretty good accuracy. I often wondered how many people were killed on the other end because our intelligence section chose them to receive the artillery barrage.

The mini-Tet Offensive of February, 1969, cost about 250 American lives and more than 3000 Viet Cong lives. The VC attacks did not make any sense at all. The North Vietnamese government had ordered that another offensive be conducted with VC units. During 1969, many of the VC divisions were starving to death and were complaining to their higher headquarters that their men were eating grass and leaves.

The North Vietnamese Communists ordered the 5th and 9th VC Divisions to attack Bien Hoa and Long Binh. The goal of these attacks was to overrun the American bases at Long Binh and Bien Hoa and feast on US soldiers rations. This absurd attack order from higher headquarters further proves my point. These attacks further weakened the traditional VC Divisions, and North Vietnamese were used to backfill the units again. By the end of our involvement in Vietnam, NVA Army regulars were staffing traditional VC leadership positions. It is also interesting to note that the South Vietnamese Communist military leader was reportedly killed in a B-52 attack. How very convenient for the North Vietnamese Communist Government. Now all forces fell under the North Vietnamese Supreme Commander, General Giap.

Col. George Smith Patton Junior was the Commander of the US 11th Armored Cavalry Regiment, the Blackhorse Regiment. Patton wore ivory handled revolvers, just like his father. There was a meeting with high brass officials just prior to the attacks against Bien Hoa, February, 1969. Patton listened intently to the briefing being given by a US general. The general said that the Thai army would hold

Patton's left flank, the US garrison (11th Armored Cav) would be in the center of Bien Hoa, and the ARVN would be on his right flank. This would be the 5th ARVN Marines. The plan was that the ARVN would collapse towards the base and draw the enemy into the airbase.

When all was said and done Patton replied, "Well general, I see only three things wrong with your plan. First, as long as the PX is open, you can't count on the Thai's to be on-line. Secondly, if ARVN feign a withdrawal onto my position they will be shot because I can't tell one of those Zips from another. Third, and most important, the airfield is not the target."

 He further explained that he felt the base would be hit by a regimental sized unit, but that Long Binh was the primary target because of its logistical supply caches. He surmised that Long Binh was lightly defended and ran along Highway Route 1. He cited intelligence reports that the attackers were encouraged to wear P38 can openers on chains around their necks and were more interested in feasting on captured rations than taking an airfield. This little story substantiates my claim that the Viet Cong units were eating bananas and cooked jungle grass; they were starving to death.

Intelligence reports indicated that there was a large and general movement of forces southward from the Cambodian border areas located northwest and north of Saigon. We knew the VC and NVA forces were running out of food. Additional reporting said that some units were complaining bitterly to their higher headquarters. They were making soup made of greens found in the jungle. One report indicated that the communist honchos had convinced the VC units that by taking Long Binh and Bien Hoa Army bases they would have a 'great feast' on our field rations. According to Special Forces personnel that recovered weapons off the battlefield, they said that many of the Communist dead had P38 can openers on chains around their necks. Prisoners indicated that one of the main objectives was to kill all the GI's and capture our food supplies.

Regardless of their motive for attack, our intelligence section knew the enemy was coming at us. The 5th VC division moved east of Long Binh, into the War Zone D area. The 7th NVA Division moved down Highway 13 out of the Fish Hook area into the Michelin rubber plantation. The 9th VC Division moved southeast toward Tay Ninh City out of the Parrot's Beak area and was operating between Bien Hoa and Tay Ninh City, a distance of only 70 miles. Marine Corps assets contacted 9th VC Division elements in the Elephant's Ear area north of Phuoc Binh Provincial capital.

On one night, prior to the February attack, I was assigned as the tower guard. Tower guards pulled a 24 hour shift, two hours on and two hours off during the night, with one guard staying awake in the tower all day the next day. During the night, I spotted about 50 enemy troops moving through a local rubber tree plantation approximately 900 to 1000 yards away. It may have been a test to see if we were able to engage them or see their movement. That night I was using the starlight scope. The starlight scope was large and heavy, but allowed you to see the night as daylight with a green colored tint. On that occasion the TOC scrambled a helicopter gunship that engaged the enemy and killed several of them.

Throughout January and February, 1969, the 5th VC Division relocated from Cambodia to the southern part of War Zone D, approximately 30 km northeast of Bien Hoa Air Base. On 15 February elements of the Division moved to forward positions to the north and east of Bien Hoa Air Base. Throughout the week, prior to 23 February, the number of contacts with the enemy within 18 miles of the base was light, and the size of the enemy units were mainly squad size or smaller. Agent reports and prisoner of war interrogations confirmed that a pending offensive was planned to begin on or immediately after the 1969 Tet holidays.

In February, 1969, I witnessed a very large battle for the air base at Bien Hoa, Republic of Vietnam. I had just turned 21 years old on

February 1st, and had been in-country for only six months. I was assigned to the 175th Radio Research Company, a signals intelligence unit, as the Combat Order of Battle Analyst. I learned quickly to tell a difference between outgoing artillery fire from Fire Support Bases Caroline and Daisy, and incoming 122 mm and 107 mm rockets. Moreover, I learned the difference between incoming rockets, which are very inaccurate, and incoming mortars, which are very accurate.

As early as 17 February, intelligence indicated that the weekend of 23 February was a critical time. The security at Bien Hoa was beefed up and augmentation forces were put on alert. Bien Hoa had 245 Security Police augmented by 65 Stateside Security Police trained in crew-served weapons, 53 Sentry dogs and 145 Air Force personnel that could be called on if necessary. Stationed at Bien Hoa was the 145th Aviation Battalion that had 60 fighting positions in the integrated portion of the southern perimeter. Two helicopter firefly teams, one lightship and two gunships were available. In addition, there were: the 11th Armored Cavalry Regiment, the 23rd ARVN Defense Force Group, the 57th ARVN Regional Forces, and the 5th Republic of Vietnam Marines. Army and Air Force K-9 units using German shepherd dogs provided additional security.

On 9 February, 1969, our intelligence section knew we were going to be attacked sometime on the 22nd or 23rd of February. Our assessment stated the Viet Cong and North Vietnamese enemies would attempt a series of simultaneous assaults on various provincial capitals in order to influence the Paris Peace talks and to attempt to capture a provincial capital in order to bring a quicker closure to the campaign. Moreover, some of the analysts I worked with felt that the VC and the NVA had set up their military regions like spokes in a wheel with Saigon as the hub and all other military regions spiking out from it. This allowed the VC and the NVA units to always concentrate their efforts towards the capital city, Saigon.

On 20 February, 43 enemy soldiers were killed in the Binh Duong Province, 18 miles northwest of Saigon. This area was believed to be the area of interest of VC and NVA forces for conducting their attacks against the South Vietnamese and US forces. Tay Ninh City was very close to the Parrot's Beak and Long Bien and Bien Hoa, the two largest military bases within easy striking distance of enemy forces camped in Cambodia.

Bien Hoa was a crowded base with more than 17,000 personnel, 350 aircraft, not counting the helicopter's owned by the Army. More than 70,000 air movements monthly meant the base was the busiest airport in the world. Fuel consumption was estimated at 8000 gallons every 24 hours. COSVN or the North Vietnamese could not ignore the importance of Long Bien and Bien Hoa. These were large complexes, staffed by troops considered to be rear area forces and not combat soldiers. The communists considered these complexes as an easy target to attack and overrun.

On 21 February, 1969, enemy activity throughout Vietnam died down to a whimper, from a total of 89 countrywide incidents a day to only fourteen on Wednesday and four on Thursday, just prior to the attack on our base.

The level of US activity of the 'bomb and sweep with the infantry' resulted with more than 197 US soldiers killed during the week. It was not much of a strategy, but Gen. Abrams was testing out new methods of engaging the enemy. The ARC LIGHT strikes would hit suspected VC or NVA command centers and the infantry would sweep through to do a ground Bomb Damage Assessment and attempt to capture or kill the VC and NVA headquarters personnel.

On 21 February, the US urged the North Vietnamese and Vietcong to seek 'common ground' for negotiations with the US and South Vietnamese at the Paris Peace talks. During the 21 February meeting, the South Vietnamese delegation called for an exchange of prisoners of war, but the North Vietnamese and the VC government representatives remained silent on that point. The Peace Talks weren't going anywhere.

On February 23, at 0210 hours, guard tower number ten reported incoming rounds from the east and northeast, about 3 miles from the base. These rounds were the 107 mm rockets that leave a distinct golden shower of sparkles as they go up into the sky. The warning siren was sounded and I hit the floor and rolled under my bunk. You only had 3 to 9 seconds to react. Because I felt we are going to be hit that night, I went to bed fully dressed with my boots laced. I had my helmet; rifle and flack vest in bed with me. At 0214 hours a second volley of rockets was reported incoming. Most of Bien Hoa City and the base lost all power as a result of impacts.

The augmentation guard had been called to report to the orderly room when the second volley hit. The pitch black base became hauntingly scary as we were ordered to take up fighting positions within our own company. At 0220 hours additional incoming rounds were reported. The number of rounds hitting our base precluded an accurate count; the barrage was the worst I had ever encountered in Vietnam, and I have encountered quite a few attacks. My guess at the time was between 50 and 100 rounds of 122 mm and 107 mm rockets. It is hard to count when you are taking a pounding.

By 0250 hours tower number 6 on the south perimeter reported that it was receiving small arms fire from the direction of 'Turkey Row,' a road lined with shacks that runs parallel to the perimeter and part of Bien Hoa City. This was an old VC trick; they would attack the base's perimeter using civilian homes as cover. Tower number 8 also received fire from Turkey Row.

All units in the southern perimeter were ordered by Air Force Security Police to open fire on the incoming fire. One Sherman tank and one APC were moved up, and opened fire. Security Police reaction forces were deployed behind tower number 8 as well as at sentry dog post number one and in the vicinity of base gate 3. Tower

177

number 6 and tower number 8 reported observing the enemy establishing two mortar positions and one machine gun position along Turkey Row. US Army helicopters were on the scene in the area. The APC vehicle responded to the vicinity of the tower number 8 and opened fire on the suspected enemy locations. All of these positions were eliminated, meaning the enemy was killed. Seven individuals were observed by tower number 8 crossing Turkey Row toward the base's perimeter, but suppressive fire by base Security Police diverted them and they were forced back to their original positions inside the civilian houses on Turkey Row.

During this time frame our augmentation guard was ordered to go to the bunker system as soon as possible. In the pitch black of predawn our 20 man team climbed into deuce-and-half trucks and moved at a snail's pace towards the northern perimeter. When we approached the bunkers not much was said by anyone. Everyone was awake, alert and all weapons were locked and loaded. Augmentation of the bunkers meant that some of us would have to remain outside and dig foxholes into the perimeter berm rather than go inside the crowded bunker. I dug a fox hole into the berm and set up my ammo for easy reloading. I had no plan for a retreat or place to run to; as a matter of fact, I had made a commitment to stay and fight until captured. Under my armpit, in a leather holster, was an 11 mm pistol intended to end things very quickly if necessary, that is, committing suicide. I had bought it for $13.00.

At 0345 hours the battle quieted and ceased. At 0430 hours security supervisors checked their areas and reported incoming rounds over the radio. The siren was sounded. A number of rounds impacted south of the base, probably into Bien Hoa City. At the same time small arms fire erupted again from Turkey Row.

By 0700 hours all firing ceased. Sweeps were made with negative results. There were four WIA among the Americans. We remained in place for the next five days. Meals on wheels had a new meaning. We were brought a pretty good box lunch every day and rotated in for a hot meal once a day but spent the night on the perimeter. Since the water supply was knocked out, we forgot about showers and shaving. Of course, at age twenty one I could have gone for a month without shaving; who would know the difference?

Three for the Ditch

By Andy Anderson

Mike Zeitschel and Roger Boyce and I were going to midnight chow at Engineer Hill in Pleiku, South Vietnam. We were with the 330th Radio Research Company at the time. We left a secure compound and were walking up the road to the mess hall to partake of some of that fabulous Army food and cooking. The term road is somewhat misleading here, as it was nothing more than a path made out of the hard packed red Pleiku dirt with water drainage ditches on either side of it.

It was pitch black, as only Vietnam could be, and I was using a flashlight to make sure that we stayed on the road. About two thirds of the way to the mess hall, we heard the lovely, melodious, WHUMP, WHUMP, and WHUMP of mortar rounds being cut loose. We had no idea where they were going to land until the ground started to erupt very close to the portion of the road that we were currently occupying.

OK, THREE FOR THE DITCH!

Mike was on my left, Roger was on my right, and we dove into the drainage ditch alongside the road to try to get our sorry asses as low as possible. Rounds continued to fall and explode for about two years, or so it seemed. We continued to lie in the ditch until we were sure that the last of the rounds had gone off. After we were sure that it was over, we cautiously got back up and started to look around.

About that time I heard Mike say something like "Ah Shit." I turned on the flashlight to see what was going on. I thought that maybe he had an encounter with a snake or rat, but was not prepared for what I saw. Mike's baseball cap had come off when we dove for the ditch, and when we got back up, Mike had run one of his hands through his hair. It came away bloody, and that's what the 'Ah Shit' was about. It turned out that a piece of shrapnel had hit him in the scalp, breaking the skin, but doing no further damage. The piece of shrapnel was still tangled in his hair. I asked him if he was okay, and after telling me that he was, I said, "It's a good thing you have red hair. I can't even see the blood except on your hand."

We decided to hit the mess hall for chow, and when we got into the light, Mike noticed a spot of blood on Roger's jungle fatigue shirt. We figured that it was from Mike until we remembered that I was between Mike and Roger. That prompted Roger to take off his fatigue jacket, and there was blood on his T-shirt. We checked under the T-shirt and, and found a pinhead sized wound in his chest. We were ordered to go to the dispensary on Engineer Hill to have the wounds looked at and cleaned.

Mike had the piece of shrapnel that cut his scalp, and the piece that got Roger was still in his chest. People at the dispensary said that the piece that hit Roger was so small that they weren't even going to remove it. The wounds were cleaned up and bandaged and they both came back to the maintenance shop a while later.

We forgot all about it until about a month later when we had a company formation. Awards and promotions were being passed out, and we were all surprised when they called out Mike and Roger's names. The dispensary had taken names of all personnel that were treated after the mortar attack and submitted the names for Purple Hearts. We all had a laugh over that, and thought that was the end of it. But, it wasn't!

When we arrived in-country we had to list next of kin, and people to be notified in the event that we were wounded or killed. Mike and I had elected notify only in the event of death or something like that, while Roger picked notify for everything.

About three days after the Purple Hearts were awarded, Roger got a letter from his mother, and she was pissed! It's seems that the Army had sent her a telegram saying something like: Dear Mrs. Boyce, (yadda, yadda, yadda, blah, blah, blah, Army speak). Your son, Specialist 4th Class Roger L. Boyce has sustained multiple shrapnel wounds to the back and chest. (More Army speak).

All that we could figure was that it was a standardized telegram that they sent out when somebody was hit by shrapnel. She thought he was hamburger until he got back home. And that's the way it was.

Snake Eater Duty
By Andy Anderson

No shit, there I was, at the 'Snake Eater's' compound in Pleiku. For those unfamiliar with the term 'Snake Eaters', that's a term of endearment that we used to describe the Army's Green Beret troops. When they go through Special Forces training they have to learn to live off the land and eat snakes, for crying out loud! Now whether or not these particular Green Berets ever ate snakes was none of my business, and I sure as hell wasn't going to bring it up!

Never in my wildest dreams did I think I would wind up with the green beanies; the Snake Eaters; Special Forces; or any of the other dozen or so nicknames that these guys had. Oh sure, we had them in the secure operations compound at the 330th Radio Research Company where I really should've been, and they were there to assist with identification, triangulation, radio traffic analysis, and all the other jobs that went on at the 330th. I was used to working with them and even got to know a couple of them a little. They were all Staff Sergeants. At least that's what it seemed like to me.

Anyway, there I was, courtesy of the Snake Eaters, my Signal Maintenance OIC, and my company CO. I was called to the orderly room one day and told I was going to be TDY for a while. The Snake Eaters had pitched a story to the CO about how their radio repair man had rotated back to the States and how they really needed a body to fill in while they waited for a replacement. Since they were helping us out with our jobs, the CO and the OIC of Signal Maintenance figured that we could return the favor; I was it.

183

These guys turned out to be really nice to me. They made sure that I had every piece of clothing that I was supposed to have, they took all my shirts to the local tailor and had the Special Forces patch put on in place of the First Field Forces Vietnam patch, told me that I could drink whatever happened to be in the refrigerator without paying, gave me a Jeep to use, and even presented me with my very own Green Beanie! I was beginning to think 'I might like being in this outfit!'

After about a week at treating me like a mascot, and me enjoying every minute of it, they brought me a PRC-25 radio and asked me to fix it. I looked at it and said, "I can't fix this *effin'* thing; it has a bullet hole through it and needs to be DXed!" DX stands for direct exchange. That's where you take a piece of equipment that can't be repaired to the depot, and they'll direct exchange it for a new or rebuilt one. That cuts down on repair time and gets a working unit back out to the field a lot quicker.

"And by the way", I said, "What the hell happened to the guy who was carrying this?"

"Well", one of the Snake Eaters said, "Our radio repairman was carrying it. That's why he was sent back to the States!"

It finally dawned on me that I would be doing double duty, fixing and carrying! Damn, I needed a building, repository, waste, 4-6-8 or 10 position, with receptacle, cleanable, removable/replaceable right now!

I thought I was going to pass out, and then they told me later that I got white as a sheet. I couldn't catch my breath and my vision started to blur! Hey! I damn sure didn't want to carry a friggin' PRC-25, with its long antennae, around in the bush for Charles to use as target practice! I didn't want to be rotated back to the States with a bullet hole in my back! I didn't want someone to hand the next radio repairman the radio that had been on my back!

About five minutes later one of the Snake Eaters said, "Andy, calm down, it's a joke man; we do this all the time." At that point I headed for the shitter and didn't know if I would make it or not! I did make it but just barely.

It turns out that the Snake Eaters couldn't have been nicer to me. I did my job and kept their radio equipment repaired for about three weeks. They got their replacement maintenance man, and I got to go back to the good old 330th Radio Research Company again. The story about how I had almost soiled my OD green skivvies had beaten me there, however, and it was a while before the harassment quieted down.

I kept the Green Beret and had taken it to work to show a fellow Vietnam Vet one night after I'd gotten out of the Army. It was in my left jacket pocket as I stopped at the grocery store on my way home. Some asshole came at me with a razor blade box cutter. It just so happened that he was right-handed and when he slashed at me it came at my left side. He sliced my jacket, sliced the Green Beret, but missed Andy! I still have the Beret, slice and all, and every time I see it, I smile, remembering what it cost me to get it.

Who Threw the F***ing Railroad Car?
By Rick Hayden

Towards the end of 1969, my job of performing the certification inspections on all of the Secure Voice installations in Vietnam was getting insane. On top of the normal workload that kept me traveling to the far-flung corners of South Vietnam, as well as occasional forays over to Thailand, it was compounded by the pullout of the Marines. I was in the middle of my 97th straight night of undergoing rocket and/or mortar attacks. It seemed that no matter where I went, even if it was supposedly 'quiet,' they got hit. Paranoid, hell no! It's not paranoia if they are really out to get you. But then that's another story.

I had been spending a lot of time flying in and out of remote sites that the Army had inherited as the Marines moved out. All of the installations that were required to remain operational had to be re-certified. When I got back to the 57th Signal, Phu Bai Secure Voice Cord-board Manual switch, one evening after a few days out re-certifying installations, Stumpy Barton, the NCOIC came running up to me in a panic. It seems that no one had figured out that when the Marines had pulled out of Dong Ha the Secure Voice Cord-board (SECORD) facility was now located outside of the new perimeter. It was getting too late to get a chopper flight and the next scheduled 57th Signal courier flight wasn't until the next afternoon.

My ass was dragging. I had figured on a hot shower, a good night's sleep in one of the trailers at the 8th RR Field Station and a well-deserved case of cold beer at the club. I told the 57th troops to call the Automatic Secure Voice Switch at MACV Headquarters when they were ready for inspection and I would be there.

All of a sudden I was lifted off my feet and propelled into the CONEX container that served as the SECORD's personnel club. I was unceremoniously dumped on a barstool and told to shut the fuck up. Now I wasn't used to that kind of treatment by these guys; usually they bent over backwards to support me. My mind raced and my already parched throat got a little bit dryer. I looked at Stumpy and saw blood in his eyes. I said to myself *'self what the fuck have you done now, you gonna get your scrawny ass kicked.'*

Stumpy produce a couple of beers from the refrigerator behind the bar and proceeded to tell me that they had to get the thing moved in the next 24 hours and to make matters worse the two shelters that they had set up for the facility had been put in place and then the bunker built around them. After the bunker was completed, the troops had mixed concrete and coated the whole damn thing with it. No one ever considered that the equipment would have to be removed and it was doubtful that the case parts of the Cryptographic Equipment would fit out the door and through the blast entrance.

I immediately started to let my battleship mouth overload my row boat ass and asked who the stupid bastard was that built the bunker with such narrow entrances.

Stumpy's reply was, "I did it on my first tour and as long as I could get in there, it was big enough."

By that time we had consumed several more beers and I thought a quick trip to the latrine would afford me the chance to escape up the road. Unfortunately, Stumpy had the same idea. I never did get to sleep in that nice air-conditioned trailer.

The next morning at first light I climbed into a Jeep with Stumpy and two of his repairmen. By the time we got to Hue my eyeballs were ready to fall out of my cheeks. The greasy eggs, bacon and tomato juice I had for breakfast were rolling around in my stomach, threatening to come up and Kemtone the inside of the Jeep. We stopped at the MACV Compound and I drank a glass of instant breakfast (Alka-Seltzer) and gulped down a not-so-cold beer. I have to mention that I was not alone in this venture; Stumpy and one of the repairman were just as bad off, but I had been convinced that this trip could not be postponed.

We hooked up with a convoy going to Quang Tri. Oh, the joy of swallowing dust and trying to look like the most unimportant vehicle in the convoy. Actually, my asshole pucker factor was one notch above tight. I had been hit a month before in a convoy going from Pleiku to Kontum. It was an uneventful ride and once we were at Quang Tri we grabbed some chow at the MACV Compound. By the time we arrived at Kontum we were beat to hell; but the best was yet to come.

The on-site repairman had installed equipment racks in the Artillery's underground Tactical Operations Center. When we pulled into Dong Ha we dropped off the repairmen that came in with us and the equipment cases off at the TOC and proceeded to the SECORD site.

I had never inspected the site but Stumpy's description of it didn't even start to do justice to the construction effort that went into it. If I ever have to build a bunker, I'm going to get Stumpy to help. Instead of the normal one blast shield on top, it had two and the front entrance blast shield was more than three-feet thick.

Upon entering the facility, there were two shelters sitting side-by-side. The one to the right was the one used as sleeping quarters by the repair man and the site operator and contained a soundproof booth for the common user Secure Voice Terminal. It was equipped with one hell of a refrigerator and a hot plate.

The site personnel had started to dismantle the installation but it was slow going since only one of them was certified on the equipment and the other didn't know shit except how to operate it. To compound matters, care had to be taken so the wiring could be reused. With our arrival, there were three qualified KG-13 repairmen plus me that could help dismantle the facility. We started dismantling the facility and had to do a little work on the walls with sledgehammers and the entranceway to get the equipment out. By the end of the day we had just about removed everything except the huge Western Electric Modem and two of the equipment racks that we had to dismantle to get them out of the entrance.

It was dark and we decided that we had best stay put for the night. Three of us stayed in the facility and the others went back to the TOC to get as much done as they could. The 155 mm Artillery started a fire mission and the ground started shaking. The site repairman said that we could count on that off and on all night. We took our time getting the racks disassembled and sliding the modem over by the shelter door. One of the men from the TOC came back and said that they were ready for the modem but Stumpy told him that there was no way that we were going to light up the area to get that heavy piece of equipment loaded tonight. He said there was plenty of beer on hand and we could settle in for a good Pinochle game.

There is an unwritten clause in the MOS qualifications for 32F Fixed Cyphoning Equipment Repairman, that you must know how to play Pinochle and every facility, no matter how small, must always have a double deck of cards on-site.

We were getting ready to call it a night, so I went over to the quarter's shelter and broke out a beer while the others finished up. I had no sooner gotten my beer when we started taking incoming artillery fire. Now I'd been through rocket and mortar attacks, but this was the first time that it felt like somebody was throwing railroad cars at me. The entire shelter was shaking. The guys had told me earlier that this was a regular thing, but they would stop before our artillery could fire counter battery fire at them. They also told me that we didn't have to worry because artillery batteries were the targets, not us.

Well, somebody should have told the NVA gunners because all of a sudden I was knocked off my feet and thrown against the back shelter wall. The fluorescent tubes crashed to the floor and shattered. I couldn't hear shit but felt it when the second round hit the facility and knocked me on my ass again. Now I was getting scared. I mean, *why are they targeting me?* The old paranoia thing was setting in. I know it was only a few minutes from the time the first shell hit the base until it was over, but it seemed like hours.

We had lost power, but the guys in the other shelter used the remote starting hookup to fire up the diesel generator located at the rear of the bunker in a sandbagged shelter. This did nothing for me except to get the air conditioner going again; the only lighting I had was from the emergency light on the wall. I got up and went to the entrance door. I undid the latch and pushed on it to open it; there was no give at all. I hollered to the rest of the guys and heard muffled sounds but couldn't understand what they were saying; my hearing wasn't worth a shit.

Fortunately, the shelter was equipped with a fire ax as all COMSEC shelters are. I got the ax and attacked the door. After about 15 minutes, I was able to break through the door but all I got in return was dirt, cement pieces, and I could see part of a shattered railroad tie and twisted PSP (pierced steel planking). I started digging, but the more dirt I pulled in the more filled the void. I had about a quarter of the shelter full of dirt and didn't seem to be getting anywhere. I thought that unless we got outside help we were screwed once the generators ran out of fuel and we lost our source of air.

I gave up and decided to have another beer when I saw the guys from the other side cutting a hole through to my shelter. I got my ax and started on my side to help get some of the separating walls cut away. We had been in there for almost an hour when we were once again altogether. They had tried to dig out their door but met with the same result that I had.

The discussion ranged from, hell does anyone besides the repairman in the TOC know that we're here, to what if he got hit and was unable to tell anyone that the facility wasn't completely vacated. I asked about the back wall and Stumpy told me that it was as thick as the front. Well, hell, there goes that idea. Then Stumpy and I both had a 'brain fart' at the same time. These were COMSEC shelters, not regular communication shelters. The air-conditioners were mounted from the inside with bolts every 2 inches. We crawled back into the equipment shelter since that's where the tools were and then attacked the bolts on the air conditioner. Once we got the nuts off the bolts we took the fire axes and pried the flange loose. Since it was hardwired to the van we cut the power at the switchbox, took an ax to the power cable and dumped the unit on the floor. Hell of a waste of good trading material.

 The smallest repairman took one of the emergency lights and checked to see if we had a way out through the generator shed. When we got the word that there was, the rest of us went into the other shelter and rescued the beer and Pinochle cards. All of our pockets were stuffed with beer cans and we handed the remainder to the man in the generator shed. After we crawled out past the generators, we stopped and relaxed for the first time in almost 2 hours.

The damned artillery unit opened up with another fire mission shaking the ground but for some strange reason it soon sounded one hell of a lot better than it had two hours earlier. We all opened a beer and proceeded to walk around to the front of the bunker.

There was a crowd attacking the bunker with picks and shovels along with jeeps and chains. We walked up to a Captain and asked what was going on.

He said, "This bunker took two direct hits and we're trying to get to the bodies inside."

'Stumpy and I looked at each other and said, "Captain you need a beer." Stumpy handed him one and told him to stop digging; I added that the report of our deaths has been exaggerated. And TANS, That Ain't No Shit. Now if I could only stop the damned nightmares.

The Tall and the Short of It
By Randolph Willard

I was born short; Short of brains, short of height, short of wealth; short a parent, but mostly short in stature. I was not a dwarf, but had been called one. I have also been called: Shorty, Midget, Shrimp, Pee Wee, Short Stuff, Half-Pint, Tiny, Squirt, little man, Leprechaun, Hobbit Gnome, Pygmy and a host of other names identifying me as a short person. My mom named me Randy. I always told folks I was named after Randolph Scott, the actor.

Money was short and my mom was not a nursing type, so I was given plenty of coffee to drink and a lot of oatmeal cookies to eat. All of my life I have been a heavy coffee drinker and a cookie enthusiast. I don't know if nutrition was a factor in my lack of height. Mom was only 5 foot and most of her relatives were short too.

I was the lad always chosen when the school carpenter was building a stool for the water cooler. I imagine I made a pathetic sight climbing up and trying to work the lever and scratching the finish on the water cooler with my belt buckle. My big brother, a boy of normal height, would often meet me whenever he could, lifting me up in his powerful arms so that I could get a good drink of water and not faint from thirst in the hot days of a West Florida sun. By the time I moved on to junior high, the custodial staff at Warrington Elementary called stools a 'randy'.

As with many short insecure boys, I took offense at being called anything but by my name. By the fifth grade, I had a reputation as a feisty, mean SOB. I took plenty of lickings, but even bullies get tired of taking a punch to the knee every day. I also had a best friend who was the best street fighter in Pensacola. It was like being the sidekick to a gunfighter.

With such a history, I was surprised to find myself in the Army Security Agency as a 72B20.D1. Wow, a Communications Center Specialist. I always suspected it was because they found I took typing and was a whiz with keystrokes. So impressive were my typing skills that I met my minimum word requirement the first day of the two week typing portion of the advanced training in the Cage at Fort Gordon, Georgia. I was naïve as to the mixed blessings of Army standards. Instead of being impressed, the sergeants found me a job raking sand and performing other menial details for a week until the other fellows in the course passed 35 words a minute so we could move on to some new phase of training.

I was surprised that they gave me a Top-Secret Crypto clearance. I came from a long line of scoundrels and felt that surely they would hold this against me. Several years later, a former supervisor told me that when the FBI came asking about me, that he only told the truth and not to hold it against him. I guess he thought I was some in some sort of trouble to have the FBI coming around asking questions, even though they assured him it was for the Army.

I was assigned to Davis Station in Vietnam as part of the legendary 509th RRCUV. I didn't know it was legendary at the time, but I did know it was in-country as many referred to Vietnam. I told people back home it stood for Ranger Recon Commando Unit Vietnam. It actually stood for Radio Research Communications Unit Vietnam. And to this day, I don't understand any of it.

Upon arrival I found I had a new name. It was NUG. I kept correcting those who got there before me that my name was Randy Willard; it was not NUG. In no uncertain terms, I was told that NUG was a derogatory acronym for No Good Useless Guy. In the Army, one quickly learns that to be called a name is a regular feature of life. I kept my head down and my mouth shut and soon enough, as is customary, a real screw-up arrived and the bullies moved on to this poor fellow.

As time went by, those men that had worked with me began to take note that I did not drink alcohol, smoke, play cards or spend any money that was not absolutely necessary; and worst of all, I did not go to Saigon to visit with the bar girls. I don't know why this was such a problem with those people. There were plenty of guys in the unit who did not go and toss their money on booze and women. When some people get an idea in their head, they just can't let it go.

The ragging begins; I was used to ribbing, having suffered a slew of it by being the last one chosen during all of those ragamuffin years at Low-rent, Florida. Two factors were at work here. One, I knew the value of a buck. I knew a dollar in the wallet was better than not having a dollar. I'd known too many days that ran into years where I was always the one caught short. The second factor was; why pay for something that easily could be obtained for free. I learned later it is never free.

I thought about hanging around at the Tan Son Nhut pool. Apparently, the Air Force provided air conditioning and swimming pools for enlisted men. After a few trips to the pool, it also became apparent that a round eyed woman, attractive or not, would not have nothing to do with a low-ranking enlisted man, come hell or high water.

My cousin Roxanne, a female of much beauty, took to sending her letters in scented envelopes and sometimes included a picture of herself. She was young, blond and hot. She told me that maybe my hooch mates would think I had a girlfriend back in the States. I could tell the guys that I was saving myself for her and I was expecting her to do the same. This ploy did not work because I was ratted out by my oldest Army buddy who told someone the letters came from my cousin.

The proverbial last straw happened when Skate decided to print a roster of everyone on his Trick with their first name, last name and their Comm. Center nickname. With much chagrin, I was shocked to find my handle was 'Cherry Boy.' This would not work and it most certainly could not go on. I was getting prone to throwing a punch or two and messing up my perfect record of being a pleasant and compliant soldier. I protested that I was not, but to no avail. I had not yet learned to not let people know that what someone was saying was getting my goat, and calling me a cherry boy sure was. Being called a 'mean-spirited midget' did not sound so bad after all.

I decided on a plan of action. My plan was simple. I would go to Saigon and the bars on Tu Do Street. I had been on Tu Do Street for sightseeing, gawking and looking around. Since I did not cruise bars and really had no idea how one went about procuring a whore for the night, I asked the man from the unit who had a reputation of being a man about Saigon. Bruno had extended his tour several times and it was rumored that he did so because of love found on Tu Do. I asked Bruno if he would take me to town on one of his sojourns and show me the ropes. He agreed, and I thought he took too much delight in the fact that he would be the one to take me, the cherry boy, to experience the charms and pleasures of women.

We worked long hours in the center , and it was like working in a cave. Depending on your Trick you could go a month without seeing much daylight except during lunch when we walked to the mess hall. We were given three days off each month as the two tricks rotated from days to nights, and this was opportune for me to accompany Bruno to Saigon and the world of sin.

We caught a cyclo outside the gate and headed for the Tu Do Street bars. I had heard that some GIs would hire Saigon cyclos and race them down city streets, but I had not personally seen such a race. I did use them frequently as they were cheaper than a cab and faster than a bus. As a matter of fact, they were a downright amusement park ride.

My head was filled with visions of the flesh. I'd hoped that I would get one of the French-Vietnamese girls. Every one of them that I ever saw was beautiful and for the most part spoke fairly good English. Then I thought that they might cost more than the going rate of $20. I knew I had to buy the Saigon tea and I did not know how many I would have to purchase so that the girl met her quota. I also would have to pay for a room. I would order my customary Coke and nurse it as long as I could.

I knew nothing about whores. The few girls I had dated most certainly were not. The girls that I had heard other boys call whores were not whores, either. Usually, these were those girls who had a flirty nature, or who were recent break-ups or had turned a fellow down. The closest I had come to a whore was on an elevator at a motel near Fort Jackson, South Carolina. I was on my first weekend pass in Basic. A couple of barrack mates and I had rented a room at a local motel in Columbia. While boarding an elevator there was a nicely dressed and attractive woman. I was thinking tourist or business woman? One of the fellows asked her, "How much" and to my amazement she said, "How many?" I didn't wait for the answer because I was sure not going to be the sloppy second or third sex route. I exited and headed for the street.

Once on the main street of Saigon, Bruno and I entered a bar where Bruno met his regular girl and told me to take a seat and soon a B girl would join me and I could take it from there. I was on my own. Bruno and his gal went up the stairs presumably to a room and I knew that I would not see him until day light the next day.

I waited a few minutes and after I was confident that Bruno would not come back into the bar area, I left. I could not go back to Davis Station as the word would get back that I had chickened out and the hazing would be that much worse. I was thinking I could find a rack at the hotel St. George if I could find the St. George and could talk a rack out of them. Or maybe I could just find a cheap room someplace in which to rack out for the night.

I headed towards Cholon because that was the area of the city that I knew best and where I went on most days off. I thought I would find a café and eat dinner. It was early yet and I did not eat beforehand on the day of my big adventure. Many restaurants had display dishes in their windows and this was how I would have to order, not being fluent in Vietnamese, to order food without making a mistake. I always ordered meat that appeared to be chicken as I was afraid of the hamburger. I had been warned that it could contain a rat or two.

Then I saw her! A round-eye. The woman looked sad, but managed a little smile when she saw me looking at her. Many times I had seen a woman that I wanted to speak with and I always shied away. Nervously, I said hello. She said hi and told me that the food artists could make the display food looks so real. I agreed.

For the first and only time in my life a woman said to me, "Want to buy me a drink?" I was shocked to say the least, but managed an okay. Why would round-eye even talk to me - an E-4?

She was an older woman. I had just turned 20 and I was thinking she was about 35 or so. She was a faded blonde which led me to believe that maybe the cuffs did not match the collar. She was thin but not skinny. Not big on top, just enough to let everyone know she was a woman. She was also one of the most beautiful women I had ever seen. I could not have imagined when the day began that I would be sitting at a table in a restaurant with an American woman. Especially a woman who was so beautiful. She was wearing slacks and a safari type jacket over a T-shirt. After she took a drag on her cigarette, she said, "My name is Trisha." I told her mine.

I told her that I was from a small town in Florida named Warrington. It was in West Florida near Pensacola. She had heard of Pensacola.

She told me that it had a Navy Base that trained aviators. When she said aviators instead of pilots, I knew she knew a little about the military. Trisha told me that she was from Iowa. I told her that Wyatt Earp was from Pella, Iowa. Trisha asked me how I knew this. I told her, I knew much about nothing and nothing about anything. Anyone who knew me could tell her that. I also told her that I knew John Wayne was from Winterset, Iowa.

She told me that she was a photographer and a freelance writer. A Stringer for some rags in the States. She did not say which ones and I did not ask. I had recently purchased a new Minolta Hi-Matic camera and I was interested in both photography and writing. She saw my MACV patch and asked me what post I was on. I said Tan Son Nhut being careful not to mention Davis Station.

She asked what I did. I almost blurted out that I was in the ASA, but remembered my instructions that one did not tell of ASA or the mission. I told her I was a teletype operator for Signal Corps. She asked no more questions about this. Apparently she was well-versed in all military matters.

We talked about little things until our rice came and then she ate in silence. Afterwards, she lit up another cigarette. I didn't smoke and it never bothered me if anyone else did. It was a common practice for almost every male I knew. I was thinking of what I should say now that the meal was completed. This was a new experience for me and she knew it too. She broke an awkward silence and asked me if I would like to walk around the town with her for a spell. We walked, looked at people on the streets and talked about many different things.

It was getting late and she asked me, "Don't you have to go back to the base?"

I could not go back and I floundered for an answer. I knew that some people lie when the truth would do one better, so I told her why I was there and that I had chickened out and was going to find a place to sleep, but I had not found a hotel. I was not familiar with renting rooms in hotels.

She said, "Why don't you just come to my place? You can sleep on the couch. I will wake you early and you can get back and no one will be the wiser."

"You don't really know me," I replied. She said that she was a good judge of men and that I was not the type to cause her harm. She got that right. I was spooked enough as it was.

I agreed and we walked some more. I was trying to remember the turns and all, but soon I was lost. I had not ventured too far astray on my few trips to Saigon, fearing ambush. Shortly we came to a hotel. I failed to notice the name. We entered and walked past the desk where a woman was reading a paper. We walked up one flight of stairs and she stopped at a room and unlocked the door. We entered and I was wondering just what I got myself into.

I thought of 'Sands of Iwo Jima' when Sergeant John Stryker took a woman up to her room only to find that she had a baby in the room, but was out of money and needed canned milk for the baby. I did not see a baby and she did not say she had run out of booze, but she did say she had noticed I was a coffee drinker and would I like a cup. I never turn down coffee. Coffee to me is what cigarettes are to others.

The room was small. I saw no bed, only a couch. I was beginning to think that she was no Stringer at all. Always protective of my wallet, I clandestinely brushed my hand along my pocket to see if it was still there. I had to go to the restroom and I saw nothing that look like a door to a bathroom, so I asked her where it was and was told it was down the hall. It was a dingy hole in the floor as I had already found to be customary. Afterward I walked back to her room. She had left the door cracked open. If she had not done this I was ready to flee to the stairs and bolt out into the night. Instead I stepped back into her little one room apartment.

The coffee was instant coffee. It had a strange taste and I was thinking she slipped in a Mickey Finn. She noticed my look and laughed telling me that she had sweetened it, holding up a bit a pint of Early Times™. I thought of Charles Bronson doing the same for Henry Fonda in 'Battle of the Bulge'. It was good and I have done this since on occasion.

We sat at the little table and talked for hours. I was drinking joe and she was sipping whiskey. She asked me if I had a girl waiting back in the world. I told her no, that I never really had a 'for real' girlfriend. I had dated, but never the same girl more than a few times. Feeling melancholy, I told her of one girl that had stolen my heart, but she never knew it. We had dated and I was such a fool and she soon fled and would not have anything to do with me. I had heard she moved to California and married a Marine.

But the drink was taken its toll on her and she started to talk of herself. Yes, she said she did have a camera; she did write but had not been very successful as of late. That she'd been married to an Army Captain. He was in ROTC at college. She was a student there but did not graduate. Instead she and her beau married on his graduation, but knowing that he was going into active service. At first they were at Fort Benning in Columbus, Georgia, but then he was sent to Vietnam. I noticed that she was tearing up. I told her I was born in Columbus and had family there.

She continued her story: While he was gone, I was kind of loose. I was bored and lonely. I was a looker and men noticed. They did not care if I was married or not. All they wanted was what all men want. What do you want? Pussy. It's all that men ever want. To a man it is what makes the world go around. For some women too, I guess.

I was at the commissary and kept running into one officer, a Major. He was married too, but it didn't seem to stop him from striking up a conversation with me and asking me out. I relented and we met for drinks, then we had an affair. The Major was shipped out and by then I was his whore. I took another lover, another officer and then I started seeing enlisted men. Young men like you. I was just so lonely and I missed my man. Trisha looked at me with the saddest of faces. I looked at her intently. She was beautiful, but looked like she'd been rode hard and put away wet, as the saying goes.

Trisha went on with her tale: One day, I wrote a letter to my husband. I wanted to clear my conscience. I told him that I had been unfaithful and I was through with that now. I wrote him that I loved him and this would never happen again. I posted the letter. He never got the letter. It was among his things that the Army sent home to me. It was unopened.

I heard a car out front. I looked and saw two officers coming up the walk. As everyone knows, when the soldiers come to the door and do not send a telegram, they carry the worst of all news. The two Captains did not tell me that my husband was dead, just missing. How could a modern army lose a man? They stayed with me for several hours. One of the Captains gave me a number and said to call if I needed anything. I asked if he would come. He said, "Someone will come."

I was looking at her in a different light now. Goodness, she was beautiful. She was a woman men dream to take to bed. Yet I had talked with her for hours and not so much as touched her hand. I'm alone in a room with a beautiful woman who I know has just been wedded and bedded and has been drilled more than a Texas oilfield. I just sat there and listened to her ramblings as I had done with my father when he was drinking.

Her cover was the writing and the photography. At first she was somewhat successful, getting some stories through and some photos.

The money was not good and certainly not enough to keep one afloat in Saigon for long.

I learned that after her husband was reported missing, she left North Carolina and made her way to California. She wound up in Tustin where she was plying bars, finding men that would buy her drinks, meals and keep her company long into the night. Much like I was doing now, I was thinking. She took off for Hawaii as it was a stopping off point for so many GIs.

She said one day she found herself in Saigon. Short on money, she started working the clubs. White women were a rare thing to find in Saigon bars that were not part of the hotel and military clubs. Often she found herself in those places where she met the high and the powerful. She was not short on the attention of these men. They vied for her and some fought for her attention.

Somewhere her game started to come apart on her. Was it the drinking, and the lying, or just being tired of playing a fool's game? As the night wore on, she tired and I was wired. I was a night person, one who thrived in the dark. Eventually she headed for the john down the hall and I wondered what it is that I should do. Make a move? I don't know how to make a move on a woman 15 years my elder. A woman who would know I was a novice and all the matters related to sex and love. The mechanics I knew well. The techniques not so well. A clumsy lover, I would not want to be and I didn't think that anything I did would compare to those who had conquered her in the past. My experience had been dating high school girls. None of which were eager to share the treasures below their waist. I was with a grown woman. Trisha was a real woman, a woman who had been around the block and more than once at that.

I drank my joe. She returned, poured me another cup and added to her drink. As she sipped it, I pondered my move. She stood up and motioned me to do the same. I did. She came closer and put her arm around and pulled me into her body. I held her tight, but nowhere near as tight as she was holding me. I kissed her. She accepted and kissed me back. I'd kissed girls. This was the first time I'd ever kissed a woman with passion. A grown up woman was kissing me. The woman who knew men, real men, not some boy barely 20. It was unlike any kiss I had ever experienced. I held her and kissed her. She held and kissed me back. I placed my hand on her breasts. Unlike the girls I had dated, there was no slick hand move on her part to slide it around her back. She left it there and gently I squeezed. I lost track of the minutes, but this embrace ended all too soon. She'd spoke in a soft voice, saying she needed to lie down for a minute.

Trisha sat on her well-worn couch and looked up at me with those sad eyes of hers. I sat down beside her, eager to renew my assault on her virtue. She laid her head down on the arm of the couch and closed her eyes. I touched her arm. She did not notice and she snuggled her face into the arm of the couch. I sat there and watched her for a while. I did not know if she was asleep from exhaustion from a long tiresome day or too much whiskey. I moved back to her table and sat, drinking my coffee and continuing to look at her. A more beautiful woman I had never seen.

I thought about stripping her and taking her. I thought about stripping her and not taking her. I thought of stripping her and taking pictures of her nakedness. I did none of these things. I wanted to know what it would be like to make love to such a beautiful woman. I drank the last of my coffee and stood up.

I am a frugal and thrifty man. The people who know me would call me tight or stingy. I took out my wallet and looked at it. It was fairly new, made of elephant hide. I had purchased it soon after my arrival in Vietnam. I took out $60; it was all I carried. Having US $60 was a violation to a soldier who was ordered to make do with script or local currency. I took out my piastres too. I had $30 worth. I took the money and laid it on her table, taking her ashtray and anchoring its corners so that she would spot it when she awoke. This is all the money I had. A Specialist Four in 1969 did not make much money. I looked at the money on the table and thought of picking it up and keeping it. I left the money on the table.

I stepped outside into the hall; I made sure that the door would lock behind me. I glanced back at Trisha. I could go AWOL. I could stay with Trisha, I could become her lover. I would love her so that she would forget her troubles. Then mine would just begin. I walked back into the room, kissed her on the forehead and retreated back to the hall, securing the door behind me.

 It was early, but I had daylight as I came out into the street with no money. With no money, it would be a long walk to Tan Son Nhut and Davis Station. I had not walked far, when I heard someone call out, 'Willard.' I looked and saw another 72B20, and a buck Sergeant. He asked if I was headed back to base and would I split cyclo fare with him. I told him I had spent all of my money and had none to offer. The Sergeant said this was okay and I could owe him or return the favor.

The Sergeant had also spent the night in a hotel. He said he had a regular girl, a French-Vietnamese. He asked how I'd made out. I told him I did all right.

I was never called cherry boy again. The Sergeant had the word out that I had scored in Saigon and those who rag on others moved on to fresh fish.

I finished my tour in Vietnam with orders to Bad Abbling Field Station in West Germany. I never saw Trisha again. Forty two years have passed since that night in Saigon. Often at night when others are asleep, I would lie in bed or sit in my chair, a book in hand, but not reading. I think back and remember Trisha. She was so beautiful and I loved her so much. I like to think she had a happy life and found someone new to love and treasure.

If not for Trisha, I never would have known that it is not how tall a person is that matters, but how tall a person stands.

Chapter 6
The 1970's

In 1971, ASA experienced the highest number of deaths of any year of the war. All of these were from our aviation units. The last two deaths of ASA soldiers occurred on March 30, 1972, on FSB Sarge during the North Vietnamese Army's Spring Offensive. It was a chaotic time in northern South Vietnam. By early 1973, ASA involvement in Vietnam ended. In the preceding years units had been withdrawn and missions had been consolidated. The Paris Peace Treaty officially ended the US combat role in Vietnam.

While the war was ending in Vietnam, ASA still had a worldwide mission to fulfill. The stories in this chapter also reflect the transition of Vietnam Veterans as they moved onto other duty stations around the world.

Getting to Ethiopia
By Randy Risener

To my mind one of the more endearing qualities of ASA was that it was not the regular Army. No doubt part of my feelings had to do with the realization that the latter would probably have had me court-martialed for one thing or another in pretty short order.

It was in the summer of 1971, that ASA managed to lose me, lock, stock, and barrel, and I was forced to make the supreme effort to hunt them down just so that I could follow orders and report in.

The story began back in Vietnam when I filled out my Dream Sheet, the form where one put in their request for the next assignment. We had been told that one of our first three choices would be honored since we were coming out of a combat zone.

Given my general attitude towards Army rules and regulations, I figured that my self-interest would be better served by staying as far away from those regulations as possible and in my mind that meant volunteering for the world's shit holes.

When my orders came down they were for Asmara, Ethiopia, a part of the world I later came to love and hated to leave, but at the time I knew nothing about the place and had assumed it would be some god-forsaken corner of the world and as such, would probably be relatively devoid of military brass, rules and formalities.

Fortunately, the last part turned out to be a correct assumption. Basically, the orders just said to be there by such and such a date and that while on leave I would be contacted with the particulars regarding itinerary and plane fare. The only thing I had to do was obtain a civilian passport.

It was only a few days after coming home that I was ready to leave again. My sweetheart and wife to be ended our relationship. She no longer knew me; I could not relate to her and to others I had known much of my life; the girl and I seemed somewhat like strangers. The war had changed me. Roaming around East Africa seemed a good way to bury my memories of her and I couldn't get there fast enough.

Unfortunately, ASA was not in such a hurry and was not to be heard from even though I had done my job and obtained a passport. There I was all dressed up with somewhere to go but no way to get there. As the days dragged on with still no word from the Agency, my anxiety levels kept going higher until I finally decided to put in an appearance at the ASA Field Representative's office in St. Louis.

When I walked into the place there were potential recruits sitting in chairs to the left and a Lieutenant behind a counter to the front. I walked up to the Lieutenant and proceeded to tell him my sad story. He didn't let me finish. I was hustled immediately to a Sergeant in a back office. I wasn't sure if the haste was due to the Lieutenant's efficiency and dedication to duty or whether he was scared to death that I might say something unkind about the Agency in front of the potential recruits.

The Sergeant and I recognized each another - he had been at Nha Trang for a while. After I filled him in on my situation he spent several minutes on the phone with Arlington Hall, our administrative headquarters in Virginia. With a satisfied look on his face, he hung up and announced that everything was taken care of. All I had to do was just show up at JFK international and go to the military liaison officer who would have tickets and supplementary instructions.

At JFK the military liaison was a nice enough fellow, but, unfortunately, he knew nothing about me and had never heard of ASA. He called information; he looked through both of his public military directories. No ASA was to be found.

Further complicating matters was that our orders said nothing about ASA using, instead, the cover name Radio Research. He wanted to call regular MI and was further confused by my explaining that while we were 'military intelligence' we were not part of the regular Military Intelligence Corps.

The situation was deteriorating to the point that he was becoming a little suspicious of me. There I was in dress greens with MI insignia but saying that we were not with regular MI and claiming to be with an organization he had never heard of and carrying orders under yet still another organization, one he had never heard of. I was half expecting him to call the MPs and have me carted off.

It was always said that ASA comprised the top ten percent of the Army, intellectually speaking. At that point I decided it was time to put my ten percent brain to work. There were ASA Field Reps in New York I was sure, but I assume that even if I could find them they would probably just call Arlington Hall. It then occurred to me that there was an ASA processing detachment on most Basic Training bases so I asked the officer where the nearest base was. Fort Dix, he informed me.

There was a small reception station at Ft. Dix where the limo dumped us. I walked up to the MP at the reception desk and asked him if he could call the ASA detachment for me. As a frown came over his face while pawing through his directories I realized that I was, once again, in trouble.

Again I was forced to go through the dreary rigmarole of explaining that we were intelligence but not part of regular MI. He wanted to know if maybe I was with CID (Criminal Investigation Division). I assured him that I was fully cognizant of who I was with. That my orders read 'Radio Research' instead of who I said I was with was not improving the situation either.

I decided that before he arrested me I probably should have do something and thought to myself, who on an army post knows where everything in every unit is? With that, I thanked the MP, picked up my bags, went outside and asked the first cab driver I saw if he knew where the ASA Detachment was.

"Oh, sure, Hop in", he replied.

At first I did not believe the cabbie when he announced "here we are." The building was what appeared to be an old World War II barracks in the field. There were no signs, just an unpainted building with weeds growing up around it.

I went to the door and it was locked. After banging on it a few times, someone finally opened it and I asked if this was the ASA Det. There was a slight hesitation so I thought it advisable to state briefly who I was and why I was there.

They all were in civilian clothes and everybody including the Captain who was in charge of the unit practically laid out the red carpet for me during the four or five days it took for them to get things straightened out with Arlington Hall.

Once again I was back at JFK.

At this point in the narrative it should be noted that tensions in the Middle East were running pretty high. Airplane hijackings and other terrorist activities were on the rise and diplomatic relations with Egypt had been severed.

The standard procedure and orders for ASAers traversing those parts was civilian clothes, civilian passport and if one was carrying dress greens they were to be turned inside out in the suitcase so that to an onlooker hanging around customs it would not be readily apparent that it was a uniform.

The final instruction was that if the airplane developed trouble and had to land in Cairo for repairs or were moving passengers to another plane, we were not to leave the plane without escort by Swiss Embassy Diplomats.

The trip from New York to Asmara entailed a layover in Athens. ASA was very generous in not counting extended layovers against leave time and any legitimate expenses incurred would be reimbursed.

Sitting in the lounge waiting to board the plane, there was nothing to do but look at the other passengers who were also looking at the other passengers. One of those passengers was a fellow about my age who appeared to have Arabic features. There probably were others of similar appearances among the passengers but I noticed him mainly because we were seated facing each other.

Upon arriving in Athens and after making it through customs and exchanging some money, I realized that I had another problem. There was a hotel in Athens that our government had an arrangement with whereby military personnel did not have to pay anything - just show up and present one's orders and that was it. It wasn't obligatory to use it but it was certainly the least complicated way to go.

However, in keeping with the pattern, I was by that time establishing a wallowing of complications. I had somehow gotten out of Fort Dix without any contact information. It is possible they had given it to me, but if so, I had lost it.

At an information desk I was steered to one of the public telephones where they had English language directories. Given that I would be reimbursed for any expenses, I saw no reason why I should not stay at the Hilton.

Calling the Hilton, though, turned out to be a bit more complicated than I anticipated. While I had no trouble locating the listing in the directory, I couldn't find any coins that easily fit into the slots. So it was that I was trying unsuccessfully to force a coin into the slot when there appeared on either side of me two Athens police officers.

Damn, I'm going to get thrown into some foreign jail for breaking into a pay phone, I thought. Once the officers realized that I was simply ignorant of the fact that these phones required special slugs instead of coins of the realm, they graciously escorted me to the counter to purchase them.

Finally I was at the Hilton's check-in desk. They wanted me to turn over my passport. Whoa, Nelly, I thought. What's this about giving up my passport? Fervently I glanced around and noticed that others were turning theirs over. Nobody had told me anything about passport control.

By late day I was comfortably installed in the cheapest room - I was always cognizant of the need to save taxpayer money, especially when I didn't have an abundance of cash to spend in the first place.

The next day I set out to explore Athens. Being young and adventuresome, my style of tourism was to roam about unshackled by guidance. And so it was, that in less than an hour, I was hopelessly lost.

I hailed a cab to get me back to the Hilton and was extremely grateful to the driver for not swindling a hefty fare out of me by driving all over the city and I gave him a nice tip being that the actual fare was very paltry since I had been lost only a block and a half from the hotel.

The following day I decided to try an organized tour and while meandering about the ruins of the Acropolis, I noticed that Arabic looking fellow from the New York to Athens flight was also roaming around. In fact, throughout the day he seemed to be popping up.

The following evening, my exploratory confidence restored by a street map specifically produced for people like me who had no idea what they were doing, I set out once again on my own. As I was sitting in a nice sidewalk bar I happened to notice this Arabic looking fellow sitting two or three tables away from me.

Mild concern was starting to develop about this guy as he was constantly popping up but there were more important things at the moment. My funds are getting low so I thought it time to go ahead and follow orders and report to Asmara. As I was standing on the tarmac at Athens International waiting in line to board the Ethiopian Air Lines flight to Asmara, who should join the line but this Arabic looking fellow. Now, what had been a mild concern was starting to turn into something much more serious - that coincidences of him showing up became a little too much - especially for the tenor of those times and in that part of the world.

I told one of the attendants who was standing nearby that I've forgotten something in the lounge and would be right back. I walked back, then turned around and rejoined the line at the end. I didn't know who this guy was or what if anything was on his mind but thought it best that from then on that he be in front of me.

The flight was uneventful until the pilot came on the intercom and announced that down below on the right, under the clouds, was the City of Asmara and that we would be landing in Addis Ababa at such and such a time.

It took a moment for the full impact of his words to sink in. Damn, I thought. If this trip hasn't been screwed up enough already, now I've gotten on the wrong airplane.

Hailing the first flight attendant who passed me, I somewhat sheepishly explained that there might be a slight problem; namely that I was supposed to be going to the city we were passing over and was unsure as to how I might have boarded the wrong plane. She assured me that all was well; that this was an Addis Ababa flight that normally stopped in Asmara but couldn't do so because of the cloud cover and that anyone who was ticketed to Asmara would be flown back up at no extra charge.

There was some time to kill in the Addis Ababa airport and I happily noticed that my Arabic looking traveling companion was nowhere to be seen. I dug out a two or three week old *Time Magazine* I had been carrying around and was sitting in a waiting area reading it when the movement of a passerby caught my attention.

I looked up and my old traveling companion was seated directly across from me. Every muscle and nerve in my body was spring taunt.

Finally, in what I hoped was an even voice I said, "Excuse me. I don't wish to be rude but you seem to be showing up every time I turn around. May I ask who you are?"

"Well," he replied in a Texas drawl, "I'm in the Navy and trying to get to Asmara."

I was practically rolling on the floor in laughter and relief.

After arrival in Asmara we parted ways and I never saw him again. I suspected he might be in the Naval Security Group. If that was so, he might have suspected I was ASA. And if that was the case it would account for why neither of us ever inquired as to what the other was doing there.

The following day after a refreshing night's sleep I met with the First Sergeant of Company A. After initial pleasantries, he informed me that they had no word or notice that I was coming.

Secret Agent Man
By Randy Risener

I don't drink much anymore, but back then, to commemorate my first and only Christmas in Vietnam, I decided to forgo the punch bowl and go for the real stuff - Bourbon. Now, Bourbon was the only way to honor that Christmas in Vietnam. Some of us Hawgs had decided that it would be almost a form of blasphemy to celebrate with just the run-of-the-mill beer, especially considering that we still had to work the mission.

Some of the details are kind of hazy but I remember we got some of the whiskey on the black market in Nha Trang and some of it on the air base.

I had been a rock n' roll and blues guitar picker before going into the service, playing with amateur bands in the St. Louis, Missouri area. So I provided the music. All I had was an acoustic guitar but that was just fine.

We actually did begin to do some Christmas music but none of us could remember all the words, so wasn't long before I was doing the stuff I had been used to.

Musically, I had grown up in the Chuck Berry rock-blues type of environment. Berry was a fixture in St. Louis in those days and today he lives quietly on his farm in Wentzville, Missouri, which is about 40 miles or so west of St. Louis.

I'd even played back up behind him once. It was sort of an accidental thing. He had a habit of showing up where amateur bands were playing and doing a few numbers with them. And so it was that one night I was with a group doing a gig on the south side of St. Louis when Chuck comes up and says "Can I jam with you?"

I know that he had some human imperfections but he was a hell of a musician and a fun person to be around.

So, that night in Vietnam in preparation for going on mission, and no, we did not get the holiday off, I played a lot of Berry stuff.

But one number we did several times was not a Chuck Berry song-it was Johnny Rivers' 'Secret Agent Man.' I still like that song.

So, with 'Secret Agent Man' ringing in our ears and flasks of whiskey stuffed into our fatigues, we went roaring into Ops when the appointed time came, ready for any shenanigans the enemy might toss at us. The night went well, as you can imagine.

The Last Seven Days
By G. Duane Whitman

407th Radio Research Detachment

Quang Tri, Republic of Vietnam

What can now be viewed as the beginning of the end of the US involvement in the Vietnam conflict started with the North Vietnamese Army's Spring Offensive of 1972. The territory north of Hue, South Vietnam, which was lost during this massive push southward, encompassed all of Quang Tri Province, the northernmost province of South Vietnam, and the majority of Thua Thien Province on the southern border of Quang Tri Province.

Our unit, the 407th Radio Research Detachment, which provided intelligence support to the remnants of the 1st Brigade, 5th Mechanized Infantry Division, was headquartered just north of Quang Tri City on the Military Advisory Command, Vietnam Three Star Compound, and was deactivated following the evacuation caused by the invading North Vietnamese forces. In addition to our Headquarters element at Quang Tri, we had elements located on two fire support bases: SFB Sarge, overlooking the Khe Sanh Valley from a mountaintop west of Quang Tri, and FSB Con Thien (The Hill), also known as 'Alpha Four', which was located on the eastern edge of the demilitarized zone.

Everything seemed pretty calm during the third week of March, 1972, almost too calm. Most of us in the 407th, including the guys at both fire bases, were short-timers, with less than two months remaining on our tours in Vietnam. Johnny, one of our personnel at FSB Con Thien, had recently returned to the Hill after a few days of relaxation with us at the Detachment. All was running smoothly in the 407th Radio Research Detachment, Quang Tri, Vietnam.

We had taken sporadic incoming rockets in the preceding few days, but none that caused any concern, or any change in our normal routine. One of the attacks however, that has always stuck in my mind occurred one evening while Johnny was at the detachment with us. Johnny was playing cards with a few of us in the hooch and had just gone out to our 'two-holer', when two or three rockets hit about 300 m to the northwest of the compound. We all just sat there for a second looking at each other, waiting for the attack siren to blow, when into the hooch hopped Johnny, dragging up his drawers! It obviously wasn't very funny to him at the moment, but his retelling of the incident later always drew a good laugh.

Our first tangible indication of an impending attack had come a few days prior to the initial attack on the fire bases, when the refugees began their frightful retreat to the tenuous safety of the Imperial Capital of Hue. The sad and weary faces of every member of the seemingly endless parade were a picture I've never forgotten. Men, women and children alike wore the masks of fatigue in battle, burned onto them by decades of war. This trek to the South was not new to them, nor would it be their last. Too poor to afford the luxury of motor driven vehicles, each packed what they could carry, some even pulling two wheeled carts filled with what they deemed their most important possessions, quite possibly their entire existence. A few, the more affluent ones, had water buffaloes to pull their carts stacked high with the goods, and the backs of the buffaloes also provided a place for their children and elderly relatives to ride. This surging flow of displaced humanity continued unabated throughout the NVA offensive, despite the indiscriminate artillery and rocket attacks that severely decimated their ranks. Around the 27th or 28th the rocket attacks seemed to be a bit more regular, but still it was nothing to really get uptight about. It was probably the 29th when everyone got hit really hard for the first time.

It appeared that frequent attacks were here to stay, at least for a while. I found out firsthand on the morning of the 30th, after about 25 or 30 hours without sleep, exactly how Johnny had felt a few days before, but it didn't seem so funny now. Since the afternoon of the 29th, the fire bases were getting hit at least on the top of each hour. Chief Warrant II Wilson, our Detachment Commander whom we referred to as Willy, along with our upper echelon Chain of Command, who were fortuitously at the detachment on a routine visit, began to seriously consider an evacuation of at least the two fire bases. Throughout the morning, while our superiors discussed their evacuation decision, we continued to communicate with FSB Sarge and Con Thien, relaying any new information. More and more sightings of NVA and VC were coming in over the radio, and sometime between 3:00 and 3:15 PM, I held our last contact with two people on Sarge. We were to find out later that a 122 mm rocket with a delayed fuse had penetrated their reinforced bunker before exploding, setting off the built-in destruction devices of their classified equipment. They never knew what hit them.

Our efforts now focused on keeping in touch with Con Thien. I knew that we would never have contact with Sarge again, but had to evade the constant queries from Con Thien on that subject. We were extremely anxious to get the guys off Con Thien by nightfall - we didn't want to lose them too. It was extremely frustrating for us trying to understand what was taking them so long to decide to extract our people from Con Thien. There was no apparent reason for delay. Were there no evacuation choppers available? What was taking them so long? What was I supposed to tell Con Thien when they asked me where was this chopper?

Night fell, and we doubled our vigil at the radio. Fifteen minutes between contacts was as long as I would permit. By this time, they had had in excess of 200 rounds of assorted ammunition thrown at them, including 122 mm rockets, 81 mm mortars, 240 mm rockets, and 130 mm artillery shells. The fire base had approximately 300 more rounds to absorb before we had them evacuated to Quang Tri Combat Base, home of the Army of the Republic of Vietnam's Third Division.

The frequency of the attacks decreased, but never stopped throughout the night. The rounds hitting us, now included artillery shells, came sporadically, making it impossible to catch even a few minutes of sleep. The morning of the 31st brought only what turned into a routine: cloudy skies, and continued attacks on Quang Tri and Con Thien. "What was taking so long getting us evacuated? Any word from Golf Whiskey, phonetic initials we used over air to identify each other, and Charlie on Sarge?"

These two questions were constantly asked by the guys on Con Thien, when passing the continuous updates on their status. I wasn't permitted to tell them we already knew that we would not have contact with Sarge again, and it seemed we would never get the go-ahead to evacuate. We were really getting tense over the evacuation decision. Con Thien had reported that morning that they were the only ones still on the hill - the ARVN Infantry Company charged with their security, had pulled out during the night! Finally, around noon we received word that the decision had been made, and that a UH-1 Huey had been laid on, along with an escort of two Cobra Assault Helicopters for the evacuation of Con Thien. The long excruciating minutes were just beginning.

Call words for the choppers and last-minute instructions to destroy everything except their portable PRC-25 radio were passed to Con Thien. The birds were in route, now all we could do at the detachment was sit and listen. The last words we heard from Con Thien before they destroyed their main communications equipment was an urgent call to the choppers to hurry - NVA troops were at the perimeter!

We were all clustered around the radio, listening intently to the one-sided conversation of the helicopter pilot. Our ears were fine-tuned to the radio, all heads bowed as one in an anxious prayer for our guys on the hill and the chopper crews.

We knew what the procedure would be: the Cobras would go in first and 'dust off' the perimeter, and then the Slick would move in and touch down only long enough for the guys to jump aboard. Timing had to be near perfect - errors could result in the deaths of the chopper crews and our men. When given the word by the pilot of the Slick, the guys would have to sprint approximately 100-150 m down a rain rutted road to the pad, all the while both the landing chopper and them would be fully exposed to enemy fire.

The seconds seemed like hours while we waited for some word from the chopper pilot. Weeks seemed to pass in my mind when finally we heard from the radio: "Grab your radio and run!"

Time stood still as we waited for the guys to reach the helipad. One-by-one the pilot of the Slick counted as they scrambled aboard his ship, finally announcing, "Got eight aboard and am coming home."

Relief overwhelmed us. No one moved for what seemed like an eternity. Then, as if on command, we all started shouting and carrying on as though our favorite team had just won the Super Bowl, and rushed out of our operations building to meet them at the helipad.

After the arrival and subsequent departure for food by the guys from Con Thien, the die was apparently cast by the NVA for the conquest of Quang Tri Combat Base. The largest attack on us so far hit shortly thereafter, and we began preparing for what now seemed inevitable: our own evacuation. We destroyed everything except those materials needed for a day-to-day existence, and tried to settle down for a few restless hours of sleep, only to be awakened every hour-on-the-hour by a rude barrage of eight-to-ten 130 mm artillery rounds.

The early morning hours of April Fools' Day brought little relief from the nightmares of the preceding week, but by daybreak, there appeared to be a lull in the enemy's efforts. Incoming artillery and rocket attacks were fewer and farther in between, but all volleys seemed to be hitting our small Three-Star Compound. Mid-morning brought us no relief from the bad weather, meaning once again, little or no Tactical Air Support. The attacks became more intense. We began to measure our time as the span between each attack, with some moments longer than others.

Chief Warrant II Larry Wilson, our Commander, was not one of whom, on first impression, we would have chosen to lead us under fire. He had appeared to us as a technically qualified and competent officer, but lacking that charismatic combat leader image that we young troops thought was important. We weren't far into our crisis before we began to see his leadership abilities emerging. His recently acquired trademark, an unlit, eight inch stogie, reflected to me the metamorphosis that had occurred between the man-in-charge in peace, and that leader under fire. We were seeing a new side of Willie: a little fatherly instinct, calm decisive leadership, and a morale lifting sense of humor. His cold, wry humor, which we hadn't seen before, often put us at ease during this time of extreme stress. By the time Easter Sunday was over, we would all hold a deep respect for him.

Around noon, another lull set in, with only 20 to 30 rounds hitting from then until 5 PM. Jovial plans for our evacuation were passed around, trying to convince each other that it would never actually come to that. At the stroke of 5 PM, the sky caved in. In the next 30 minutes, more than 500 shells of assorted sizes impacted and detonated setting off numerous secondary explosions of ARVN munitions.

Time froze once again, that half hour lasting an eternity, with the barrage ceasing as abruptly as it started. It was probably the first shell of this attack that hit the compound's generators, knocking out our electrical power, forcing us to crank up our 'rat van', a non-armored radio/teletype communications van, and put our communicator in it to keep in touch with our parent unit at Phu Bai. Throughout the night of the first and until noon of the second, Bill remained inside this tiny cubicle, maintaining contact and passing periodic updates to the command from there. It was a miracle, and an incident of unsung heroism on his part, that he maintained his vigil and emerged from it in spite of the numerous shrapnel holes through the van when we left it.

At 5:30 PM, when the heavy barrage was lifted, we resumed destroying all that was not an absolute necessity. Concentrating on this destruction made the night seem to roll on faster. Simple acts like putting documents into our destruction barrel took on the studied movements of a drill team. All that could be destroyed prior to our action evacuation had been completed and wiped out by 10 PM, And Willie told us to sack out on the floor, something that by now was not unusual. How long had it been since we had slept in our bunks in the hooch? The incoming rounds continued, not really fast or heavy, but steady. The cold concrete vibrating beneath me from the concussion of each exploding shell caused another night of fitful sleep filled with nightmares of what could happen.

The night dragged on. Flashes of life back home, my family, friends, and images of school days were intermingled with the dream interrupting eruptions of incoming artillery. Drifting in and out of fitful sleep, realistic scenes flashed through my mind of a telegram at my home, a funeral, muted family and friends. Would this night ever end? Oh, for a couple of hours of uninterrupted sleep! Loneliness and fear began to creep over us as the noose tightened around Quang Tri.

The realization was sinking in that two of my friends, one of whom had flown to Vietnam with me, would not fly home with me. How much longer did I have? Hour after endless hour of lying face down

225

on the concrete floor, wincing at every whistle and each thump of incoming artillery, hearing the stones and the sand rattling off our thin tin roof reminded me of how very near I really was to joining Chuck and Gary. During those last few hours, I was oblivious to the others for moments at a time, concentrating on people and places back in 'the world.' What kind of news was reaching into that faraway place? The expressions borne by the others told me that I was not alone in my thoughts.

This would be an Easter not soon forgotten. With the rising of the sun, the nightmares of the previous night were temporarily forgotten; we tried to keep busy until the time came for us to leave. The shells came quite a bit more regularly, but now there was more than just 130 mm artillery and rockets. The morning had brought with it mortars and 90 mm recoilless rifle fire, meaning only one thing: the NVA were getting closer and closer. Close enough now to use the 90 mm direct fire weapon and begin accurately targeting their short range mortars at anything that moved within the compound. At the Quang Tri Detachment, the only casualty occurred during this period of time, when one of our Military Policemen was superficially wounded by shrapnel from a 90 mm round while on an excursion outside of our operations building to survey damage. Every round seemed to get nearer and nearer to our little 15' x 30' building. The only thought now crowding our minds was, 'why aren't we gone yet?'

By noon, we all had our most prized possessions crammed into our duffel bags, which we had to leave behind anyway, and we were ready to pull out at a moment's notice. Actually, we had been ready for a long time, but now it was just a matter of getting the order to hit the helipad. The second day was by far the worst day for us. There was apparently no end of the NVA munitions. Over the preceding week, there had been in excess of 2000 rounds of assorted ammunition dumped on us alone.

Around 2 PM, Willie told us to set up for final destruction, get out of the building and head for the perimeter. We set trios of thermite grenades on each piece of equipment, and dumped diesel fuel inside the building. When I thought that everyone was out of the structure, I yelled inside just to make certain, and not getting an answer I pulled the pin on the last thermite grenade, and tossed it inside. The exploding grenade ignited the fuel and above the roar of the fire, I heard frantic screams for help from inside the building! Bill and Joe were still in one of the back rooms, and hadn't heard my call to them: I had just sealed the only exit!

Our building was surrounded by a ten foot high blast wall with walkways at the front and rear ends of the building. Surrounding the building, about 6 feet from the 4 foot thick wall was a 6 foot high anti-personnel concertina wire fence. The fence had only one opening - the one I had just sealed. Running to the end of our fenced in area, the realization of what I had just done struck me, rendering me helpless as I watched Bill and Joe scramble from the rear of the blazing building, escaping from the fire through the rear opening in the blast wall. Simply climbing over the fence that stood between us would have resulted in multiple lacerations to them from the thousands of tiny razor-like barbs on the fence. Looking behind them, the fence appeared to be the less threatening choice. How they did it, I don't know, but within seconds both of them were up and over the fence, with only injuries being a crotch-to-knee rip in the leg of Bill's pants and a corresponding superficial scratch on his leg. We then headed for the compound's perimeter to await the chopper.

The Three-Star Compound's only helipad had been demolished during one of the attacks, so we would have to catch the chopper outside the perimeter. The short wait was filled with last-minute destruction of anything and everything in sight that the enemy could conceivably re-use against us.

In the distance the characteristic sound of a Chinook helicopter could be heard, and we moved outside the perimeter to meet it. Following the MACV Directive, the Deputy Senior Advisor, MACV Team 155, sent the eight of us RRD members out to meet the helicopter, followed by the MACV Team personnel that would be able to fit into the Chinook. When all available space was filled, the bird lifted off and headed south, to Phu Bai, or so we thought. We had been airborne for only a few minutes, when the chopper landed at a small POL point, and we were told to empty the craft. We assumed that we were at a safe landing zone (LZ), but as we soon found out, we were only a couple miles south of Quang Tri City on Route QL 1, at the small hamlet of the La Vang. Within a matter of seconds after the chopper left us and headed back north, we heard the sound of mortars leaving the tubes, whoosh overhead, and explode just south of our position. This definitely was not a safe LZ.

Willy assumed command of the groups of GIs from Three-Star Compound, which numbered about 35, and moved us out to a row of ARVN bunkers along the south edge of the POL point. Needing no encouragement, we all sprinted for their relative safety. Making sure that everyone was undercover, Mr. Wilson then left to try to contact Phu Bai to check on another chopper to take us further south.

About 20 minutes passed before he returned, going bunker-to-bunker telling us to be prepared to move out to the pad where the chopper had left us. At his order, we broke cover at a run, forming a staggered single file line, trying to ignore the ominous eruption of small arms fire and mortars as we high-tailed it toward the helipad. The Chinook picked up extra passengers from somewhere, not leaving enough room for all of us to fit. The pilot informed Mr. Wilson that five men would have to stay behind and wait for the next helicopter. Pointing to four of us, and indicating that he would be the fifth, Willie advised an Engineer Lieutenant as to where the remaining RRD personnel were going. After conferring with the pilot, he rejoined us in the grass along the east edge of the helipad, and told us to make tracks for the bunkers again while he went to find out about another chopper.

We were barely underway when a firefight broke out, with us caught right in the middle of the helipad! Faster than we thought possible, we hit the grass along the south edge of the pad. A quick inventory told us that we were in bad shape: we had a total of about 80 rounds of assorted .45 caliber and M-16 ammunition among us, and the ARVN bunkers were about 40 m to our rear with a concertina wire fence between us. The firing was left-to-right across the helipad with none coming from behind us. We could see M-16 tracer rounds, and hear the distinct 'pop' of the NVA AK-47 rifles coming on both sides of the pad. Which side was 'ours?'

Realizing that we were not the targets of the firing, we hugged the ground waiting for the crossfire to cease. As soon as there was a perceptible lull in the firing, we made our break for the bunkers to our rear.

It wasn't long before Mr. Wilson located a radio and once again contacted Phu Bai to get us another bird. His return brought some disheartening and frightening news: we may have to remain there in the bunkers overnight. The idea of staying there was not too appealing to any of us, even though we now had more ammunition than before: the ARVN troops that had vacated the bunkers while we were at the helipad had left theirs behind. While explaining the situation to us, Mr. Wilson was interrupted by an ARVN officer who informed him that someone was trying to contact him on their radio. With only about three hours of daylight left, we all had our fingers crossed that we would be leaving the area before darkness fell. No one wanted to spend the night at La Vang, knowing, based on past ARVN performance, that by morning we would be the only ones remaining.

Mr. Wilson had been gone for only a few minutes, but with the mortars and small arms fire continuing, we were all concerned that he wouldn't return, and wondered among ourselves who would assume the responsibility for the others should something happen to our commander. The few minutes that he was gone felt like hours. When he finally returned, we were informed that a chopper would be there in a few minutes to pick us up just behind the bunkers, but due to a lack of room, he would stay there and wait for another one. Once again, we assumed that this ride would terminate at Phu Bai. Within minutes, we could hear the approaching helicopter, and left the cover of the bunkers, moving into the bushes behind them to wait. At the pilot's gesture, one at a time we broke cover and scrambled into the hovering helicopter. Airborne for the second time, we all breathed a sigh of relief, carrying with it a silent prayer for Willy's safety.

Again we were headed south, this time on our own. Flying barely above the ground at more than 100 mph, the chopper suddenly banked sharply to the left, and it appeared that we were headed out to sea. Were we being taken to the US fleet that was off-shore instead of to Phu Bai? But no, stopping as if on a dime, the pilot brought the chopper to a hover over a rice paddy and told us to get out! Get out? Did he really want as out?

Frantic thoughts raced through my mind. This whole day was a bad dream. We were extras in a John Wayne flick doing a combat assault jump into a rice paddy that was probably deeper than I was tall. Any minute now I would wake up in my bunk at Quang Tri, pick up my pencil, and mark off another day in my 'short-timer's calendar.' Snapping out of my daydream, I was the first one to jump out of the hovering Slick to the paddy below, which proved to be only a couple of feet deep, but still leaving only my chest, shoulders and head above the short rice stocks. From our vantage point there in the rice paddy, things were looking rather bleak. None of us knew where we were, where we were supposed to be going. We could see a road from the paddy where we stood, and headed for it.

Upon reaching the road, we noticed a small compound off to our right with a very comforting sign hanging above its entrance: US MILITARY ADVISORY COMMAND, VIETNAM. Inside the compound, we located the Commander and informed him who we were, where we were coming from and where we were supposed to be going. We told him that we were expecting our Warrant Officer to show up soon, and asked him to please check and see if he could find out what happened to him. Promising to check for us, and to try to get us transportation to Phu Bai, he sent us to their mess hall for Easter Dinner. Easter! We had completely forgotten what day it was. While eating our first real meal in several days, we saw familiar faces of personnel from MACV Team 155. Worried about the other members of the 407th RRD, we asked about them, finding out that we and Mr. Wilson were the only ones who hadn't gone directly to Phu Bai from the POL point at La Vang.

After finishing our meal, we headed for the compound's bunker line, resigning ourselves to the likelihood at staying there for the night. We were issued additional ammunition and began cleaning our weapons to occupy our time. We had no sooner gotten our weapons broken down when Willie came jogging from bunker-to-bunker, with the now familiar unlit stogie in his mouth, in search of his displaced troops. He told us to grab our gear and get out to the main gate, unless we wanted to spend the night in the bunkers there. I never before, nor since, reassembled an M-16 as fast as I did then.

En route back to the rice paddy where we were dropped off, Mr. Wilson informed us that another bird would be there shortly to take us further south, and that he would remain there at the MACV Compound until morning and join us at Phu Bai the next day. Back into the rice paddy we sloshed, sure that this time the next ground we touched would be the familiar turf of Tri Bac Station, home of the 8th Radio Research Field Station, Phu Bai.

Once again airborne, and in high spirits, we watched the ground slip swiftly beneath us. Seeing the settled Citadel of Hue, we knew that it would be only minutes before we reached Phu Bai. Our hopes were dashed again - as the pilot reined the chopper in, and landed across the river from the Citadel, informing us that this was where he was told to drop us off and that someone would be along shortly to pick us up. Bewildered, we watched the chopper take off. Standing there in a daze, we didn't have time to speculate as to what we should do next, when a Jeep pulled up and the driver informed us that he'd been sent to pick us up and take us to the MACV Compound there in Hue.

Apparently we weren't expected, or they weren't expecting what they saw. Into the compound we tramped, in clothes that we had been wearing for at least a week, soaking wet, covered with mud, decked out with the gear that we had acquired throughout the day, ammunition threatening to fall out of our crammed full pockets, Bill with his pants torn from the crotch to the knee: and there they were in their freshly starched fatigues, khakis or clean civilian clothes, wide-eyed and mouths gaping! What a sight we must have presented!

Finally, for the first time in a week, we were out of the immediate danger area. The Team Commander ushered us into his office where we could contact Phu Bai to let them know where we were and that we were all safe. He told us to make ourselves right at home, anything we wanted was on the house, and to let him know if there was anything that he could do for us. The others returned to the lounge area with him while I put through the call to our parent unit. It took several minutes of concentrated effort to get through on the antiquated telephone system, but finally I reached the Commander of the 8th RRFS and informed him that the four of us were fine but that we were concerned about Mr. Wilson's whereabouts and safety.

Colonel Powers, the CO, told me that the other members of the 407th, including Mr. Wilson, were safe and sound at Phu Bai and instructed me to insure that we abstain from the luxuries of Hue so that we would be ready at the crack of dawn to meet a helicopter at the helipad by the river. I assured him that we would all be bright-eyed and bushy-tailed in the morning - under no circumstances would we miss the chopper ride!

It was over. It wasn't long before we were all sound asleep and joining the long needed restful slumber. There were no nightmares that night. We were out of the immediate grasp of the crushing NVA offensive. In the morning we would be in Phu Bai, and leaving Vietnam within the month. The long-awaited sight of the 'Freedom Bird' winging her way across the Pacific filled my dreams.

Sp 5 Bruce A. Crosby, Jr. and Sp 5 Larry P. Westcott were killed on FSB Sarge, 30 March, 1972. They were the last ASA soldiers to die in Vietnam.

Lieutenant Bar
By T.H.E. Hill

The summer permanent change of station (PCS) season brought in a shipment of new faces as more slots were filled to cope with the growing tasking requirements. One of these new faces was Lieutenant Butter Bar. He was a man with a mission. Unfortunately, it was not the collection of intelligence. His full nickname was Second Lieutenant Butter Bar, NRI, USAR, OD, green in color, unit of issue 'each,' but everybody called him Lieutenant Bar for short, which he was. Lieutenant Bar didn't drink, didn't smoke, didn't cuss, and didn't go out with fast women. He was sure that all those who drank, smoked, cussed and went out with fast women were going to hell in a hand basket with a ribbon tied to the handle. His mission was to stamp out all these vices among his troops. He had promised his mother that he would.

By some perverse turn of fate, Lieutenant Bar ended up with the ditty-boppers. It might have had something to do with the fact that he knew Morse code because he'd been a ham radio operator before he became a Lieutenant, but that implies a logic that was normally lacking in military decisions. Still it cannot be ruled out that someone somewhere had a flash of lucid insight.

Lieutenant Bar was appalled when he first met his subordinates. He had never seen such a collection of depraved souls before in his life, but that was only because he did not come through the scribe shop on his way to the ditty bay.

"I'm sure that you will enjoy working with the men," said the Major when they reached the door to the bay. "A finer bunch of collectors would be hard to find."

The Major opened the door just as 'Mad Dog' set off the carbon tail that he had put on 'Jimmy the Greek.' There was a brilliant flash. Jimmy jumped up cursing Mad Dog for all he was worth and chased him out the door past the Lieutenant and the Major.

"A lively crew," said the Major, whose mission in life was the collection of intelligence. "You'll have to watch out for carbon tails yourself."

"Carbon tails?" said Lieutenant Bar with his mouth hanging open in disbelief.

"That's right. We work with six ply paper here. There are five sheets of carbon paper in it to make the extra copies. The carbon paper burns so fast it almost seems to explode. It's just hot enough to wake you up, but not cook your goose."

They walked into the bay. Nobody reacted to their presence. The staccato click of typewriters echoed the sound of Lieutenant Bar's highly polished shoes on the floor. About halfway down the row of positions they came to Sergeant Schlaff.

"Best damn Morse Op I ever knew!" screamed the Major. The sound of twenty-six Morse positions with the volume turned up so loud that some of the Ops just had their cans hanging loose around their necks made it impossible to talk in a normal voice. The Major walked on, not wanting to wake up the Sergeant.

Sergeant Schlaff was asleep with his head resting in the key well of his mill. He never kept the cover on because he typed so fast that the keys got stuck all the time and he had to reach in and free them up. That also meant that when he crashed on position, which was every time he sat down practically, his head fell into the key well. The letters from typewriter keys marched across his forehead upside down.

'That's a priority one target in cast-iron," said the Major "I wouldn't want anybody else on it."

"But, he's asleep," said Lieutenant Bar in disbelief.

"I know," said the Major. "It's an exhausting job."

The Major left. Lieutenant Bar was alone. He felt that he was the only sane man in the loony bin.

"Don't let them see that you're afraid," he said to himself. "Demonstrate that you are their superior. Yes, that's what they said at OCS."

He needed a daring plan. He tried to think, but the cacophony of dits and dahs made it hard to concentrate. One by one, all the circuits fell silent. The silence in the bay was deafening. One of the Ops finally restored a sense of normalcy to the bay by tapping out some code absentmindedly with a cigarette lighter against the metal table that held his mill.

Dit-dit-dah-dit, dah, dit-dah, tapped the Op slowly over and over again. The letters 'FTA' wormed their way into Lieutenant Bar's consciousness, and he remembered that he could copy Morse code too. He was very good at copying Morse code. He would show them that he was better than any of them at copying Morse code. He'd show the Major that they don't need that drunken bum Schlaff - he had smelled the scent of liquor as they passed the position.

Lieutenant Bar wondered what FTA meant. Must be a pro-sign that he didn't know. He would have to look it up, but right now he had to be a man of action. He pulled a typewriter table next to Sergeant Schlaff and grabbed a pair of cans and plugged into Sergeant Schlaff's circuit. He needn't have bothered. Sergeant Schlaff had the volume turned up high enough to wake up the dead. Lieutenant Bar could have copied the circuit at the other end of the bay.

The circuit was silent.

Lieutenant Bar looked at his watch. He'd been sitting there for eight minutes and 35 seconds. It was exactly 2 o'clock in the afternoon. "What time is that in military time?" he asked himself.

The Russian Op in Wuensdorf looked at his watch. It was 14:00 local time. It was time to make his schedule with MOD, Moscow. He reached out his hand and leisurely sent his call. Sergeant Schlaff rose up from his mill like a man possessed. He didn't open his eyes. His hands flew over the keyboard:

KNDV KNDV KNDV DE SGGF SGGF SGGF QTC 5 IMI KK

Lieutenant Bar was so surprised by Sergeant Schlaff's sudden metamorphosis that he missed the call up.

The Russian Op in Moscow woke up, looked at his watch and answered.

Sergeant Schlaff's hands flew over the keyboard once again:

SGGF SGGF SGGF DE KNDV KNDV KNDV QTC 3 QRV KK

Lieutenant Bar got that.

Russian Op in Wuensdorf moved the text of his first coded message over next to his speed key and began to send the 365 mixed five number-letter groups in the message, the lazy speed of his call up forgotten. The sooner he got the traffic out, the sooner he could get back to his book. At his normal 45 groups a minute, it would only take him about eight minutes to send this one.

Sergeant Schlaff's hand raised high in the air and smashed down on the keys of his mill like a flailing machine. The springs behind those keys were heavy and you needed to hit them hard. The ten mixed five number-letter groups marched across the page in rows of ten followed by a carriage return that hurled the page all the way back to the right and made the table shake. It was a good thing that the mills are heavy, otherwise it might have flown off the table.

By the thirtieth group, Lieutenant Bar was in trouble. By the fiftieth his fingers hurt. By the ninetieth yes, he had stopped trying to keep up. Sergeant Schlaff, on the other hand, was still blindly smashing the keys of his mill to the beat of the dits and dahs of the Russian Op in Wuensdorf.

Lieutenant Bar sat there staring in disbelief. Watching over Sergeant Schlaff's shoulder, when he could sync up with the Russian Op and his speed key, which was about one group in five, Lieutenant Bar, could see that Sergeant Schlaff wasn't missing a beat.

The sched ended at 14:37 local time. Sergeant Schlaff slumped back down into his mill. Jeff, the duty analyst came over and carefully tore off the copy, so as not to wake Sergeant Schlaff. Lieutenant Bar looked at Jeff in disbelief.

"Does he always do that?"

"Yes, Sir."

"Find out what he drinks. I'll bring in a case for everybody else tomorrow," said Lieutenant Bar, and then left the bay in search of the Major. He turned out to be an OK officer.

See You July 1st
By Harold Castle

It started in 1978, I guess, when someone decided I might be a good candidate for a special collection program. I was permanently stationed at NSA on a four-year assignment that was frozen, meaning the Army couldn't touch me until very late in 1980 or early 1981. I was sent on temporary duty for a quick four-week trip, to Djibouti and The Afar, tucked between Somalia and Ethiopia on the Horn of Africa, and got a good commendation letter from the Chief of Station on my return to Fort Meade.

About two or three weeks later, I was approached and interviewed about my knowledge of worldwide communications, with no emphasis on a particular area, but about both Morse and Non-Morse usage. Since I had been working for more than two years on some of those problems, and had been a search Op for a long time, I passed that part of the process with no problems.

The next thing I was asked was if I would be interested in a six month temporary assignment starting the beginning of July, 1979. As was typical of the times, when everyone had to act like everything needed to be cloaked, compartmentalized, hidden and kept behind 'the Green Door,' I was told by the interviewer that it would be in a location that cannot be revealed until you make a positive commitment.

"I guess there would be some crummy place, wouldn't it?"

"How do you know that, SFC Castle?" he asked.

"We NCO's talk to each other, and three have already been used." I replied. "No shithole tours for the NSA civilians who demand extra pay, so you guys are using cheap labor who can't say no."

"Hmmm, I have to take this up with some other NCO then, since you are such a wise-ass."

"Not being a wise-ass, just truthful. NSA uses the military where the civilians don't like to go, like in Djibouti. We understand that, and don't have a problem with it. NSA is after all paying for us. Because of our experience we are a whole lot better than the GS-9 and 11 folks you have, trained up at 'Friendship Airport Annex."

"That's a given."

"I've talked about the possibility with my wife. I am willing to go wherever needed, for up to six months."

Evidently my answers satisfied him, or at least the shadowy figures I could catch a glimpse of through the not quite perfect one-way mirror behind him. Little did I realize what the future would bring, and didn't think much of it. I just did what I was told for the rest of the clearance, which included a really comprehensive physical, financial background check, evaluation of any strain the TDY might put on our budget. My wife was also a SFC, so that wasn't a problem.

The polygraph test came next.

That wasn't much of a problem, but the dumb engineer, working on a person eager to get it over with, almost made it one. The counterintelligence part went smoothly, and most of the lifestyle part until the examiner got to drinking and sex. My answers were straightforward, but I tended to embellish during that part of the questioning. And like all poly sessions, this one was monitored by another interrogator and another person behind a one-way mirror.

"Do you like to drink, Sergeant Castle?"

Yes, a lot in fact - all Hawgs kind of take to it like fish to water."

"A lot?"

"A lot, no ambiguity there now is there?"

"Can you not drink for a long period of time?"

"Yes, if required to, not a problem."

"Are you sure?"

"Yes, I'm positive. Doesn't the cute twitching little machine confirm what I'm saying?"

"Okay, next I want to ask if you enjoy sex."

"Yes, a lot. No ambiguity there either."

"Do you have sex often?"

"Yes, often."

"Very often."

"Yes. I'm 34 years old, in great shape and have a wife who is five years younger than me, anything else?"

I didn't don't know why, but questions about sex on the personal level have always bothered me, and caused me to walk out of a polygraph exam in 1970 - an exam I needed to pass to qualify for the Fairfax County Virginia Police Department. Maybe it is just a part of my personality that when I give an unequivocal reply to a question, I get really impatient having to answer the same questions over and over again, even if it's couched in slightly different terms when repeated to me.

Can you go six months without having sex with your wife?

"Yes."

"Without having sex with any other woman?"

"Yes."

"Without having sex with a man?"

"Yes, shit-head, I can. I don't do dope and I don't do men. Anything else?"

"Are you sure?"

"Sure of what, punk. I have answered all your questions truthfully and if you don't like it, you can jam this machine and the program where the sun doesn't shine."

"Sergeant Castle, your attitude doesn't look real good at this moment."

"Fine, fuck-head, I'm done whether you are or not. And it is Sergeant First Class Castle to you, civvy!"

I was starting to leave, ripping the leads and contacts off my fingers and arm, when a man in a rumpled suit came into the room. He told the examiner the interview was terminated, and that he didn't need his input to make a decision. He introduced himself as an Agency psychologist, and it was his final recommendation and that would be the go/no-go for the selection to the program.

"So you really want to go in the program, Sergeant First Class Castle, regardless of which shithole it might be?" The second man asked.

"Yes Sir, I do. I like hard work in my field and believe I have a good time doing a tour or two."

"And just how will you deal with the issues of sex while there; the same way you did in Shemya?"

"If you know about Shemya, why did you let that creep keep up his crap so long, and yes the same way."

"We have to screen our examiners while they are screening interviewees, and he is fairly new. He may last, he may not. You however, have passed."

You could have folded me up like a cheap cardboard suitcase at that moment, because I was absolutely sure I had blown the chance, and second chances for that kind of assignment never come around.

In late February, 1979, I had an interview with a US Army Colonel. He knew a lot about me, having talked with some of the senior officers and NCOs at Meade and Arlington Hall, and by looking at my records. He also talked to some of the troops who worked there at NSA HQ. He asked me some very technical questions which were a little surprising. Most colonels wouldn't have known a BFO knob from a knobber at a steam and cream. I answered them fairly easily, though.

"So, can I call you Sergeant Rock; I know a lot of your troops do?"

"Sir, you can call me anything you want. You know why they call me that?"

Because of an incident that occurred in Vietnam, and because you have a reputation of being pretty hard, although fair. I want to give you a job, but can't tell you where it will be. You've got to accept it and me as your boss, before we can talk anymore. The work will be right up your alley, since you like to work hard and can handle different kinds of signals. The hours will be long and there won't be a lot to do when you do get some time off. But we'll have fun, I'll guarantee you."

"I think I'll take the job. I've spent most of my life in the Army working 12 and 12 or worse for weeks at a time, and I'm getting kind of lazy here at B-ROF."

"Great," he said, and then slipped on his greens coat, with ribbons and badges showing a long career. I'm Leland Holland and I'll see you July the first, for a six months tour. The folks here will make all the arrangements; you just have to do a little prep, like study some language tapes."

I had a thousand things going through my mind - how many razor blades will I use in six months; how much underwear to pack; how many hours a week between now and July could I devote to language tapes; not a thousand but a million questions. Then I realized I hadn't asked the key question.

"Where will you see me, July the first, Sir?"

Little did I know that but for the caprice of the Carter Administration's failed foreign-policy regarding Taiwan, and the need for the Army to flex some administrative muscle and show NSA exactly who owned soldiers, I would have been taken along with the 58 folks; being held a captive for 444 days, beaten, tortured, starved and possibly wound up dead. I know myself, too well at times, and would have taken great pleasure in sending as many of the hostage takers to God as possible.

"In Tehran, Iran, at the US Embassy." Colonel Holland said.

Marg Bar Amerika and the Pig's Head Caper

By Harold Castle

In early 1979, Jimmy Carter angered the Taiwanese by canceling official relations with them, and embracing communist China as the sole voice for all of China. The Taiwanese told the US to get all its equipment off the island, including the stuff at Shu Lin Kou Air Station. They were not nice about it, either; the order was to have it done by a certain date, or they would do it for us. The China-Vietnam war of that spring delayed it, but after that was over, the site was shut down, putting a couple hundred folks out of work.

The Army figured that if we didn't have jobs, and there were SIGINT personnel shortages, all bets were off on the locked-in assignments. My wife at the time was not on the locked-in tour, and the Army wanted her with her clearances in Germany. She was to be available to go into the tunnels at Massweiller if war broke out. The Married Army Couples program kicked in and at the end of March, 1979, we were off to Field Station Augsburg; forget the trip to Iran.

April turned into May, May into June and on the first of July I wondered what Colonel Holland and the folks in Iran were up to, but only briefly. I was the NCOIC of the main Manual Morse collection effort and had a lot to keep me busy. We were preparing for a very busy fall, so I didn't dwell on missed opportunities or TDY's to strange places for NSA.

Fall came and disaster struck the US Embassy in Tehran - the Field Station. Augsburg Communications Center was keeping everyone informed of what was happening there and we were watching the Bear to the East to see if there was any reaction. Finally, the Embassy fell, and the news started carrying photos of Iranian 'students' holding up banners that said '*Marg Bar Amerika*' - Death to America - on them, along with pictures of the bound and blindfolded hostages being dragged through the streets, and being beaten and stoned by women in chador's.

It struck me really hard to see those pictures and see the TV footage on the German channels. It reminded me of the stuff the North Koreans used to release of the Pueblo crew, and how I felt being denied the chance to go on that cruise.

I realized that but for the whim of some anonymous clerk at the Army Personnel HQ, I would have been one of those hostages. And I was pretty sure that had I been one I probably would have died trying to take a few of them out with me, because of my rash hard-headedness.

Not long after they were taken, I had to pick up some people at the Munich International Airport, as their Official NCO's Sponsor. If you never have been there, it was a very long, single-story building. The international arrival and departure area is at the extreme right end of the building. From the counter area, going to the right, you passed a few bars and food stands and other businesses, then some utility rooms on the left and the public restrooms.

As you passed the restrooms on the left, tucked into an odd corner was where Iran Air had their counter, remote from the rest of the airport for some odd reason. Guess they didn't want their folks exposed to too much Western decadence. On the right, directly in front of their counter was an entry/exit doorway to the parking lot across the street.

Because of work pressures in trying to keep troops working 12 and 12 energized, the Embassy hostages hadn't been on my mind much that day or for a couple of weeks. I was stunned to see the same '*Marg Bar Amerika*' signs and copies of the offensive, to me, photos and the newspaper pages plastered all over the Iran Air station. I asked the German Border Patrol Policeman (DGS) hanging around why they were there.

"It's their government's orders and their right to say what they think. We may not like it, since the States are our friends but there is nothing we can do."

"You mean they can make those statements, and Germany can't stop them?"

"It's kind of like your Freedom of Speech Constitution, Oberfeldwebel Castle."

I got my arrivals and escorted them to the baggage claim, through customs and into the VW van I owned, steaming and fuming all the time. The new guy, another SFC and his family told me how the folks in the States were reacting to it, that there were those who thought it was cause for going to war and those who thought that the Iranians were right in opposing the US that way.

Over the next several days my responsibilities as a sponsor, and to my troops, kept me really busy, but I continued to brood on what I considered to be an outrageously vulgar and inflammatory display against my country. Munich, like the rest of Germany, had hundreds of thousands of Islamic followers living and working there as 'Gastarbeitern' or Guest Workers.

Finally a time came when I could take a couple of days off and a group of us, with our wives, went to Munich to visit the famous *Bierhallen*. The plan was to drive there, get a cheap room at the guesthouse on McGraw Kaserne where the 66th MI group was headquartered, then do the town by taxis or by bus and streetcar.

We started far too early the first day. By three or four in the afternoon several of us had already drunk too much beer. I was getting madder and madder at the Iranians and not being much of a party guy at all. One of the guys with us who didn't drink suggested that we all take a break, go grab a shower and maybe a bite at the local Wienerwald restaurant by McGraw and start over by going down to the Munich "*Fussgangerzone*," or pedestrian shopping area. It was *Langzammersmastag* (Long Saturday with extended shopping into the evening) so we all said okay.

Back in our rooms, Roger, an old friend going back to Vietnam days, pulled me aside. Roger was a qualified Vietnamese, German and Russian linguist and we worked together for the Field Station S3, and we had an extensive network of German DGS, Army and Anti-Terrorist Police acquaintances,

"Hal, you are obsessing over this," he said. "Kelly has talked to me about it, or how much you wanted to go to Tehran, and how you feel about the Pueblo crew in North Korea. You have to do something to get it behind you."

"Can you drive?" I asked him.

"Sure, only a couple of half-liters of Lowenbrau™, I'm fine."

"Let's go, then."

"Where, what for?"

"I ain't sure but come on, we'll take my van."

My wife did lay down to take a nap, not because she was drunk - she drank a little - but because she had worked late the night before, getting ready for Colonel Mike Schneider's upcoming Change of Command Inspection. He was a prick and a stickler for *net-noy* things, like having all filing cabinets and safes dressed and covered, ordered by number of drawers and color. I told her I'd be back soon and left with Roger. I had no idea what I was going to do or when, but he was right; I needed to do something.

The street that crosses in front of McGraw Kasserne leads to the route to the Munich airport, east of the city. We started down that, and I was drinking a half liter of Spaten Helles™ as we went along.

"What are you going to do, spit beer on them? They abhor alcohol, you know. Makes them unclean."

"Unclean? Those stinking, goat-screwing, camel-humping barbarians? Unclean?"

We were just going past a very large *Metzgerei* - butcher shop - and in a flash I was yelling, "Unclean! You want unclean, I'll show you unclean! Stop right now!"

I stumbled out of the van and ran inside. There were three or four whole pig's heads in the refrigerator case and they had what seemed to be reasonable prices. The way I felt, anything would have been acceptable. I told the guy I wanted the biggest one, and he wrapped it in butcher's paper.

"Do you have any fresh blood, pig's blood?" I asked him in my limited German.

"Sure, naturally," he replied.

"One moment."

I ran out to the van and grabbed a plastic, collapsible 5 L water can, and ran back inside. I asked him to fill it and he did. I paid for it and stumbled back into the van, threw the head and its wrapping down on the bench and sat the blood at my feet.

"Drive, dammit, before I change my mind!"

Roger started the van and off we went in the direction of the airport. I told him that when we got there I wanted him to park at the very right of the lot, directly in front of the entrance of the building.

I should mention that the van was a used one I had purchased from the Bavarian *Maltaserhlefdienst*, the equivalent of a volunteer rescue or first aid group. It still had the Maltese cross painted on it, but the blue flasher was gone from the roof. Most cops and traffic control folks didn't look at the roof, they just waived me through to wherever it was that I was going. It worked for the controlled parking space I wanted us to go to.

"You coming with me or staying here?"

"I believe I'll stay here and keep the motor running; if you do what it looks like you intend, you just might need a fast getaway, cause you could have Iranians and DGS both after you."

"Nah, the rag-heads will be in too much shock and the DGS will just stand around, saying it is a job for the regular police, "it's not a border problem."

"Well, just in case, give me your knife."

"What?"

"Your damn knife, give it to me."

"Oh."

A habit, a very old habit I had was to carry a 'rigger's' knife, with a sharpened Marlin Spike, with me at all times. That was for opening beer bottles and cleaning out the odd bit of ear-wax, mind you.

I went in the door, and standing right in front of it was the DGS officer, Sergeant Zuber, whom I had met several times at the big firing ranges on Lagerlechfeld, the German Air Force Base south of Augsburg. We had shot together, exchanging weapons, and afterwards drinking the bier the Germans provided and the Old Grand Dad™ that we brought. For some reason they really like that particular brand of Bourbon.

Our conversation lasted about 15 seconds or so.

"Guten Tag, Oberfeldwebel Castle, how does it go with you?"

"Guten Tag, Sergeant Zuber, it is not going well. Those damned Iranians with their signs have really torqued me off."

"And, so, what for is the hog's head and what looks like blood? Them maybe?"

"Yes, for them."

"So, man must piss."

He started towards the restrooms and you could have bent me like a worn out playing card after way too many games of Pinochle. By then, my anger - and good German beer - was really taking control of my thought processes.

I started towards the Iranian Air counter, holding the pig's head by one corner of the wrapping in my left hand; I flung it at one of the computer monitors, and unscrewed the top of the water container. I had it open by the time I got to the counter, and started pouring it all over everything I could reach, all the while yelling every foul thing that came to my mind about the "spawn of a mating session between a diseased camel and the Ayatollah" and yelling *"Marge Bar Khomeini, Marg Bar Iran, Marg Bar Iraq"* in the rudimentary Farsi I had retained. You always learn the dirty or insulting words and phrases first in a new language, if you recall.

One of the men ran from the office behind the counter, pushing a pretty woman dressed in Iran Air colors with a pale chador, out of his way and towards me. Another man just stood there with a look of shock on his face, arms spent and palms up, as if saying "What?"

I managed to get some of the blood on all three of them.

When I had finished I was limp from using so much adrenaline. The DGS officer came up to me, took the empty water container from me and threw it in a construction trash container inside the controlled area of the terminal.

"You go, Commerad," he said, using the familiar *Du* instead of the formal *Sie* pronoun. I think he meant it as a complement instead of an insult.

I went back out to the van and my friend drove us away. I was still not thinking about what I had done, only how good it felt.

"So, who was the DGS guy in there? I saw his uniform through the window."

"Zuber, you remember him."

When we went to those ranges we took the 'training ammo' to the Germans, who had a hard time buying it in common US calibers, like .38/.357 and .45 ACP.

"Oh, yeah, the guy with the new DGS issue Glock."

"Yep, Him."

"Think he'll say anything?"

"Don't know; he went towards the latrine, then came and told me to leave. Let's get back to McGraw; I'm sobering up and need something to eat."

"Okay, I think Sergeant Zuber is a friend of Paul's, so if I see him I'll talk to him."

Paul was one of the elite Bavarian Anti-Terrorist Police, and he liked to hang around with Americans, even joining the Augsburg German-American Square dance club. He was a friend of mine, Roger's and Rodney Barneycastle. He always knew what was happening, but at that point, I didn't care, and hadn't thought through what the consequences would or could be. I had just acted viscerally, maybe stupidly, and it felt great.

At the guest house I took a shower while my wife was fixing her hair. "So, where did you guys go while I was napping, Forty-Mark Park for Roger's sake?" she was laughing because Roger was single and had a reputation for liking German women.

"No, to the airport. I think I'm over being obsessed with the Iranians. And maybe I am in trouble."

I told her what I had done, and although she paled, she smiled and said, "That sounds just like the Sergeant Rock I married. The same kind of guy who would drop trousers in a whole bar full of 'legs' and shout "Asshole, you want to see asshole; I'll show you asshole!"

The Iranians filed a terrorist incident report, and thought their attackers might have been Turkish or Kurds who weren't as strict Islamic fundamentalists as they were. I guess that at the time, with my dark hair and big, dark mustache and tan from being in the mountains the previous week; I could look like one to them. One of the investigators was my friend Paul, and he reported that Zuber couldn't have seen anything because of a sudden need to go to the restroom, and had been absent during the event.

Much later I used to worry about whether what I had done caused the hostages any additional grief, but from what I've read and been told, it didn't. They intended to hold them as long as they could to embarrass the 'Great Satan,' and treated them really badly from the very beginning. I also thought what could have been the consequences if I had been caught. It could have been one hell of an international incident, embarrassing both the German and the US governments.

But, it felt so good that I didn't dwell on that. At least not until my company CO called me to the orderly room. He closed his office door, turned to me and said "You dumb shit, you big dumb shit! I know what you did; Roger told me," in a voice that sounded filled with rage and disappointment.

I started to sweat a little, because Captain Lent was one of the best CO's I had ever had, and if he was pissed, he would do the right thing. Visions of court-martial went through my head. In my mind I imagine I would be drummed out of the service, with the sleeves of my uniform in tatters where the stripes had been ripped off.

"Yes, Sir, Hal, you are known to have all the balls of a Day Room full of pool tables, but sometimes you just let your mule headedness overrule your thinking brain. Next time, use a car that has German plates, not your own van with US plates. Dismissed." He said it with a big beaming grin. I knew I was home free.

I never did get around to talking with Colonel Holland about Iran before he left this mortal plane. After his release, Inauguration Day, 1982, the Army kept him out of sight for a while. He had some serious medical problems, including cancer. When he became Commander of Vint Hill Farms Station, I was off in Central America a lot. I did get a copy of the book 444 Days signed by him, which I cherish to this day, but at the time he was busy with a lot of other folks at the VHFS Officer's Club, and we'd just chatted for a couple of minutes.

From what I've read and heard about his resistance to the Iranians during his captivity, and being the subject of the most abuse, I hope he would have approved of my 'gifts' to the Iran Air counter personnel in Munich, in late 1979. I believe so, and that ain't no shit.

ASA and A Box of Rocks

By Harold Castle

An Army chaplain was explaining to a group of ASA soldiers how to have a full life. For illustrative purposes he had some props, which he intended to use. The first was a Plexiglas cube or box, filled with sand. He also had some rocks and pebbles and piles next to the cube.

"If you only concern yourself with the small things in life, represented by this sand, there is no room in it for the really important things," he said as he demonstrated by trying to place some of the rocks and pebbles in the box, but none would fit. He then dumped all the sand out in a pile, and placed the rocks in the box.

"If you take care of the most important things first, such as your spouse, children, religion and so on, your life will be much fuller" he said.

"Who thinks that this box now represents a full, satisfying life?" he asked.

A 98C Signals Intelligence Analyst jumped up and said, "It looks close enough to me to be full, Padre!"

"No, let me demonstrate further," the chaplain said and started filling the box with the pebbles from the pile, shaking the box as he did so, and explaining that they represented the next important things, like a good job, a nice place to live, and schools for the kids and so on. The pebbles filled in the spaces around the rocks until the box appeared full.

"Who thinks the box now looks like a full life?" he asked.

A 05D Duffy Sergeant, without his glasses, but with lots of black fishing line to measure the box from several points on the perimeter, declared the box was full.

"No, let me demonstrate some more," he said, as he began to scoop the sand into the box, and shaking it so the sand filled in all the spaces between the rocks and pebbles.

"Who thinks the box is full now?" he asked.

A 98G Linguist, just back from town and in civilian clothes, naturally, stood and said, "On close examination the box is full, Padre."

"Yes, it is and it represents a full and satisfying life," the chaplain said.

Then, from the back of the room, an NCO, a Morse Operator, stood, burped, 'adjusted' himself and strode to the table where the box was. He peered at it from all sides and from the top. After a while he reached into his BDU pants cargo pocket and pull out a can of beer. He opened the can, and slowly poured the beer into the box, letting the liquid fill in all the spaces between the rocks, the pebbles and sand, until the box was truly full, with a little creamy beer foam on top.

The moral of the story: Only a person dumber than a box of rocks thinks life is full and satisfying without a good beer.

The Tale of the Honest Hooker
By The Wolfman

To tell this tale, I need to crank up the Time Machine and return to the winter of 1973. The place was Camp Humphries, Pyeongteak, Korea. At that time I was assigned to the ASA Field Station serving my second tour in Korea unaccompanied by my family.

It's no secret that prostitution was legal in Korea at that time and there were portions of each village outside the gate of a military installation devoted to entertaining US servicemen while separating them from their paychecks. All of the village bars had their complements of willing women each ready and willing to sell their charms.

All of the bars had different themes; some played music oriented to attract Black soldiers, some played rock 'n roll. There was almost nothing to do on post so most soldiers choose to go to the 'Ville' for entertainment.

I was no different. The bar that I frequented was on the second floor of the Seoul Hall Hotel and played mostly Country and Western music and some golden oldies. While I did not go there every night I went quite frequently. Invariably, I would get propositioned by one of the working girls, usually using a line to the effect "Hey, GI you want a good time?" My answer was always to hold up my left hand pressing on my wedding band with my thumb so it would stand out and say no thank you.

That usually produced some sort of an outburst about how she was only trying to make a living and support her family. Normally, I would listen patiently and offer to buy her a cup of coffee or a

Coke™, and then just sit and listen to the music while making small talk with the girl.

As things happened, about mid-winter I caught a really bad case of the flu and was in bed for three days. Come Saturday night I really felt a lot better and decided to hit town and go to the Country - Western bar.

It was a short walk and then a climb up the stairs to my usual seat at the bar. A few words of greeting with the bartender and I settled in for a couple of hours of relaxation. All of a sudden I had a hot flash and felt extremely dizzy. That is all I remember. I woke up in the back room of the hotel with one of the working girls swabbing my forehead with a cool towel. I asked her what was going on and she said "You passed out in the bar and we brought you here so the Military Police would not get you. Mama San check you out and you really big sick. *Taksan* hot in the head."

About then I realized that I was on a futon bed under a heavy quilt and my clothes were gone. I asked where my clothes were because I needed to get back to the post. I was told that Mama San had taken them so I could not leave because in her words I was '*taksan* sick.'

I protested and Mama San was summoned and I was told in no uncertain terms that I was too sick to go out on a cold night and she would not let me leave. It was a moot point because I was too weak to even sit up.

In a little while the door slid open and there stood a little old man who looked older than dirt. He was wearing traditional male Korean clothing. He was accompanied by a youngster carrying a large wooden box that turned out to have what seem to be literally hundreds of small drawers in it. He came over to the bed and began to examine me. After my first weak protests I realized that he was some sort of a doctor and knew what he was doing, so I just let him do his thing. After taking my temperature with a modern thermometer and listening to my chest with a modern stethoscope, accompanied by much poking and prodding, he gave a gruff order to the kid with the box and a small brazier was lit and a brass teapot with water was put on to boil. As the water boiled he added various powders to it. After a period of time he poured the contents of the teapot into a coffee cup and made me understand that I was to drink it.

It smelled terrible and I refused. At that point he called out and Mama San entered and really tore into me explaining that it was medicine and I was going to drink it or wear it. At this point she came over to the bed and grabbed my jaw with one hand and pinched my nose shut and with the other forced open my mouth and began to pour. I had no choice - so I drank it.

After that he packed up his things and had a long talk with Mama San in Korean that I couldn't follow at all. He then left. Mama San then told me that the medicine would make me sleep, so not to fight it. She told me that someone would sit with me through the evening. What can I do? I just let go and fell asleep.

When I awakened in the morning I felt 100% better and ready to take on the world. As soon as it was evident that I was awake the young lady that was beside the bed called Mama San who came in immediately. I asked for my clothes and was told that I could not have them yet as the doctor had ordered that I was to take a steam bath when I awoke.

She then produced a robe and a pair of thongs and I was taken to the Korean style bath facility in the hotel where I took the bath as directed. While there, a barber was called who trimmed my hair and shaved me. At that point Mama San appeared with my uniform and boots. Everything had been washed and pressed to include a spit shine on the boots. She then told me to get dressed.

After dressing I pulled out my wallet and was surprised to find that all of my money was still there. I thanked Mama San profusely and asked her how much I owed her. Her response floored me.

"Your money is no good. You come in here all the time and you never take girls to hooch. You married and not cheat on wife. You always kind to girls and buy coffee or Coke. You never fool around and act like gentlemen. Your money is no good."

I tried to protest but I knew that the herb doctor alone had been expensive. The response was "Go home now."

 I had been completely helpless and at the mercy of anyone that came near to me. Those hookers and their Madam had responded to my simple act of fidelity to my wife and the way I treated them as human beings.

Sometimes it takes a real body slam to understand the Golden Rule, 'Do unto others as you would have them do unto you.'

EPILOGUE
After The War

Hummingbird on the 43rd
By John Klawitter

Autumn, 1989. I had an army footlocker half full of unsold manuscripts in my garage in the San Fernando Valley. At that time I was an absent minded fifty year old moonlight writer (my wife assures me I'm still that way) and a DGA director who made a decent living directing semi-brainless television commercials for way off-Broadway plays, for a major car company that claimed they had *No Unhappy Owners*, and for a cheap light wine with a touch of lime. *Lime, for a wave of refreshment!* I got to film waves at Ana Moana on the Big Island and gape at the topless girls on Waikiki Beach for that one. Life wasn't all that bad, and yet…

In the first few years after I'd gotten back from my tour in Saigon, *Pearl of the Orient*, I had furiously scribbled down anything that came to mind on any scrap of paper on hand, but as the rejection letters piled up I slowed down and took a second look, and then a third. I got a little smarter, shaved off the poetry and the nonsense, learned pacing and how to tell a story.

When I went to Vietnam I was close to a master's degree in Oriental Studies. I had spent a year learning Vietnamese and six months at the NSA's top secret 'Puzzle Palace' at Fort Meade. But back stateside after I returned to the civilian life I had yet to meet an agent, editor or publisher who liked my vision of what any of that meant. I was lectured to. I was told I was too pro-war. There was no valid reason for *that stinking mess* in the first place. The US had no business in Vietnam. We were on the wrong side of history. Nobody who actually volunteered for Vietnam had the smarts to say anything relevant about it.

Once, in a Hollywood agency on the west end of Sunset near Beverly Hills, an agent threw a copy of my first unpublished manuscript across his desk in my general direction. It slid off the end before I could grab it, pages scattered across the hardwood floor. *Talk about rejection!* Maybe he was outraged I'd asked him how he'd avoided the draft. He never did say.

I had originally titled my first novel In The Interest of National Security, and later, Nam Viet. But no matter what I called it or how many times I rewrote it, in the two decades that followed there was no sale.

I was working with animator Phil Mendez on a spec project he called Monster Tales. I was working on a pilot show with Erich Van Lowe, a staff writer for Bill Cosby's show. He'd spun off and sold a black vampire paperback titled Blacula. I was bending his ear about how I couldn't get anybody interested in my war novel, and he gave me a lesson on how to get published:

"First, your manuscript is too long. You got enough for six novels in here. Take the most rotten, horrible thing from your Nam experience and write about that.

"Don't bother with agents. It's just a damn paperback and you're unpublished and Vietnam is about as popular as a dick with venereal disease. Go directly to editors. Find a publisher doing war stuff. Write query letters praising their work. Say you're a big fan. Pour it on. And send the manuscript with it. And no exclusive to anybody. Fuck the exclusives. Everybody in the business, they're all assholes. Blast them out to everybody at the same time."

Well, I followed his somewhat pithy instructions. I knew about an incident in-country where a small, twisted band of CIA operatives was sending dope back to the states in the body cavities of dead GIs. My hero was a somewhat jaded and war weary hero who accidentally became a part of that. I called it Crazyhead.

But it was hard to find anybody actually doing anything about Vietnam at that time. After a lot of skulking around I found a few that might work, and I sent out 5 copies.

Months went by. I knew my book was on a slush pile somewhere, so it would take months. But after I got four reject letters, I forgot about it. Real life may suck, but bills have to be paid.

I was working as in-house senior writer at Home Savings and Loan when I got the incredible, impossible phone call.

"Hello, John Klawitter?"

"Yes."
"My name is Locke Wister. I work for a big publishing house here in New York, and we would like to buy your book."

"You're kidding. Who is this, really?"

"Locke Wister. And I assure you, Mr. Klawitter – we never kid."

When it was almost too late, when Vietnam fast fading into history, somebody had finally taken the bait. My first novel was set to come out in a few months, published by Ivy Press, an imprint of Ballentine/Del Rey, a division of the mighty Random House publishing conglomerate. A very big deal for me. And now I'd flown to the Big Apple to talk about writing a sequel.

So here I was walking past Macy's store in Manhattan. I'd heard it was a famous place, but I couldn't see what was special about it. It looked about like any other department store. I stopped to frown at my reflection in the window glass. I saw a somewhat frayed fellow still running 10 Ks to stay in shape, but now graying around the edges. Unfortunately, the on-the-movie-set part of me that owned the quiet but firm directorial voice of command was nowhere here to be found, at least not for the moment.

Instead, I was in the dreamlike state I tended to drift into when I was alone for any length of time. I was not like this when I was in the flow and chatter of film or vid production or the hasty grin, grab and *see ya later* of a wrap party. In those shallow, hustling and triumphant moments I had no empty, sad feelings. I caught myself looking at my reflection in the Macy's window and at the same time I was thinking about looking in the window and I was also thinking about writing about looking in the window. I wondered when this sick habit of pulling back from the moment had actually begun.

I hadn't been this way in the monochrome shades of my uneventful youth in a Midwestern industrial town. Something had happened to me in 1964 or 1965. Was it that moment of withered innocence on Le Loi Street when the ratty kid terrorist pointed an ancient revolver at me and pulled off three shots at nearly point blank range? Was it the grisly visual image of a little kid's small, neatly amputated foot with the white cotton stocking and the light blue tennis shoe still on it, lying on the sidewalk a half block away from where the car bomb went off outside the US Embassy? The human intestines hanging like prankster's toilet paper from the tree outside the shattered Brinks BOQ? There was no way for me to know, and I certainly wasn't going to see a shrink about any of that. I had ridden my luck through a bit of a chain saw movie and nothing from there could touch me. I was here on the other side now, and that bad business was in the long ago and far away.

I stared at the ghost of myself in the glass. In the little room behind my reflection real manikins in chic autumn outfits played out a scene with pumpkins and dried corn stalks. A taxi drove by in the reflection. I turned to call it, but naturally I was too late. It is also true that in the daytime, the city that never sleeps, never waits for anybody. The muggy August heat beat on my bare head. I should have worn one of my panama straw hats, that year all the rage in Hollywood. I trudged on, bearing my determined look, shoulders slouched and head forward, taking my steps one by one, the way I always did.

And then I was standing in the shiny marble floored lobby of the big skyscraper. My publishing conglomerate occupied at least six entire levels here. After all these years, I was actually hesitating, wondering if I really wanted to go through with this. I guess I slipped into my dreamlike state again. I was a character in the story of going to see my new editor, and I was writing the story. I know this sort of mental writing gave me a vacant, perhaps witless appearance, but I didn't care.

I guess I was thinking about the war again, wondering if there was such a thing as invisible PTSD, something like a functioning alcoholic, if that's what I was. I caught my reflection in the mirrored aluminum face of the elevator. The proof was in the pudding; I couldn't be something like that; I was whole, not a scratch on me. The doors parted and, having half convinced myself, I was on my way.

The appointment was on the 43rd floor. The elevator dumped me off at 30. I had to walk to another brushed metal door that silently offered an invitation to chance the rest of the way. A pair of young secretaries eyed me and then moved to the opposite corner of the little aluminum box. A few moments of silent swift rising and I was in his publisher's waiting room, a reception area with one side entirely floor-to-ceiling glass, a dramatic view looking out and down on the sheer vertical walls and cliffs of the city above the streets far below.

I saw an odd flash of color at one corner of my eyesight. There was a little bird outside, a jeweled wonder hovering motionless in the air like a tiny clown's Huey 1B. Amazing! I saw it was attracted to the lavender and cream petals of a giant potted orchid on my side of the glass. My God! I would not have believed such a tiny bird could fly so high.

I checked in with the receptionist, who pointed to stiff leather chairs in the lobby. I sat as erect as possible. It was an uncomfortable chair, low and slippery, built for show. I had to work a bit at not slumping down into the seat. I had hoped for a moment alone to settle my thoughts, but there was a lean *literary type* slouching in one of the chairs down the line from me.

The fellow made me uneasy. He was maybe forty, and was wearing rubber treaded hiking boots, khaki pants, a tan shirt and a photographer's vest with dozens of pockets. *The war reporter look.* A clothing outfit that said I'm just back from the Middle East. Just in from the Killing Fields of Cambodia. I had just turned in my story on the genocide horrors in North Africa. Inside I was moving up toward nervous. *Was this what authors were wearing these days?* The guy had a pocket full of pens and a set of round wire-rimmed John Lennon glasses perched on his beaky nose. *The savvy intellectual look.* had to admit that is how I would have cast him if he was an actor selected to do a commercial for some deodorant preferred by sophisticated men of action and adventure, *Lucky Boy Gel - takes away the smell of fear!*

My spirits sagged. I was out of place, a relic from some other time. I didn't belong in this posh and quiet lobby. It wasn't fair, but there it was. I had simply picked the wrong war, or as I'd been told by the dancing Nazi, himself a survivor from World War II, *The war had picked me.* Over the years, I had tapped key after endless key with a dogged single-mindedness, churning out the stories of my lessons learned in my war, the bad war, the wrong war, the non-PC war. I had burnished my query letters to that plateau where the rejection letters were kinder. I believed my work was better, truer, more vital now than it had been in the heat of the moment, when war's gagging outrages, waste and foolishness had me gasping for fresh air. Why did I feel this way? *What the hell was so wrong about me being here?*

A few days before, I had jetted from LAX to DC where I'd made a futile attempt to pay my personal debts with a walk through The

Wall, that hauntingly sad Vietnam War Memorial namvets have grown to love. Now it was two days later but I still felt weighed down with my memories of the time when I was a linguist-cryptographer with the 3rd Radio Research Unit. I had been young and invincible, had done foolish things and had been lucky enough to survive. Hence, the guilt.

Ironic, but the me in that waiting room on the 43rd floor wanted to be like that other guy; bright, optimistic, aggressive, a rising star, a writer on his way up. But my spirits hit a snag when my gaze fell on the purple sprig of drying flowers on my own lapel, and I could see now that even that was a mistake. I had snapped it off a wilting wreath somebody had laid next to the names etched on the wall, my small token to take back to the West Coast, something to say *Yeah, I still remember all of you.*

But too late; I was here now, waiting for an editor who was an unknown quantity, and everything was wrong, wrong, wrong. I was sweating, overheated from my walk through the busy Manhattan streets. I should have been a little quicker; I should have caught that taxi. I could feel the dampness staining the thin shirt under my *California chic* black-and-white checked sport coat. The panic was coming on strong now. *Damn, I've waited twenty five years for this!* I should have worn an undershirt. My soft leather Bally boots were wrong too, somehow so 1970's. Why was my expensive Sy Devore outfit – that was so right when I was directing on the set – why was this same look so out of place here? No two ways about it. My goddamn miserable stupid jacket was too loud, too West Coast, too wrong. My fingers fumbled to loosen my red-and-yellow striped tie, a tribute to the South Vietnamese flag that had seemed like a good idea when I dressed in my hotel room, but now felt like it was strangling me.

The lean literary type eyed me with bemused disinterest. *Get with it,* his attitude said to me. *In another few months it will be 1990. Nobody gives a crap about your stupid old war any more, if they ever did.* I shifted my weight, ready to get to my feet and bolt for the elevator, but even the timing was against me as in the next moment the elevator doors opened and a look-alike to the first literary type ambled in gave a familiar wave to the receptionist and took a seat. This second guy was lean, angular, and maybe a few inches shorter than the first, but he wore the same round, wire rimmed glasses and similar clunky hiking boots. The checkered arms of his Pendleton shirt indicated he was a woodsman and a nature buff. The newcomer sighed, stretched and nodded in his direction.

"Edward! How's the muse treating you, you old scribbler?"

"Greedy, rotten bitch. What about you, Martin?"

"Turning in my pages."

"Been waiting long?"

"Nah, maybe ten minutes. Wister's running late."

Wister. That had to be Locke Wister, my editor. I frowned and stared down at my highly polished boots. This was not going well for me. I placed my Samsonite briefcase on my lap. It was a tan hard shell, out of fashion as I could see my rival writers had soft cases that were half-backpacks. I ran my fingers over the rough spot where I'd scuffed my briefcase when I flung it into the *xe hoi* taxi and yelled at the driver to head for the hollow flat *pam!* Sound I knew by experience was a detonating bomb. I was right; I was just getting out from teaching a class at the *Hoi Viet My* and a terrorist had just set off a car bomb outside the old US Embassy. I had to see it. That's the way I thought back then: *What would Hemingway have done?*

A quarter century later, back in my brand new publisher's tasteful lounge, I clicked the Samsonite case open and took out a book I had bought earlier that day at a small shop on Lexington Avenue. The bookseller was an odd old man with a full white beard. The wrinkled oldster was wearing a white plastic construction hat with the big letters CPC stenciled on the front. *Big Apple cool.* Between the hat, which was snugged down to his bushy white eyebrows, and the beard pushing up to his nose, his eyes were like two black beans under an upside down soup bowl.

"Why are you wearing that hat?" I said.

"So nothing falls on my head."

"What does CPC stand for?"

"Canoga Power Company. You want the book?"

"How much is it?"

 "Fifty dollars."

"That's a lot for a used book."

"Fifty dollars," the invisible mouth under the droopy white mustache repeated.

Published with high quality paper with a glossy finish, it made a heavy rectangle in my hands, *A Little Tour of France*, by American Henry James. I knew his work. He was a popular and sensible writer of the Victorian era, after Hemingway and Faulkner, a guy you had to read in college lit.

At first, I didn't realize why I was interested. The opening pages noted Mr. James had scribbled batches of notes, apologized for their 'hasty accumulation', and further write that 'the author had hoped to have them published with some black and white sketches of cottages and cathedrals to be done by a man named Joseph Pennell.' The sketches had not proven forthcoming in a timely manner, so the words were published alone in 1884, and then with the sketches in a separate edition in 1900. The one I held in my hands was a recent edition, printed in 1988, and it included not only the sketches, but also color plates by French impressionists as well as color maps tracing the early routes Mr. James had taken.

And then it hit me: as I browsed through the pages, I was struck by a similarity between the lives of the rural French citizens in that golden time before the two World Wars and the simplicity of the peasant way of life in the hamlet society of South Vietnam before mortar rounds started looping in on the rice paddies.

My imagination left the waiting room in the air high above the ant-busy streets of Manhattan and I daydreamed I was back in the late 1890s, walking beside a French girl past thatched roof houses on a path along a row of birch trees beside a pleasant brook. And then I was walking with a pretty bargirl on her day off from the Cherry Bar and it was back before the Nam war really started up in earnest and I had taken her to see the orphanage my unit sponsored. And then in my imagination back to France again, only it was twenty years later and I was wondering that those simple French peasants had somehow transmogrified into companies of dinner plate helmeted troopers armed with rifles and protected from pungent evil by strangely alien looking gas masks. And that led me to a vision of poor peasant rice farmers enjoying idyllic lives in isolated bamboo villages as they are somehow convinced to spend their spare time manufacturing homemade bouncing betty's and aiming AK-47s that were made half a world away in Czechoslovakia. You do not fight tanks with bamboo rakes and water buffalos.

My mind spun idly for a time, putting down the possibility that my half-formed and disconnected thoughts could lead to anything rational or even useful. Eventually, right there in that waiting room, I did doze off into a dream where I felt rather than saw the image of two dark clouds squabbling over the best way to grow a lotus flower from a single patch of fertile soil, and in my drowsy state I thought I might be on to something but then my dream was interrupted by surface chatter in the here and now and I came back with a start to Manhattan.

"Sleepy-head is wearing a Nam Vet's pin."

The literary types were talking about me. I slid *A Little Tour in France* back in my tan briefcase and placed the case on the floor between my legs. *Hey, I'm right here and you're talking about me as if I am nothing and nobody.* But I didn't say anything yet. Maybe I should have, but I didn't.

"And a tie made out of the South Vietnamese flag," Edward, the perhaps conflict reporter, added.

"Semaphoric attire."

"He could have tried the Viet Cong flag. More dramatic."

I frowned, drawn in. I guess they had me.

"You know the flags, but you didn't go?"

The photographer type grinned and trumpeted like Frankenstein's creator, "It's alive!" But after a moment of silence when I didn't reply, he more seriously considered my simple question. I apparently can never resist a chance to spout off about what I know, and the anti-conflict war dodgers can never resist a chance to defend their position.

"Nobody went except the stupids. Nobody *had* to go."

"You don't remember John F. Kennedy, the President of the United States, asking patriot soldiers to help fight brushfire wars?"

"Kennedy was a Democrat, you ass. Republicans start wars."

"Ass, yourself. Back in 1961 JFK called on us to beat back the communists."

"Yeah, yeah, right. Something about countries toppling like Monopoly pieces. He sure got that one wrong."

The hiker type chanted wearily, "*LBJ, LBJ, how many kids did you kill today?*"

Even after the decades removed, I felt my face flush and my blood rise. "Like *dominos, double-ass!* And they did all fall, except Thailand!"

Before I could say anything that would mire me further in the old, hopeless argument, the elevator doors opened and two fat, middle-aged Jewish men in drag hopped out and flounced through the lobby and into the reception area like a dance number squeezed out of an off-Broadway musical. Their dark chins showed a two day's growth of stubble. Their cheeks were rouged. Their heavy red lipstick was a crimson mess over their lips. They were chewing dead cigars, and their nylons were rolled half way down their hairy, stocky calves. Their slips stuck out an inch or so below their knee-high skirts and big padded bras projected from their chests like the prows of twin gunboats. They wore tennis shoes, a gesture to show they didn't care a hoot that their big fat feet could never fit in high heels.

The new twosome came on with a burst of energy and a mincing dance step, lustily singing the show biz opening to the old Warner Brothers Bugs Bunny cartoon show at the top of their leathery lungs. Ta-Da-duh-da-da-dut-dut-dut-da!" The receptionist brightened when she saw them and ushered them into the inner sanctum, still singing "Ta-Da-duh-da-da-dut-dut-da!"

"So you didn't go?"

My question thudded like an brick in the silence that followed.

"Neither of you went?"

"You still talking about that? Look, Dumb-As-A-Brick Wonder-Boy, you didn't have to go. None of us had to. Bad eyes. Nerve disease.

Mental what-the-fucks aversion. You got a slip from the doc. If you were in too good a shape, he could always inject water in your knees." He grinned knowingly at me. "At least that's what got me out." The happy recollection faded from his face. "Screwed up my knees ever since, though."

"But that only meant somebody else had to go in your place."

"Yea, verily, truth. Better him than me."

The hiker type turned to the maybe photographer. His body language clearly said the hackneyed and useless discussion about Southeast Asia, such as it had been, was over.

"You notice how gays are all the rage these days?"

"The Wister has a nose for the next new thing. I don't know how he does it."

"Editors don't edit any more. They are *literary marketeers*."

"Well, I know that's true; you don't even want to show up around here without a pre-edit. That's become our responsibility now days."

"It's not fair. I'm a crappy speller so I have to pay big bucks for some schmuck to do what's supposed to be Old Wister's job."

The lingering scent of heavy perfume hung in the air. "Those queers weren't real swishes."

"Yeah, I know. Spoofer-doofers. But how long has *La Cage aux Folles* been at the West End? I tell you, our pal Mister Wister is never wrong – *light-in-the-loafers* must be the coming thing."

"I don't get it, why is butt sex such a big deal? Give a little push in the right direction, anybody could be gay."

"Maybe you should try it. Money to be made. Think of the titles: Being Queer. Gay Today. The Flip Side. The Crowded Closet. People are curious, and sex sells."

"Man's got a dick, I guess it doesn't matter where you stick it."

"The coming thing, I tell you."

The elevator doors opened once more. This time they cast out a gaunt thirty-ish girl dressed in ankle length black chiffon that swirled like Pigpen's dirt as she walked. She wore white powder facial makeup and black rings around her eyes. Her nails were purple and a large golden ring pierced one corner of her lower lip. She gave us a disdainful glare and stood in a corner, glowering at a blank wall.

"Goth," the hiker whispered, rolling his eyes with a shake of his head.

I was drowning in my old familiar sinking feelings. Both the pleasant French countryside of Henry James and the green rice paddies of the Mekong Delta were far away. I didn't want to be a pessimist, but this meeting with Wister wasn't going to go very well. Yes, I was already sure it wasn't. I got up. I was *out of here*. The huntsman and the correspondent type eyed me casually as I headed for the elevator.

Waiting for the silvery doors to open, I looked out the window and saw the hummingbird was gone. A woman who reminded me of Mrs. Wilson, my high school drama teacher, came down the hall and stood next to me. She noticed I was looking in the direction of the big orchid plant.

"They aren't real, you know."

She gave me a thin smile and dismissed the waxy dark green leaves and shoots of exotic flowers with a wave of one hand. "Marvelous imitations, though, don't you think?"

Note: John Klawitter did not publish a second war novel with Random House, though Crazyhead went on to become a cult classic. In the years since, he has written over a dozen war, action and suspense novels, and nearly as many non-fiction books. In 2009 his novel Hollywood Havoc won the coveted EPIC Author's Prize for Best Action Thriller Novel.

Vicarious Trauma or PTSD
By Wayne Munkel

It is February of 1964, the dry season in South Vietnam. The temperature is in the eighties, the sky a crystal clear blue above us without a cloud in sight.

The Company formation is called to attention as the two black hearses pull up. Two flag draped coffins are placed on saw horses. There is the usual *military business* as the pall bearers, officers and chaplain get to their places. A reporter is quickly escorted away from the scene. I see the black gaping hole in the side of the airplane that will transport the two ASA soldiers across the Pacific.

I am in the second rank of the company formation. Words are said, but I am inside my own head and don't really hear them. I am angry, sad and confused. Tears run down my cheeks and I fight to keep from breaking down. Nothing will ever be the same for me, because Wayne Glover, my friend and workmate, is in one of those coffins.

The death of a close friend has me in emotional turmoil. I just want to get even with someone. I am confused. We in ASA are not supposed to be killed. They told us we were the top ten percent in brain power. This was supposed to be an easy station. I didn't sign up for nightmares of explosions and maimed bodies. Taps echoes off the metal buildings of the airport in the distance. Finally, the black mouth of the cargo door swallows my friend into its belly and we are dismissed.

Several months later I flew home, back to the world I had left behind. But home is no longer the way I remembered it. I see everywhere that things have changed. People have changed...or, let's face it, maybe it's me that has changed. My uncle tells me Vietnam is not a real war, not like his WW II war. I replied it seemed damn real to me.

My life goes on: After a year and a half of work in construction I went back to college. After graduation I met the woman I married and we had three children. My employer helped me earn a Master's degree in Social Work and I began a career in that field. Along the way, reoccurring nightmares haunt me.

In 1980, I began what, looking back, seems to have been a second war. This time, the casualties are children who have been abused, neglected, sexually abused or assaulted and who all are suffering trauma to their bodies, minds and souls. My job is in the Emergency Room of a children's hospital. My new position coincides with my realization that more children than I could have imagined had been sexually victimized in Missouri, and abused children are everywhere. More and more of my work hours are taken up with these children. Some days it is absolute chaos. The staff struggles to find ways to help the children and to intervene with all aspects of child protection and law enforcement. I find much of this bewildering. The state of Missouri seems ignorant of what to do about the increasing numbers of sexually abused children.

I see that there are hundreds of them. Throw in an occasional murdered, abused child and I was getting a picture of a society run amok and a medical staff in crisis. Not every child we evaluated was abused but the amount of work to get to a diagnosis was the same.

Over time our overloaded staff became expert on all forms of child abuse and neglect.

I remember one case from those early years that stands out in my mind. I was called STAT to the Emergency Room. STAT means you have to be there immediately. Two girls, one four and the other seven, were in the ER with multiple stab wounds. They were found by relatives lying on the dead body of their brutally murdered mother. I spent the next two weeks, eight hours a day, working with everyone concerned with the case. By chance, my own two daughters were four and seven. So, in a sense, I was working to save my kids, too. I remember this case like it was yesterday; it was a key trauma of hundreds I experienced in all the years I worked at the hospital.

Back then, I was like a man possessed. I wanted to help everybody, save everybody, make everybody's life whole again, but I couldn't. There was a series of Dirty Harry movies beginning in the early seventies. One famous line spoken by Clint Eastwood was, "A man's got to know his limitations." I realize now that I didn't know my limitations. Being a slow learner, it took many crises for me to learn that I had exceeded my limitations. The emotional and psychological toll was overwhelming. I was a mess and my wife and children suffered for it. Some days I would come home and hug my kids. As they grew older they would say, "Another bad day at work, Dad?"

Listening to stories of the brutal treatment of children and seeing the broken bones, burns and bruises these children suffered all added up and took a toll on me. Emotional numbness and distancing were a way for me to protect what was left of me against the daily trauma. Helplessness and hopelessness crept into my thinking.

Professionals around the country were experiencing similar emotional and psychological pressures. In the early 1990's I found a journal article that described what we professional helpers had been experiencing. Lisa McCann and Laurie Anne Pearlman developed a landmark framework for understanding this aspect of professional life. They called it *vicarious traumatization*. That struck a chord with me. It was the mirror I was looking for.

Basically, what McCann and Pearlman had discovered was that the effects of repeated work with trauma victims cause changes in the way the therapist/helping professionals perceive themselves. They no longer can see the world as safe and positive. To such individuals it no longer is an orderly place. The key psychological areas that are affected are those that are most important to the person. For me, power, intimacy and imagery of memory were most salient. It was the disruptions in these areas that led to my difficulties.

To combat the helplessness I felt and my need for a better self-image, I knew I had to do something. I found that lobbying for necessary changes in the child maltreatment laws helped. Working with community groups to improve the intervention process for children helped. And writing grants that focused on specific changes that were needed in the community was another positive step I was able to take.

But it was hard, and there were many setbacks. Fantasies of what I would like to do with child molesters often involved sharp instruments on certain body parts or high speed lead encounters. I imagined breaking the bones of perpetrators in the same places they broke up little children; *How about bruises for bruises, burns for burns,* I told myself. Burns were the worst because the next step for kids was usually death. I never carried out any of this, but it became a way to cope with my anger and my feelings of helplessness.

Abuse and trauma victims experience a sense of alienation from other people and the world – a loss of intimacy. Helping professionals, through their work with these victims, often become separated from other professionals and the world in general. I learned through my experiences what that was like. I had to recognize I was in a lonely place. Comments like, "How can you listen to that all day or how can you do that kind of work?" further alienated me and others in my position. One therapist I know went to a party and was found by her husband standing alone. He said, "I see you told them what you do for a living." Such is the response from many people who are normal and decent but just don't want to hear about the reality of abused children.

I know now that many of my fellow Vietnam Veterans suffered similar anger and frustrations. Over the decades since the war, many felt alienated from the world they left behind. Questions like, "What was it like?" "Why did you go?" served to confirm their alienation.

And I think my being in ASA added an extra mental burden that many of us *Old Spooks & Spies* share. Our work was classified and we were set apart from other veterans in that we could not honestly talk about what we did. It was like taking all those days in Vietnam and putting them in a trunk or closet and leaving them there. All that time those memories are still there, festering, like an angry boil getting ready to explode. Anger is like that. Vengeance is like that. For me, intrusive thoughts kept breaking through to destroy what should have been a happy life.

After twenty eight years at the children's hospital it was time to retire. I'd had some level of intervention in thousands of sexual abuse/assault cases, hundreds of child abuse and neglect cases and tens of child homicides. My last child abuse fatality confirmed that it was time to leave. Looking at the obtunded body of that little girl, I recognized that she had most likely died from a lacerated liver or pancreas. The autopsy the next day revealed two liver lacerations.

For forty five years I'd had this awareness of wanting to kill someone. It was such that I was always the hero in doing so. Sometimes it would come in the somnambulistic state, and other times in a more awake time. It robbed me of many nights sleep. Sometime around the time I retired, I got upset that this was still happening. So, I put *the top ten percenter brain* to work on the problem. It took a while but I traced it back to that much earlier time in Vietnam.

I was not there when Wayne Glover was killed. I had gone to Can Tho to visit with Joe Kislan and to take a little R & R. I probably would not have been at the ball game where he was killed, but I felt guilty anyway. I was Wayne's trick chief. He was a friend and he was teaching me his craft. I had lived and he had died; I wanted to kill whoever had killed him. I wanted vengeance. Of course, back then I could not act on this desire. I didn't know who killed Wayne Glover, except it was the VC. I didn't know where they were. I had to continue the mission. It was not macho to cry or grieve, so I didn't. And later, I shipped out and physically left the war behind, and it was too late to do anything of the sort.

What I did was to subjugate my feelings, put them on the back burner so to speak. I went on with the war. That's what had to be done. And then my tour was done and I left it. So my desire for vengeance was not satisfied. It just festered and became that reoccurring, intrusive fantasy. Decades later I was able to psychologically *name it and claim it*, and that finally enabled me to set aside my old anger. No more nightmares and sleepless nights over this.

There was still one thing left to do and that was for me to personally find a sense of closure. In August, 2010, I attended a dedication of a bridge named in Wayne's honor in Tennessee. I visited his grave. On Memorial Day in 2011, I was honored to attend the Memorial Day Observance for the National Security Agency/Central Security Service at Ft. Meade, Maryland, where Wayne and another ASA soldier who died with him were memorialized. Five former ASA soldiers who worked with Wayne were there. I now have closure and am free of the pain of that traumatic time in my life. I know now that Wayne's death was my key traumatic memory of Vietnam.

Footnote: McCann, L, Pearlman, LA: Vicarious Traumatization: A Framework for Understanding the Psychological Effects of Working with Victims, *Journal of Traumatic Stress* 3:131-149, 1990.

Faded Souvenirs
By Robert G. Knowles

Like merchant seamen, police officers, and other folks who have led an adventurous existence, old soldiers drag a trunk full of memories with them across the years. Mine once traveled by slow boat, across the water, from North Carolina to the Republic of Vietnam and back again. It's a battered steamer trunk, spray-painted in flat olive green, with my name-rank-serial number stenciled on it in faded white half-inch characters. The trunk was shipped overseas before I left Fort Bragg, North Carolina, in September, 1967. Most of the things that I carefully selected and packed at Bragg were of little use in Vietnam. The silver framed picture of my wife and kid and a portable radio were wrecked by shrapnel. The green rain jacket I packed got torn to shreds in the same attack. After that, I sent the trunk back home. When I got back to the World a year later, I stowed the war away. The trunk sat unopened for almost 30 years in the garage over Stone Mountain house. Then one day, we were clearing out stuff my son, Ben, had left behind when he went off to Young Harris College. At the bottom of the pile, we found the old trunk.

In the top tray was an assortment of war mementos: 'O' club meal cards, shoulder patches, old uniform brass. Grace Kelly's likeness on a stack of low-denomination, pink and green, Military Payment Certificates, that were designed to look like *tarted-up Monopoly money*. In a corner of the trunk was a flare parachute, folded the size of a pocket handkerchief. Its faded white canopy was wrapped with yellow nylon shrouds, cut off short when I separated it from the flare charge, and still smelling faintly of cordite.

As I felt the nylon and unwound the shrouds it was wrapped in, the little patch of soft cloth lit a sizzling powder train of half - forgotten memories. Late one November night, at a firebase near Pleiku, I tried to pluck the sparkling flare out of the air, while it was still a few feet above the ground. I had seen it and a dozen others, descending through the blackness, lighting our defense perimeter with a jerky candle glow, in which shadows dance, within which phantoms moved. The descending flares exposed black-clad enemy raiders, called sappers, dragging bomb filled satchels behind them as they squirmed under the sprawling base's defensive barbed wire, past sandbag bagged fortifications. Seen from a quarter-mile away, the little crawling figures were quickly cut down by converging streams of stuttering red machine gun bullets.

The ground rocked to the KA-RRUMPP of bursting mortar shells. An arching stream of red tracers from a gunship hidden high overhead was followed in a split second later by the ripping sound of its rapid-fire cannon. In the stillness that followed, the only shadows still moving were from relief troops checking the wire, and medics, checking the wounded. The mortar flares cast eerie cones of flickering yellow light as they floated lazily down on us while we emerged, blinking, from behind high sandbagged walls and the 'all-clear' siren sounded.

As the darkness returned, a burning flare dropped almost on top of me. The light from the fading charge which dangled beneath the parachute was flickering out, and I thought it would be easy to catch, like fireflies back home. I reached for it, being careful not to grab the faintly sizzling charge hanging beneath. Just then, a puff of wind pushed it away.

The parachute slid beyond our area, into an unfamiliar sector of dark, unlit tents, closer to the base landing strip. I ran after it and tripped over a tent rope. The flares had blotted out my night vision. The tents around me weren't lit, and didn't seem to be occupied. I scrambled up, as the flickering scrap of cloth settled on a dark oblong shape under a rolled up tent wall. I reached out to claim my prize, and then jerked back my hand as if from a fire. The little parachute was resting just beyond my reach.

It had settled on the closed lid of a gleaming wood coffin. The hair stirred gently beneath my helmet. The battle of Duc To was being fought 30 miles away. I couldn't determine whether the dark oblong box, one of the many stacked around me in the tent, was empty, or already had become a resting place for a dead soldier, who was about to begin the long flight home. Before I could decide, the midnight wind flung the little parachute at me. I caught it in the air, stuffed it, smoking charge and all, in a pocket of my field jacket, and got away from there.

Thirty years later, as I rolled the faded line nylon between my fingers, and smelled again the faint aroma of gunpowder that clung to the shrouds, the little souvenir still had the power to return me to a long forgotten moment. I stuffed the fear I once had felt back into the old footlocker along with the rest of the Vietnam War, closing the lid on a life, and a land, far away.

Made in the USA
San Bernardino, CA
06 October 2014